PAINTING WITH EPOXY RESIN

HOW TO GET STARTED IN RESIN ART

TIPS
TECHNIQUES
TROUBLESHOOTING

CHARLOTTE STRONG

INTRODUCTION

Resin is addicting. From the first resin painting that I did I was hooked. A resin painting is glossy. It can have vibrant colors, and has a depth that is difficult to achieve with any other medium. Once you see that shiny surface and the way the resin interacts with pigments you're hooked. At least that's the way it was for me. The first time I did a resin painting with layers for dimensional effect was very exciting for me. Looking down into the painting was like looking into a river or ocean. Looking through water and seeing what was below. It's truly amazing to see that in art.

It seems that almost anything can be done with resin. It is versatile enough to be used to clear coat a finished painting; or by adding pigments & paints it can be used it as the painting medium. It can be used to embed objects into jewelry or on a canvas. Artists all over the world are creating art on canvas, and incredible works of art in furniture with resin. There are social media sites devoted to the craft.

You have likely seen resin in commercially made jewelry. There are many handmade artists making resin jewelry on Etsy and Amazon Handmade. Painting with epoxy resin is not a new concept. It has been around since the days of embedding sea shells or cereal into table tops was a thing. Now, it's gaining a customer base in modern abstract art.

Epoxy resin is a 2-part polymer that turns to plastic once cured. It requires a precise mixing of the 2 parts. Powders and paints can be mixed in, or it can be used by itself. Once cured it will dry into a very hard plastic that is glossy and glass looking. It can be colored, layered, sanded, drilled & filled again, and embedded with objects.

I got started in resin many years ago. I work in multiple mediums from acrylics to encaustics. I am always looking for a new art technique to try. It was inevitable that I would try resin. I'm always researching art techniques. I was visiting an art gallery in central California and saw an art piece that was so stunning that I had to figure out how it was done. I knew it was resin. I was familiar with the process of epoxy resin from using it on tables and crafts. But how to use it on canvas was the question. When I returned home I found a container of Envirotex Pour On resin in my garage. It had been sitting there for about 7 years. It was yellow, but functional. I had originally purchased it to finish a table. I was only using it for practice, so I decided to go ahead and make some art with the old resin. I told myself that I could always throw it out if it was bad. It worked great, even though it was really old resin. I headed to the hardware store to purchase more. I have since moved on to try many other brands of resin.

Soon, I was looking for a way to use the leftover resin mix. I found that making jewelry was a natural addition. I like to say that the jewelry bezel is a tiny canvas. So now I have both going as I paint. I never intended to become a jewelry maker. But you go where the art takes you.

I like to work in resin because it is a lesson in patience and going with the flow. You can't control resin the way you can other mediums. You can choose the pigments and canvas, but you can't always put the pigments and paints in the exact spot you want them to be on the canvas. Resin flows and moves. You can plan what you want to do for a piece and sometimes it turns out the way you plan, but sometimes not. Sometimes it turns out so much better than you expected. Because of the way it moves and flows, you have to be open to the unexpected when painting with resin. Allow it to do what it does. Go with the flow.

My hope for you, in reading this book, is that you find resin to be easier than you might have imagined it to be. I hope to provide you with tools for getting started, and take you through the process of using it. If you already have some resin experience, I hope this book will give you a few new tips and ideas for your work.

Please take the time to read through the safety section. I find that many artists don't want to think about safety when we work. Believe me I get it, art is fun, safety is not fun. Working with powdered pigments and other materials can compromise health. Safety in resin art is very important. It is important to consider safety in any medium that we are using. If you have experience in resin art, I recommend you read through the safety section anyway.

It will be helpful to gather the materials from the "Material's list" before you get started. You may find the check list on "Resin Painting Techniques", and "What You Can Do In Resin Art" to be most helpful. The "Troubleshooting Guide" is there to provide some tips on what to do when things don't go as planned. The "Frequently Asked Questions" section can provide tips for the working artist as well as additional information about resin.

Go make some amazing art.

Charlotte Strong

CONTENTS

SECTION 1
SAFETY

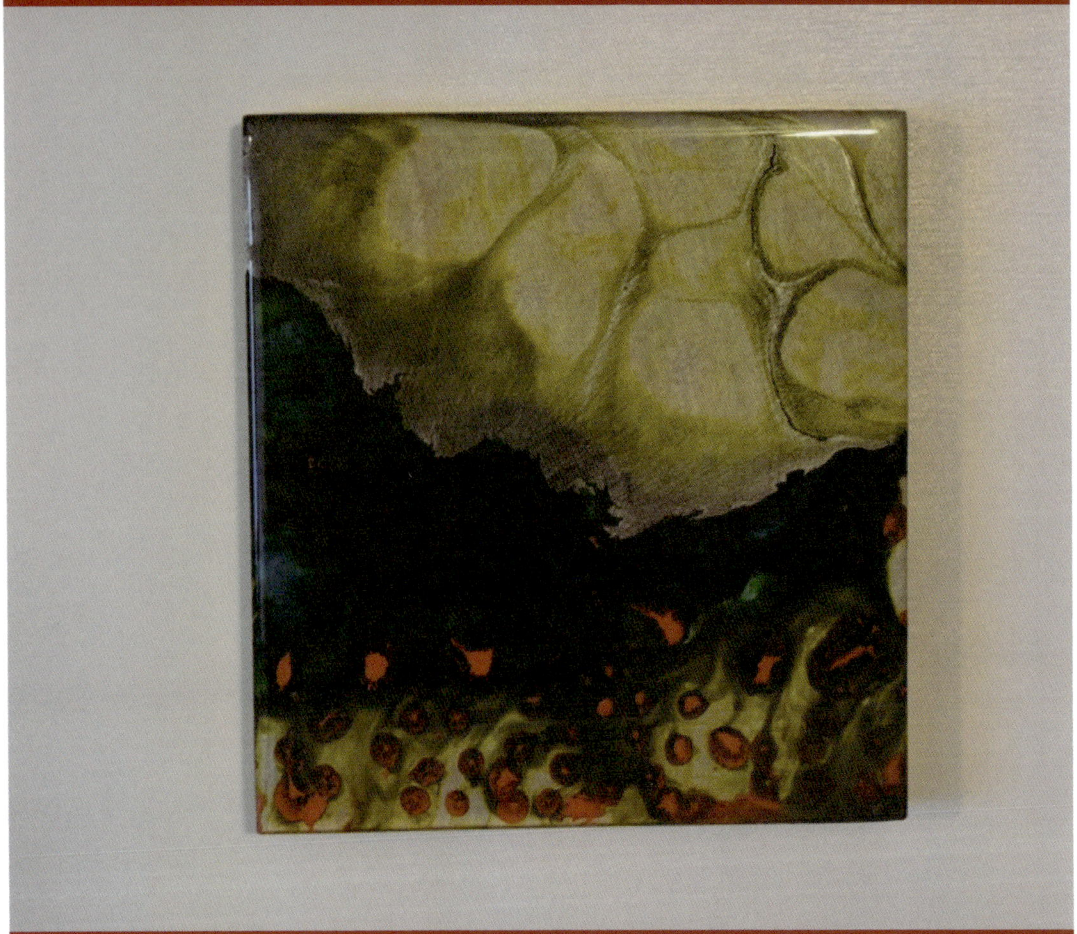

THE PATH OF DREAMING
Resin, Mica & Ink on Cradled Wood Panel
8"x8" (20cmx20cm)

SAFETY FIRST

Please read this section before reading the rest of the book. It is important that the art of resin painting be carried out with the utmost safety precautions in place. Practicing safety in art not only keeps you healthy, but it ensures that you have more fun in your art experience. There is information in this section that is crucial to working with resin. It is helpful to read up on how to clean resin from your skin before doing resin work. Have everything ready for clean up before starting to paint. That way, when resin gets on your hands, you will have it at the ready for cleanup. Read the entire safety packet that comes with the resin. Remember to always read the product information. It's fine print but it's important. It gives information on how resin works and how to be safe working with it. Many of the answers you need are in that data sheet.

While it's not an exciting topic, it is an important one. All art mediums carry potential for toxicity, depending on how you use them. That is why it is important to be safe with use. Wear a mask when working with resin, pigments, powders and torching. A full-face respirator is ideal. If it seems that I repeat myself on gloves and mask, throughout the book, it's because it bears repeating. It is very important.

Mixed resin in its liquid state is a fire hazard when tossed in the trash. Please do not dispose of resin in its liquid state. Wait for resin covered gloves and containers to dry before tossing them in the trash. They can heat up and catch fire. For this reason, allow everything to cure before tossing in the trash. Remove gloves and place them on the resin painting table, or on a non-flammable surface, for the resin to cure on the gloves. Leave any towels, brushes or rags to cure on a non-flammable surface before tossing in the trash.

Avoid using wax coated cups for mixing resin. The wax in the cup can melt with the heat of the resin. This can cause the resin itself to heat up to a higher temperature and ruin the resin. Even if it does not heat to the point of ruining the resin, it may heat enough that it adds wax to the resin and gives a finish to the surface of the painting that you do not want.

Large containers of mixed resin can become combustible when near sawdust or other materials. Large containers of mixed resin can heat up. Do not toss in the trash. If you have a large container of resin that heats up and begins to smoke, do not throw it in the trash. Set it on a non-flammable surface to cure. Once it is fully cured you can throw it in the trash. Unless you find something creative to do with it, it's a ruined batch.

If you have a resin spill in the studio use sand to absorb the resin and/or hardener. Do not use sawdust as spontaneous combustion can occur. Sawdust can create a fire hazard. If the 2 parts have not yet been mixed, try and scrape up what is spilled. If you can still determine the mixing ratio to exact measurements it can still be used.

Avoid pouring resin in any form down the drain. It will clog the drains, and is bad for the environment. Avoid washing resin mixing cups and tools in the sink. Wash these outdoors when possible. If you don't have access to an outdoor faucet, use a bucket. The method I use for cleanup is to allow the resin to harden in my mixing cup and peel it out once hardened. I use baby wipes for cleaning tools and hands. I only rinse in the bathroom sink after I have gotten every last bit of resin off my skin. Use a bucket, if water is needed. Do not pour this water down any household drains. Allow it to sit and evaporate in the bucket, or allow any resin to harden in the water, and pick it out before pouring it out. Do not pour resin, in any form, down any household drain. Do not clean resin tools in any household sink.

It is vital that you work in a well-ventilated area. A garage or studio space with open windows and a fan blowing fumes out the window is important. If possible, have an air purifier going in the room or studio where you are working. An air purifier with a carbon filter is best. There are air scrubbers made for the art studio and made for chemical use. They cost between $200 -$5000. If you can afford one, this is your best option. Find them on industrial supply websites and Amazon.com. Another consideration is activated carbon. This absorbs fumes and purifies the air. Find it in pet stores or online. If you have a fan pulling the air away from the space, place a container of activated carbon where the fan is. Don't place it where the fan blows the air. Place it where the fan sucks the air. The idea is, the fan will pull the air across the activated carbon and clean the air. You are making a floor model air scrubber. If you use this method, be sure to replace the activated carbon regularly. Replace it about once every month or so. It stops doing its job after about a month.

If you read the safety data sheet that comes with epoxy resin it states that resin should not be mixed or used near food prep areas. The resin off-gasses. If using it in the kitchen, the resin will off-gas into the food prep station and into boxes and bags of food. The kitchen ends up being an ideal place to do resin because of the very available vent above the stove. Which makes it tempting to use, but don't do it. Just because you can't see or smell the off-gassing that happens, it doesn't mean it isn't happening. It is best to do your resin work away from food prep areas.

The garage is great, if you have one. A small bedroom, set up as described above, will also work. A shed or shop works. You can resin outdoors and have natures ventilation. Outdoors provides you with leaves, dust and debris. If you work outdoors you will need a large box to cover your resin to keep debris out. You will also need to work on low wind days to avoid excess dust when you work. If you work on a covered patio, you still need to cover your resin art to avoid debris from landing on it.

Have a fire extinguisher on hand. Resin may be flammable. You will be torching the resin to remove bubbles. A fire extinguisher is a must. Always use a face mask. A full-face respirator is best. Wear safety glasses or goggles. Even if you are using resin that states that it is safe to use, and has no VOCs (volatile organic compounds), you are torching it. It's best not to breath in those fumes. The goggles and gloves are for your skin and eyes. In fact, you should cover yourself with long sleeves. Resin will cause burns if left on the skin. Even if you clean up thoroughly you may miss a spot from time to time. But if you cover up, there is less chance of resin burns, because you are keeping it off of your skin. Wear Nitrile or chemical resistant gloves.

Always follow the manufacturer's directions on all products you are using. Be aware of the toxicity of the pigments, powders, resins and mediums you are using. Many of the pigments used in art carry some toxicity. Those pigments are even more toxic when in powdered form. For this reason, gloves and face mask are important tools in the art studio, and not just for resin.

SURFACE SAFETY

Resin will cure to anything it lands on. It's important to cover your work area well. Cover surfaces with heavy duty plastic. Don't forget the floor. An option is 2mm or 3mm plastic sheeting from the hardware store. Use it on the floor and tape it down to avoid tripping. I have found 5mm plastic sheets in the craft section at big box department stores work well for covering the floor. These lay very flat and generally don't require taping down.

For the table use 2mm or 3mm plastic sheeting. In a pinch parchment paper can be used. It works well but, generally requires layering as it isn't wide enough to cover the area. Resin has a tendency flow between the layers. I used my dining room table for years as a surface for resin art. Back then I used parchment paper to cover my surface. It works for providing a surface that allows resin to be peeled from. It does not protect your table. When I finally made myself an art studio, I moved my dining table in there. It is a permanent art table now. Cover all surfaces with plastic, even if you plan to never use the surface for anything other than resin. Resin builds up over time and takes away the levelness of the surface. Plastic sheeting is easier to change than a table. It costs just a few dollars at the hardware store.

Respirator, Goggles, Face Mask, Nitrile Gloves, Baby Wipes, Alcohol, Paper Towels.

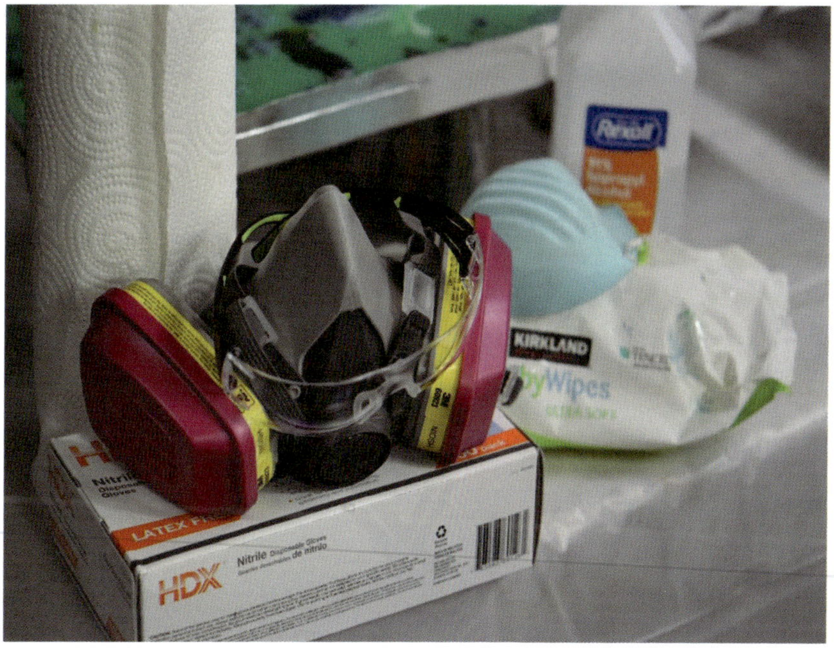

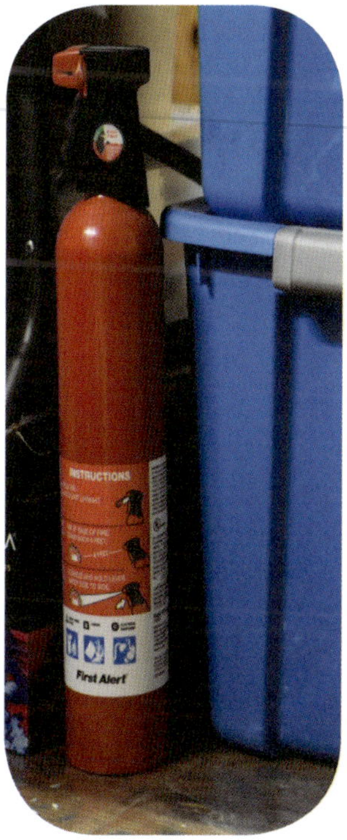

Fire extinguisher in the resin studio

SANDING SAFETY

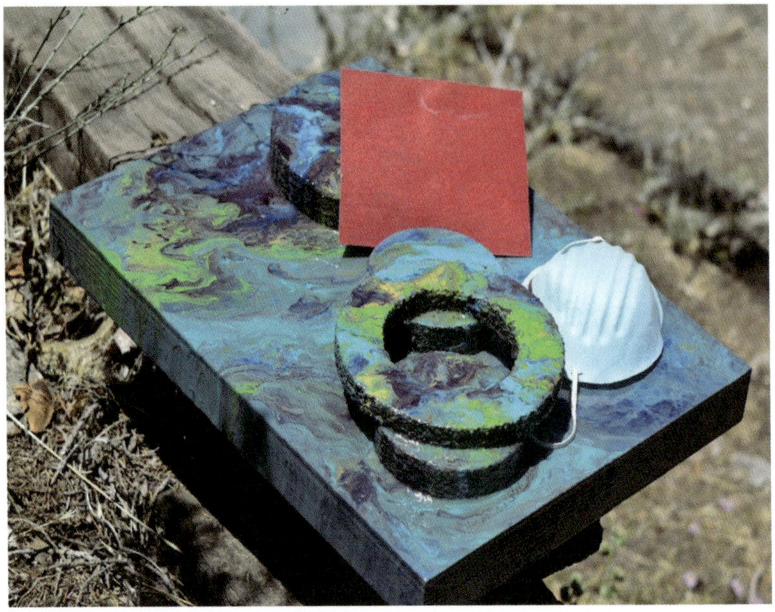

Getting ready to sand.

Caution

When sanding or scraping resin, wear a mask. A full-face respirator is best. Resin dust can cause respiratory irritation. Repeated sanding of resin without a mask can cause long term health problems. Anytime you are working with these techniques practice safety. Wear a mask, gloves and goggles. Sanding resin is best done outdoors.

FIRE SAFETY

It is important to always have a fire extinguisher close by. You are going to be working with chemicals and a torch or other heat source. Resin can become flammable when overheated. Alcohol is flammable. A fire extinguisher is a great safety precaution. I keep 2 of them in my studio.

I also keep a large box of salt near my art table. Once, when torching resin in a jewelry bezel, I caught the parchment paper on fire, that the bezel was laying on. I didn't want to ruin the jewelry with a fire extinguisher, but I didn't want to burn the house down either. I poured salt on the fire and it took care of it. I saved the jewelry and put out the fire. I changed the setup of my station so the ends of the paper would not be so easy to catch on fire. I tucked the paper under the tray I was using.

If I have a fire in the studio I want to have something I can grab quickly to toss on the fire. I want to have options. I have salt and I have a fire extinguisher. If a fire happens, I am prepared. A fire extinguisher is a must. Regularly check the date on your fire extinguisher, and replace it when expired.

HEALTH & SAFETY

While resin is said to be fairly safe when used properly, it can cause health problems if safety isn't practiced. I'm an artist, not a doctor. I don't have the expertise or training to give medical advice. The following information is meant to inform not diagnose or treat. Please see your doctor if you have concerns or questions. It is possible that severe medical problems can result from exposure to some types of epoxy resin fumes in an enclosed area. Do not use any type of epoxy resin in an enclosed room. Open a window or create air flow in the space. I was at an art fair and was approached by a person who shared a story of her mother who died from COPD. She said that her mother was a resin artist and learned that the art caused her COPD. Lung disease or COPD is even more likely to develop when sanding without a mask.

I belong to several resin art groups and there are numerous stories of people developing allergies to resin. Allergies to resin lead to rashes and breathing difficulties. Allergies can develop from exposure to fumes but are more likely with skin contact. If you have never had an allergic reaction to resin before, it doesn't mean you can't develop allergies to it. You are more likely to develop allergies when exposed to larger amounts in enclosed areas. This is another reason it is important to work in a well-ventilated area and to cover up when you work.

Choosing a resin that is low or no VOCs (volatile organic compounds) will lessen the health risks. Working in a well-ventilated area is still necessary. Use of a mask & nitrile gloves are also necessary. Just because a resin is low odor doesn't mean that it's safe to breathe in. More on VOCS in the epoxy resin section.

Resin burns and allergies are not the same. Allergies are inflammatory reactions from within the body to resin. Resin burns are a result of resin being left on the skin and curing in. I had a resin burn early in my resin art career. I didn't realize that I had gotten resin on my arm and after some time the area started itching. I realized it was due to resin and cleaned the area well but the damage had been done. By the next day it was a burn. It took weeks to heal. If you have been working with resin and a spot on your skin starts to really itch assume you have left some resin on your skin. Clean it well. See the section on cleaning skin. Then apply an antibiotic ointment or at least some lotion. If it turns into an actual burn, see your doctor. I still love resin even after the resin burn. I am more mindful now of cleaning up after I work. I practice safety with my resin work.

RESIN & PETS

It's best to keep all pets away from your resin area. Too many things can go wrong with pets in your resin studio. Plus, their fur tends to get into the resin art. I have heard stories of cats stepping in resin pieces and getting it on their paws. Dogs knocking off resin work from the table and getting it in their fur. Pet birds should be removed from the area where resin is used. Resin and torching of resin are not safe for pet birds to breathe in.

I have an area with ventilation and a purifier. I have a mask but my animals do not. I admit I have worked with my dogs in the room. But when you know better you do better. I now do my resin work in my garage. No animals allowed. Remember, if resin cures into your skin and causes burns it can cure into your pet's skin and cause burns. If by chance your dog or cat gets resin on them, grab some dish soap and slather it on. It will neutralize the resin enough to stop the curing and save your pets skin. A trip to the vet is best at that point. If your pet is like mine and is capable of opening doors, simply closing the door is not enough. You may need to invest in a lock on your art room. I have a baby gate across the door frame and the pets leave it alone.

SECTION 2
SKIN SAFETY AND CARE

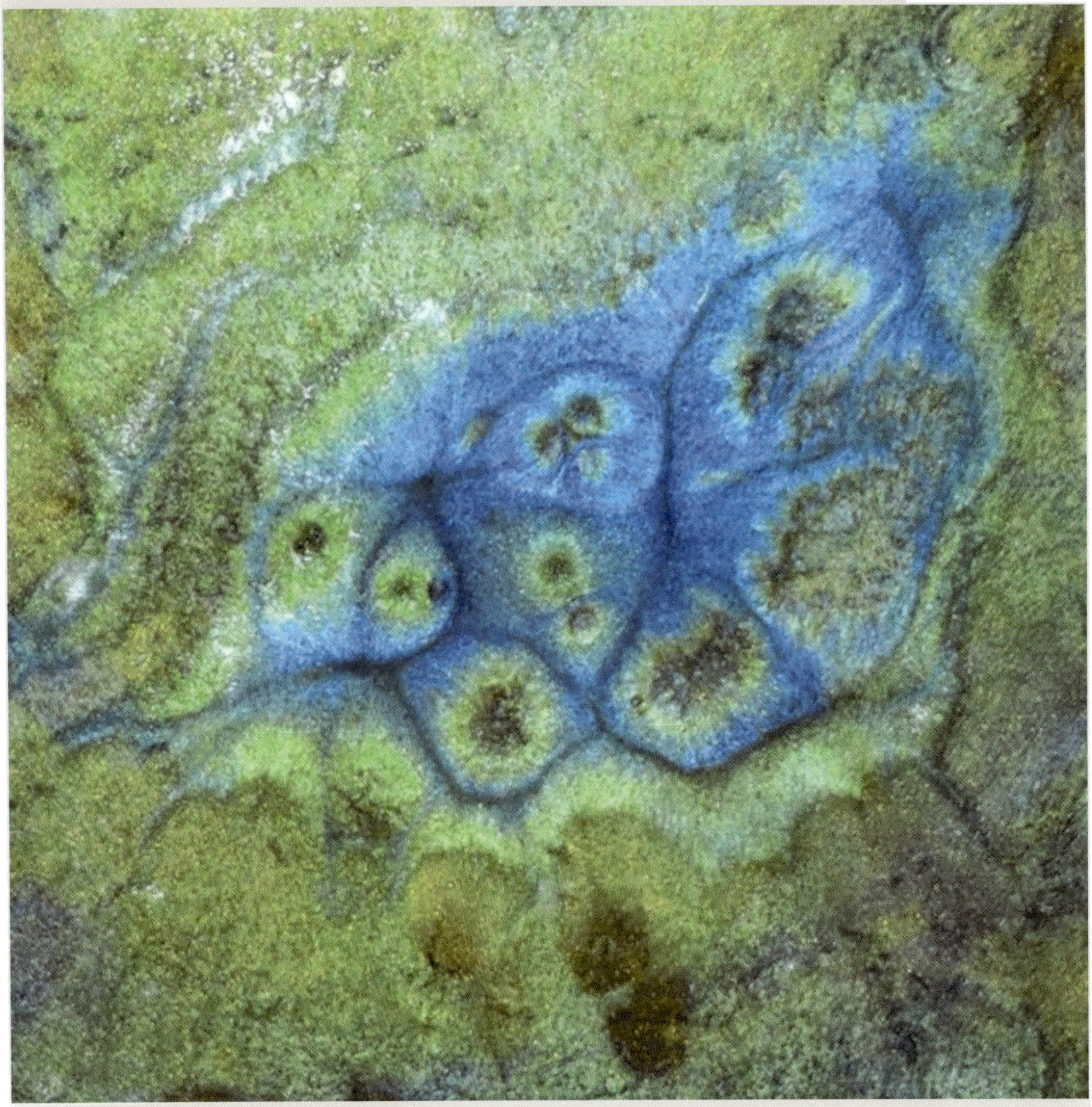

SHADOW LIGHTS
Mica & Pigments on Cradled Wood Panel
10"x10" (25cmx25cm)

RESIN & SKIN

Cover your entire body when working in resin. I use a long sleeve lab coat. A vinyl apron or vinyl lab coat is also a great option. Use Nitrile gloves or chemical resistant gloves for protecting your hands. Resin cures as plastic. It does this to any surface it's allowed to cure to. If it gets on the skin, it will try to cure into it. Imagine a substance trying to bond to your skin, permanently, and you get the idea of how much damage it can do if left on. When the skin is left uncovered it is easy to drop or drip resin onto it.

If you have long hair, put it up when working with resin. You want to avoid your hair dropping down in the resin. Avoid giving yourself a reason to brush your hair out of your face and ending up with resin on your face. Even though I always put my hair up in a ponytail, I ended up with my hair in the resin once. My ponytail dropped right into a painting I was working on, when I reached to pick something up from the floor. I didn't realize it until the next day, requiring a trip to the salon for a haircut. I could have used dish soap to get out the dried resin, but that would have taken hours and the hair would have been damaged anyway. I opted to get a haircut instead. My stylist had a good laugh.

When cleaning up, pay attention to your wrist, that's where you grab the gloves to remove them. You are likely to get some resin there and not notice. Clean any exposed areas of skin, even if you don't think resin got on to those areas.

Clean up with 91% isopropyl alcohol poured on a baby wipe. Wipe down your skin. Then coat the area with grease fighting dish soap. Any kind of dish soap will work, but I find that grease fighting dish soap works best. Use the soap straight from the bottle, without adding water. Rub the soap into the area well. Then add a little water and lather. Rinse well. Use lotion, after clean-up, to further neutralize any remaining resin.

This cleaning technique is the way that I do my clean up. After experimenting with many cleaning methods, this is what I developed. It works so well that I now use it for cleaning up after oil painting and acrylic painting as well. But, if you are sensitive to alcohol you might consider a different method.

Another method is to use vegetable oil rubbed onto the skin followed by dish soap. To use vegetable oil, massage it onto the skin for several minutes. Wipe off as much as possible with paper towels. Lather up with soap and water and rinse. Check your skin and if it still feels sticky, repeat the process.

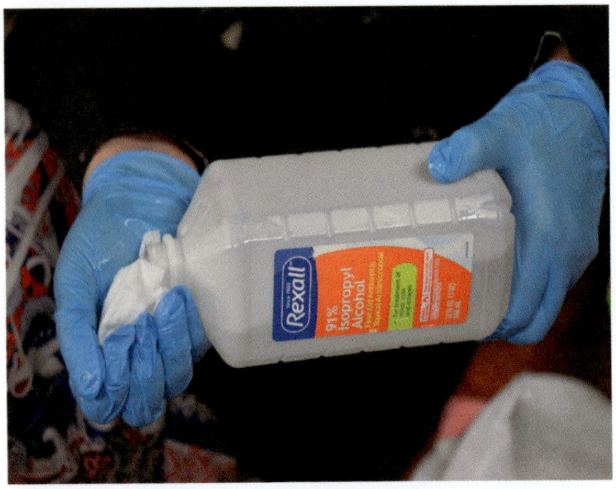

Pour 91% alcohol on a baby wipe. Keep gloves on for cleaning tools. Wipe down all areas of skin that may have been exposed to epoxy resin.

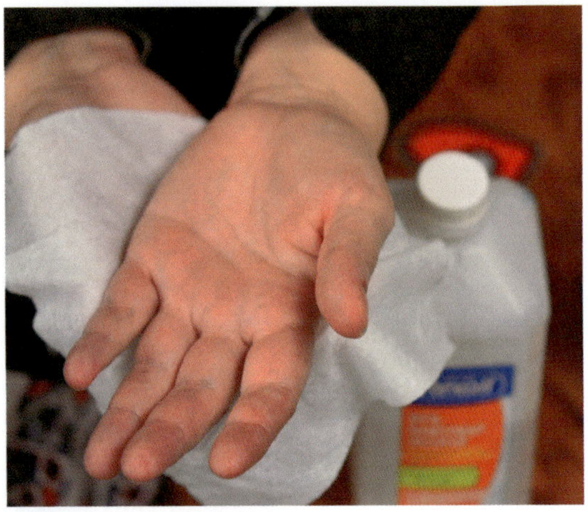

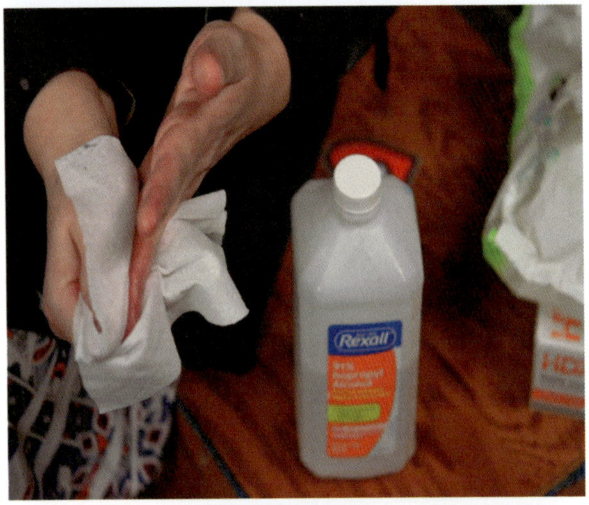

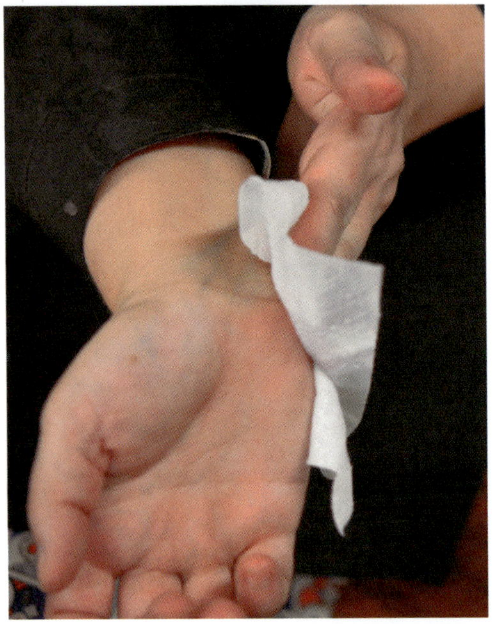

Remove gloves & clean skin. Be sure to wipe down both wrists. This is the area most likely to have resin on it from taking off gloves.

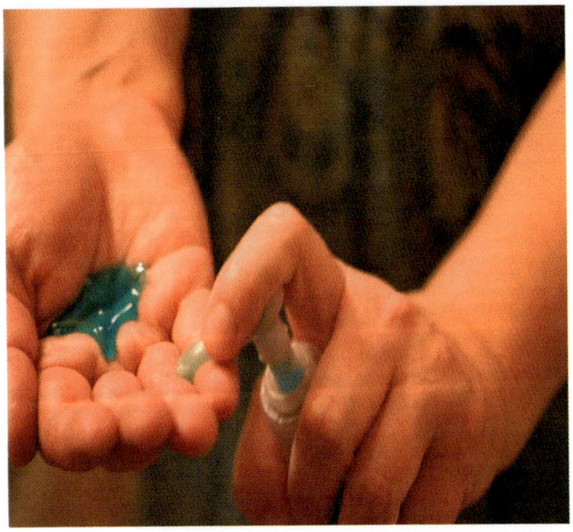

After cleaning with alcohol and baby wipes, use Dawn dish soap. Slather it on the skin without water.

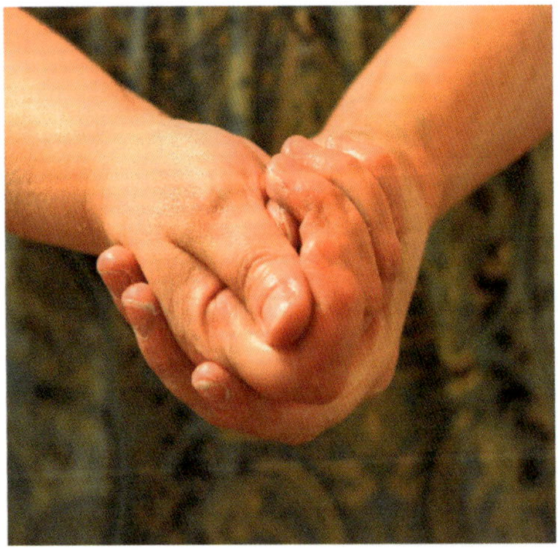

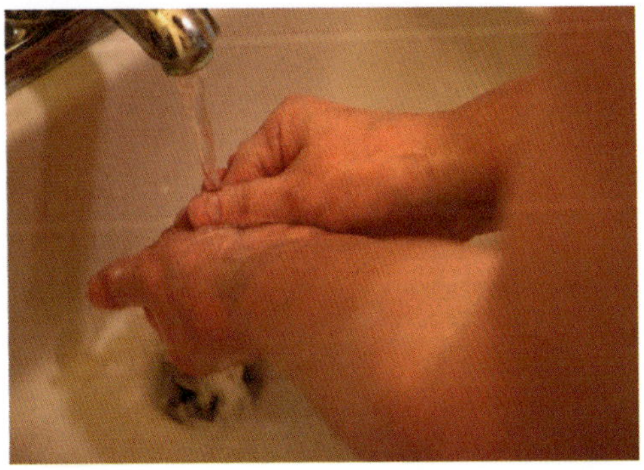

Rinse Well.

SAFETY RE-CAP

Work in a well-ventilated area.

Have an air purifier in the studio.

Wear a face mask or full-face respirator.

Never sand resin without a mask.

Cover all surfaces with plastic sheeting.

Have a fire extinguisher nearby.

Keep 91% isopropyl alcohol, baby wipes nearby for clean-up.

Never pour resin or hardener down any household drain.

Never place liquid resin in the trash. Allow it to cure first.

No pets in resin studio.

Alcohol is flammable.

Resin will smoke when overheated & is flammable.

Absorb large spills of resin with sand NOT sawdust.

Wear gloves – Nitrile or chemical resistant.

Cover your whole body. Long sleeves or lab coat.

Put long hair in a ponytail.

Clean-up with alcohol & baby wipes, followed by dish soap.

Pay attention to the wrists.

Clean-up even if you have not gotten resin on the skin.

Now for the fun stuff!

SECTION 3
WHAT CAN YOU DO WITH RESIN

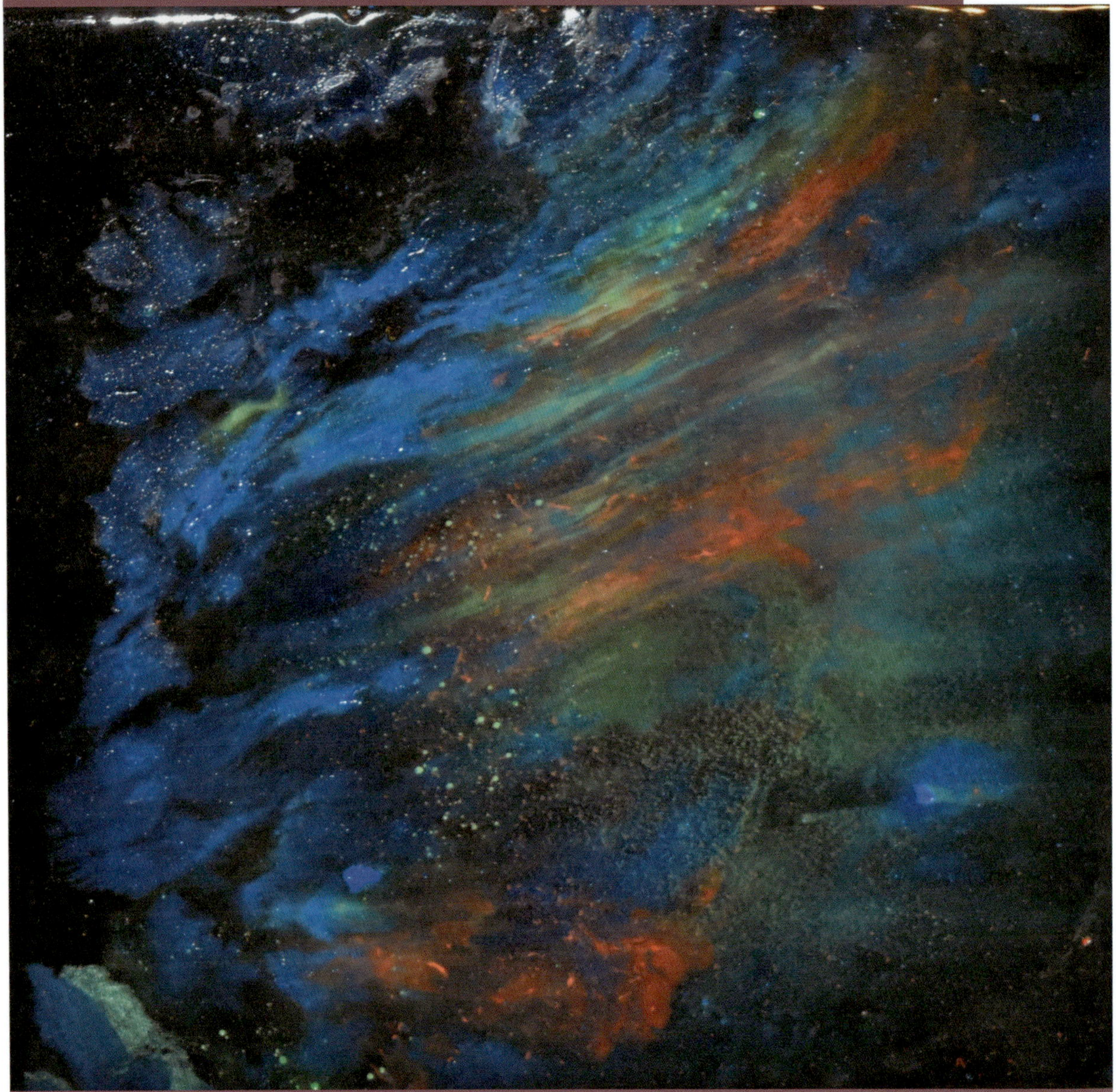

COMING OUT OF THE DARK
Resin, Pigments, Mica & Glow Powder on Cradled Wood Panel
12"x12" (31cmx31cm)

One of my favorite things to do is to visit thrift shops to look for ideas in art. I search for things to re-purpose for resin art. Removing the mechanisms from nonworking clocks creates a great base for resin art. Wood picture frames can be re-purposed by adding a piece of MDF or pine board to create a wood canvas or panel for resin art. Metal parts and frames can be used and re-purposed in resin art. I look for bits and pieces that I can re-purpose into dimensional resin art.

A visit to the craft or hobby store is great for ideas on creating dimensional art. Styrofoam works great for this and can be purchased in varying shapes and sizes at craft stores. I re-purpose Styrofoam and cardboard from shipping boxes for use in dimensional art. I save paper towels that I have used to wipe paintbrushes for use in dimensional art.

The easiest surface to work on is wood panel. Wood gesso panels can be purchased at art stores and some craft stores. Resin can be applied to linen or cotton canvas but requires supporting at the back so that it doesn't sag in the middle with the weight of the resin. Wood table rounds from hardware stores make a great substrate for resin. Purchasing MDF board or sheets of oak or other hardwood from the hardware store is another option for substrates for resin work. When using bare wood priming is suggested as excessive bubbles will result in resin on bare wood. More on this in preparing your canvas.

The possibilities are endless on what you can do with resin. Once you have the basics on how to work with epoxy resin, the rest is all about creativity. It can be used to enhance artwork you have completed; or use it as the medium for making art. You may want to take some ashes and create a memorial in a piece of jewelry. Or embed bees and bugs if that is your thing. Here is a list of ideas, and you can create your own list as you work with resin:

RESIN IDEAS

- Clear coat a finished acrylic painting.
- Clear coat a finished oil painting.
- Clear coat a finished encaustic painting.
- Clear coat a finished watercolor painting.
- Clear coat a chalk pastel. Must use a fixative before resin.
- Clear coat an oil pastel.
- Glow in the dark art.
- Clear coat a photo.
- Clear coat a drawing. Must use a fixative before resin.
- Cover a rose or other dried flower in resin.
- Cover fabric in resin (concert t-shirt, loved one's favorite tie).
- Create a geode painting.
- Preserve objects in resin (cookies, candies, flowers, butterflies, bugs, ashes).
- Clear coat a puzzle.
- Make resin jewelry.
- Make a table by covering wood or another surface in resin.
- Give old furniture new life with a modern resin finish.
- Give an old counter top an update with a resin finish.
- Create clocks out of old records.
- Create a dimensional painting by pouring layers of resin with effects in between.
- Create a beach or ocean scene painting using real sand.
- Create abstract art using pigments, mica, acrylic paint, oil paint, enamel paint.
- Use resin on almost any surface including canvas, wood, glass, metal, concrete, or cardboard. I prefer to work on cradled wood panels. It's much more of a dependable surface to work with.
- Take a trip to a thrift shop and look for things to resin on. Old non-working clocks work great. Look for anything that is wood and can be turned into a canvas.

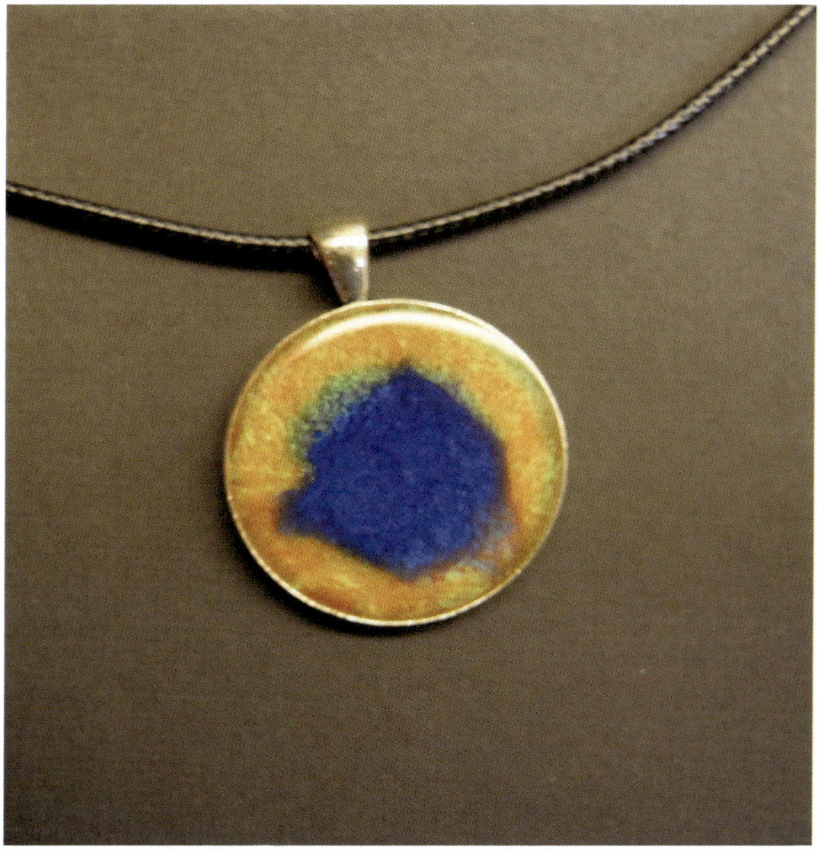

Resin & Mica
Pendant Necklace

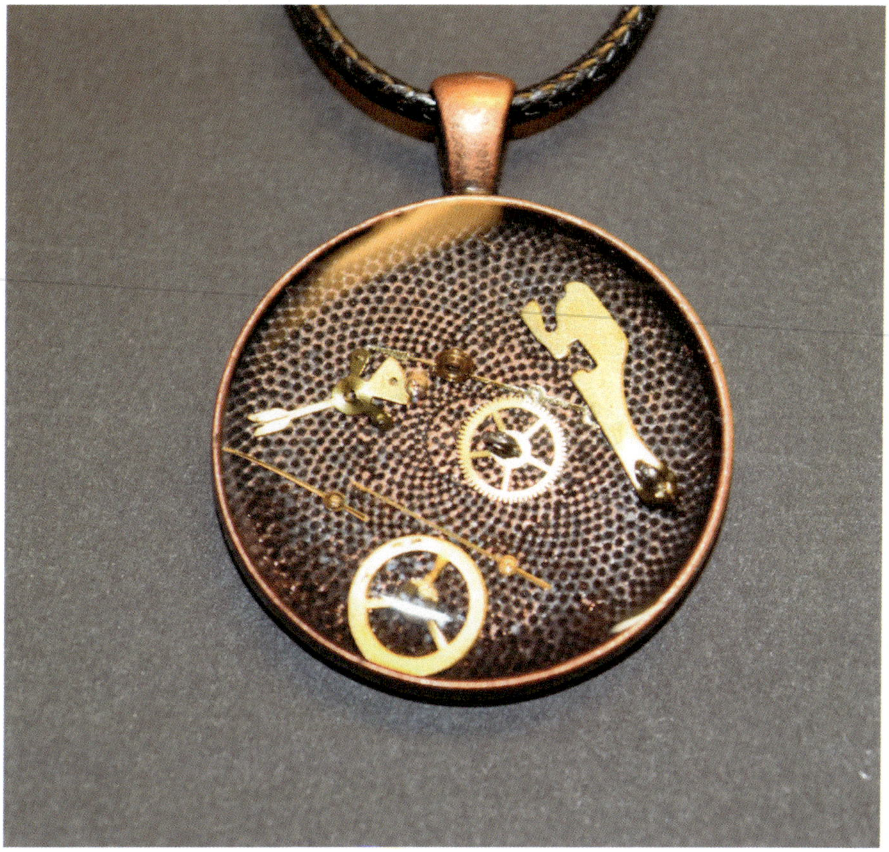

Resin & Watch Parts
Necklace Pendant

SECTION 4
STUDIO SET UP

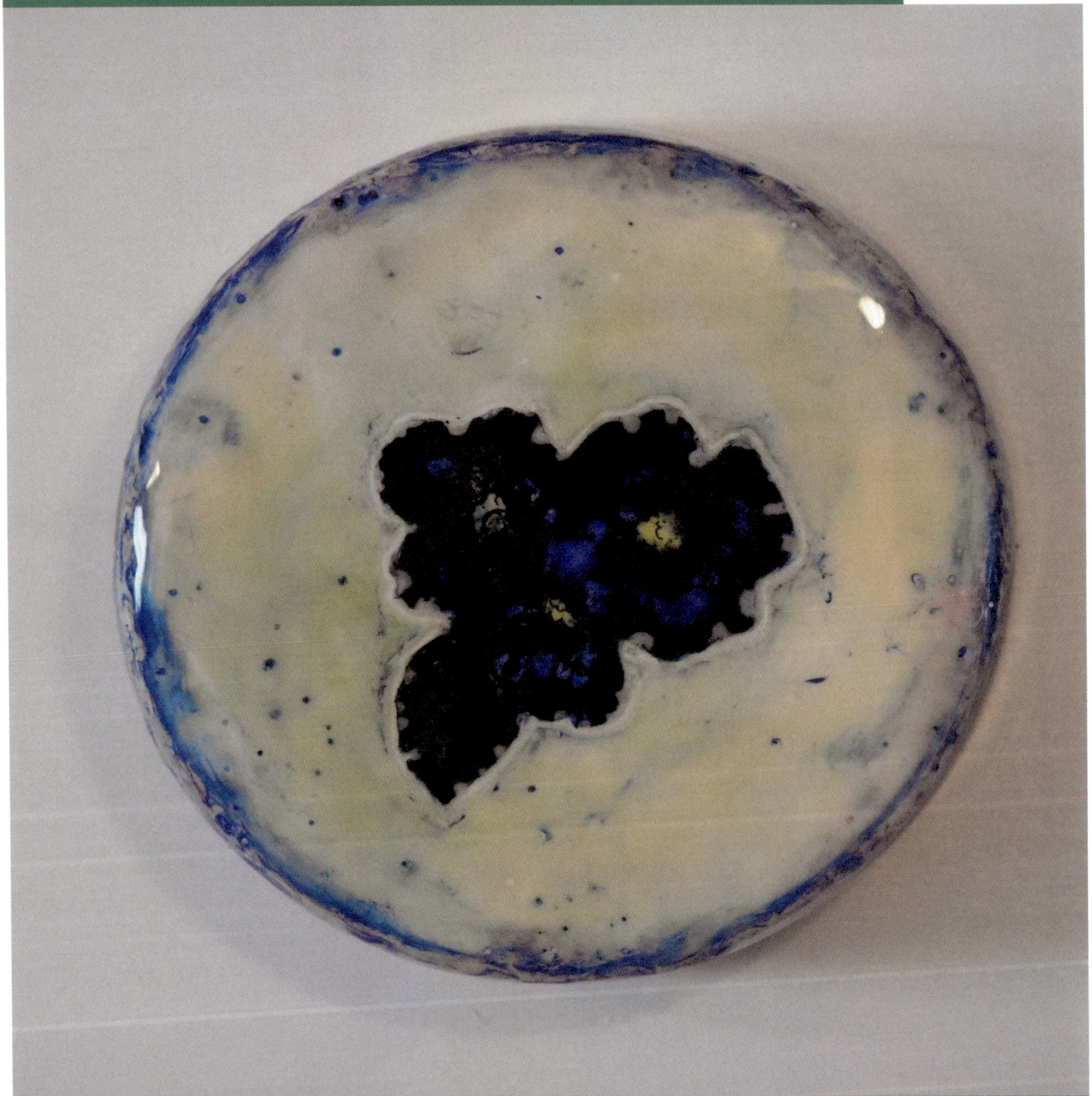

BLUE
Resin Coated Encaustic Painting on Wood Bowl
6"x6" (15cmx15cm)

MATERIALS LIST

- Epoxy resin - There are many brands of resin. Choose one that is right for your project.
- Pigments, paints, inks, and things to color your resin – See Section on coloring resin.
- 91% Isopropyl alcohol.
- Baby wipes.
- Mixing cups - silicone cups, hardware store paint mixing cups, recycled containers for mixing paint. Note: avoid wax coated cups.
- Stir sticks - wooden craft sticks, plastic rulers, coffee stirrers, gelato spoons, chopsticks.
- Extra cups for mixing resin with paints or pigments – Small plastic drinking cups, disposable condiment cups.
- HVAC tape (aluminum tape) or Tuck tape (sheathing tape).
- Large plastic cups & small plastic cups.
- Canvas or painting substrate - wood board or cradled wood panel is best but you can resin on linen canvas.
- Butane or propane torch - or a heat gun.
- 91% isopropyl alcohol in a spray bottle. Use to spray onto your surface for effects, and it can pop bubbles in resin.
- Parchment paper – Use this for mixing pigments and paints before adding them to larger resin batches. Use it under your resin paintings to avoid drips on your surface. Wax paper works too.
- Large plastic bin/storage type container for placing on top of resin to keep dust out of art.
- Plastic sheeting - 3mm from paint section of hardware store.
- Old clothes to wear that you don't mind ruining.
- Lab coat or vinyl apron to wear over clothes.
- Safety glasses or goggles.
- Face mask or respirator.
- Nitrile gloves – Nitrile is chemical resistant. Get a big box of gloves. You will use lots of them.
- Cardboard - Use pieces of cardboard or foam to place in the back of a linen or cotton canvas to prevent sagging in the middle.
- A timer or clock for keeping track of mixing and curing of resin.
- Long tweezers for removing particles from resin.
- Primer for bare substrates - I use Kilz from the hardware store, Gesso from the art store and if I am out of primer I use acrylic white or black paint as a primer.

Plastic covered table. Caddies with tools for resin. Plastic mixing cups. I use this studio for oil and acrylic painting as well. I have an air purifier in the room. The doors and windows open for ventilation. Pouring resin in a garage that opens to the outside is also a great option.

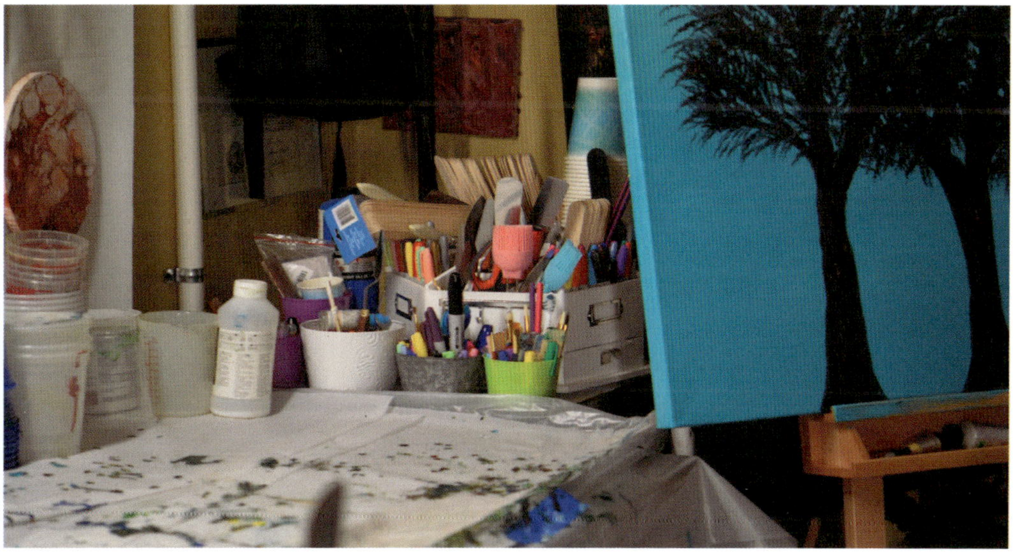

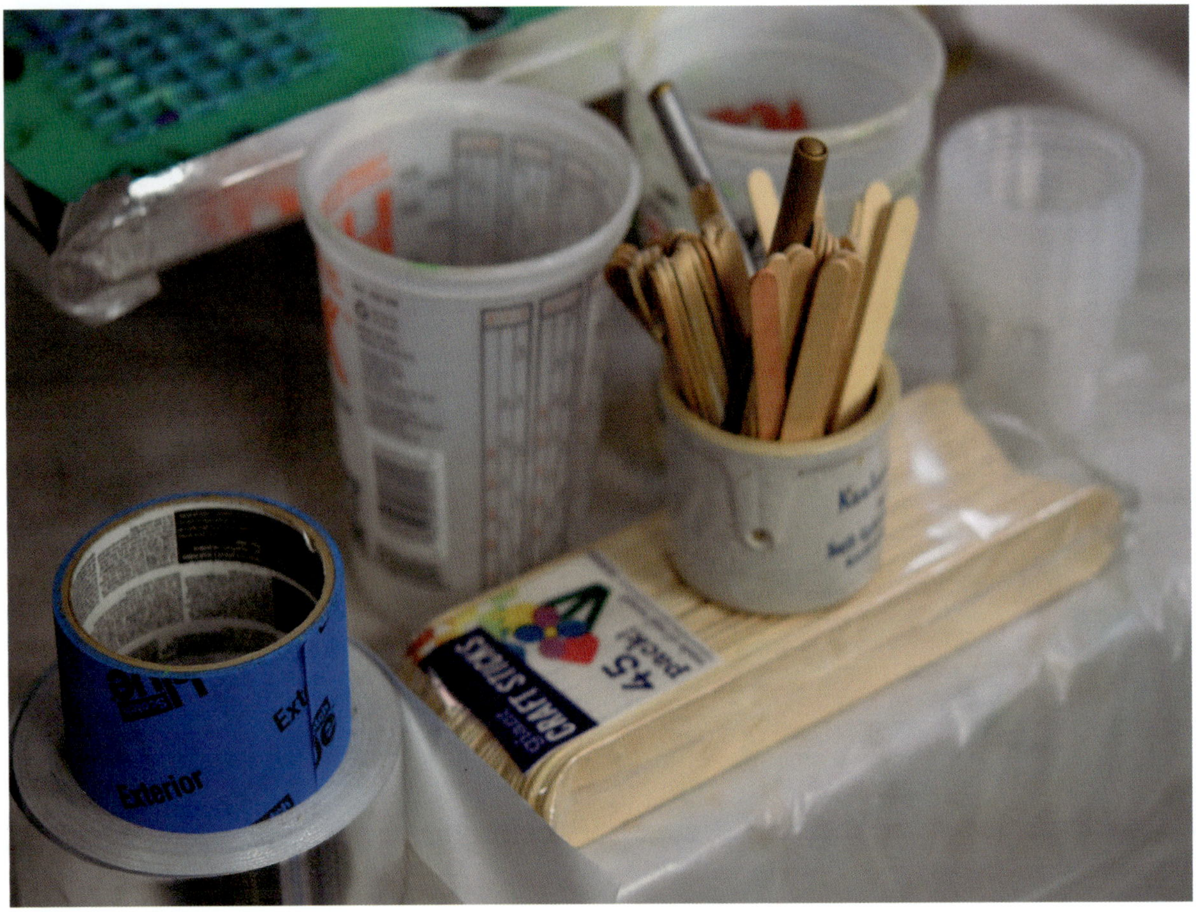

HVAC Tape, Masking Tape, Giant Craft Sticks, Craft Sticks, Paint Mixing Cups, Plastic Dessert Cups.

When working with epoxy resin it's important that everything be covered with plastic. Since resin will cure to almost any surface, floors and tables should be covered. If you are working in a space that you need to preserve the integrity of the walls, it's a good idea to line them with plastic as well. Rolls of 2mm or 3mm plastic can be found in any hardware store. This kind of plastic is a painting supply. It will be found in the paint supply section. To cover the walls, begin at the ceiling and either staple the plastic on using staple gun; or use thumbtacks. I use thumbtacks. Allow the plastic to fall to the floor. Trim the plastic at the floor, to fit the size needed, and tack it at the base or floor. Cover the floor in the same plastic or purchase 5mm or thicker plastic. A thicker plastic will not move or be kicked up from the floor.

Cover the work table in plastic. You may have a dedicated resin table or a plastic bin that you use for resin art, but it's still important to cover it in plastic. Cover the surface unless cured resin peels away from the surface to be worked on. Cured resin on a work surface will cause it to be uneven over time. A level work surface is necessary in resin art. Plastic sheeting is easy to replace. Check the table for levelness before beginning to work with resin.

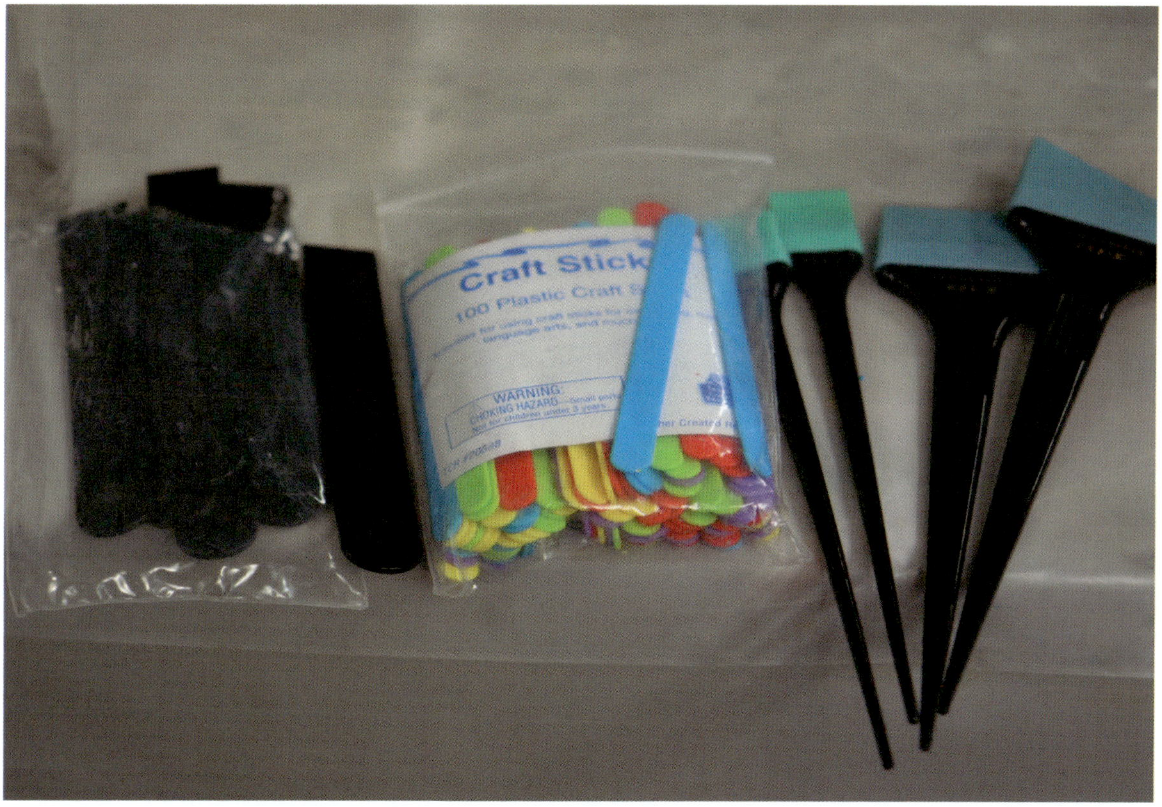

Plastic Epoxy Mixing Sticks, Plastic Craft Sticks, Silicone Hair Dye Tools. Resin can be wiped from these tools and reused, or allowed to cure to the tools and peeled away.

TIP

I use plastic kennel liners as a base for my resin art. Find them in pet stores. It cost about $50.00 depending on the size. They can be purchased in very large sizes. They are made of very thick plastic. I bought one the size of my table. They work great for all kinds of painting mediums. I drape 3mm plastic sheeting around it and now I have a tub for doing resin art. The resin will stay in the tub. No resin run off. The plastic sheeting allows for easy clean up between resin projects. It's easier to change the sheeting than it is to change the kennel liner.

SECTION 5
COLORANTS

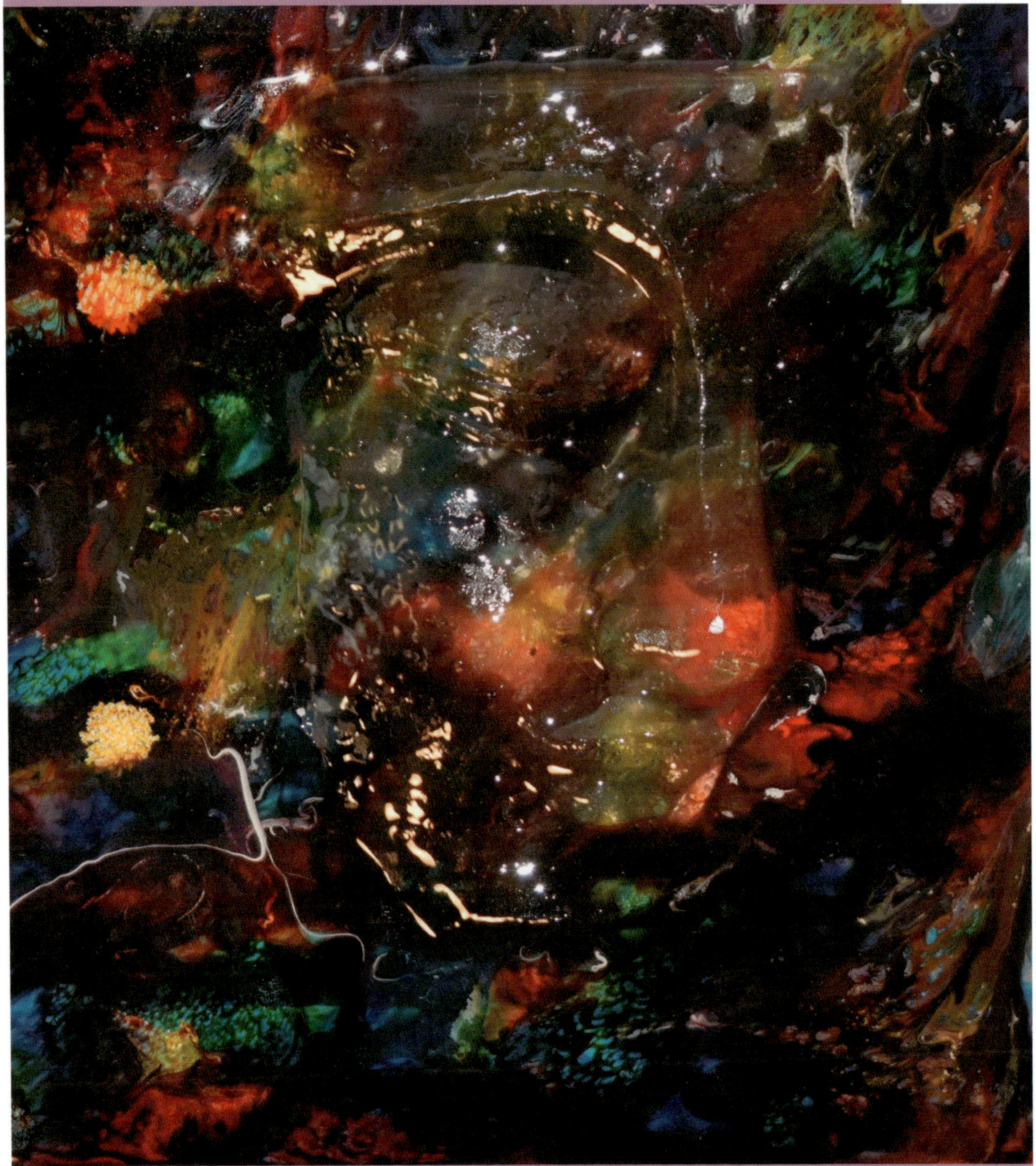

CHIONE
Molded Resin, Resin & Alcohol Ink on Cradled Wood Panel
9"x12" (23cmx31cm

WHAT CAN YOU USE TO COLOR YOUR RESIN?

The answer may surprise you. You can use so many things to color resin. In fact, I encourage you to look at my list and try them; and then get creative to see what you can come up with to color your resin. Always be safe. Think about what you are breathing in, torching etc. But be creative. Try it. See if it works.

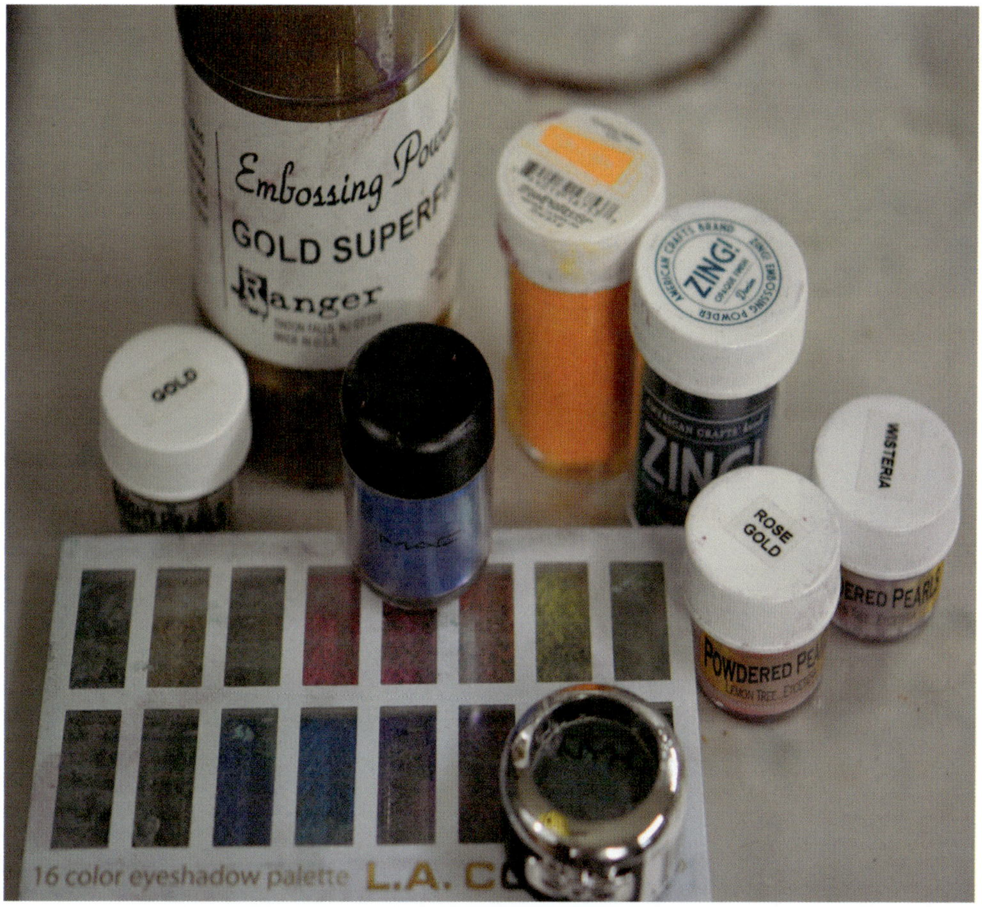

Eyeshadow, Embossing powder, and Flocking powder are unusual choices for resin but work really well.

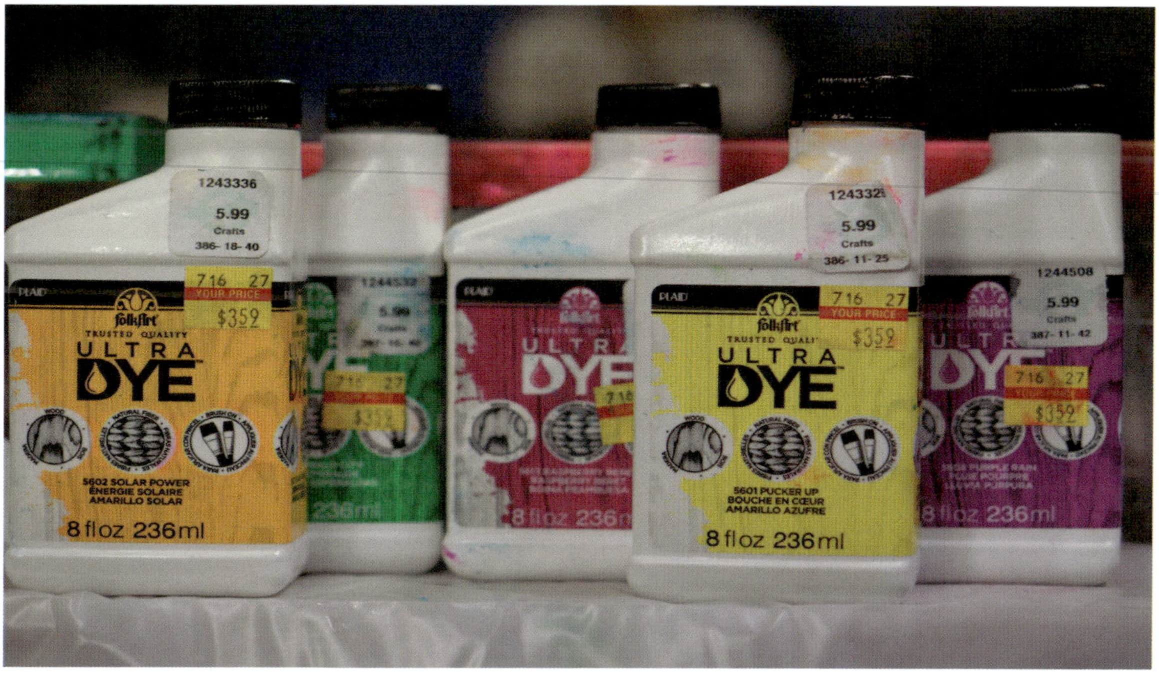

Craft Dye works great in resin art. It only takes a little to color a large batch.

RESIN COLORANTS LIST

- Powder pigments.
- Resin tints – these are tints made by resin manufacturers specifically for resin.
- Dyes (Alumilite dye, hair dye, fabric dye) Art and craft stores carry many different brands and types of dyes for art. A little goes a long way.
- Acrylic paint (10% paint 90% resin).
- Spray paint (Spray into a cup then mix into resin. Do not spray onto poured resin surface).
- Oil paint (for more details see section 10).
- Mica Powder (Pearl Ex, Perfect Pearls & Art 'N Glow do great things in resin).
- Glow in the dark pigments and paints (Art 'N Glow has great glow powder and glow paint).
- Inks (Copic ink, acrylic ink, India ink, alcohol ink, tattoo ink).
- Cocoa powder.
- Mustard seed powder, turmeric, chili powder.
- Eye shadow and blush (both are mica powders and work great in resin).
- Nail polish.
- Chalk pastels.
- Glitter.

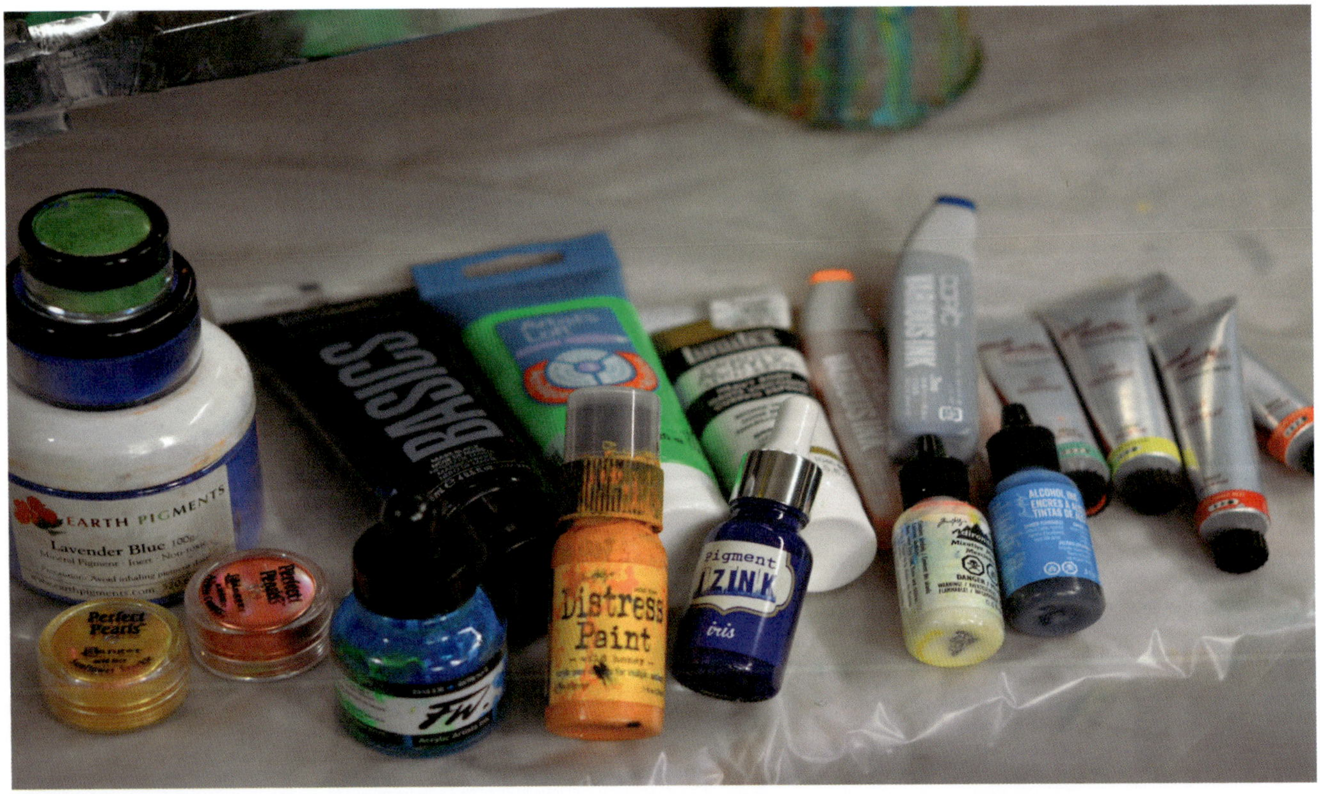

Primary Elements, Pearl Ex, Earth Pigments, Liquitex & Artist's Loft Acrylic Paint, Copic Ink, Mont Marte Oil Paint, Perfect Pearls, Acrylic Ink, Ranger Paint, Pigment Ink, Ranger Alcohol Ink

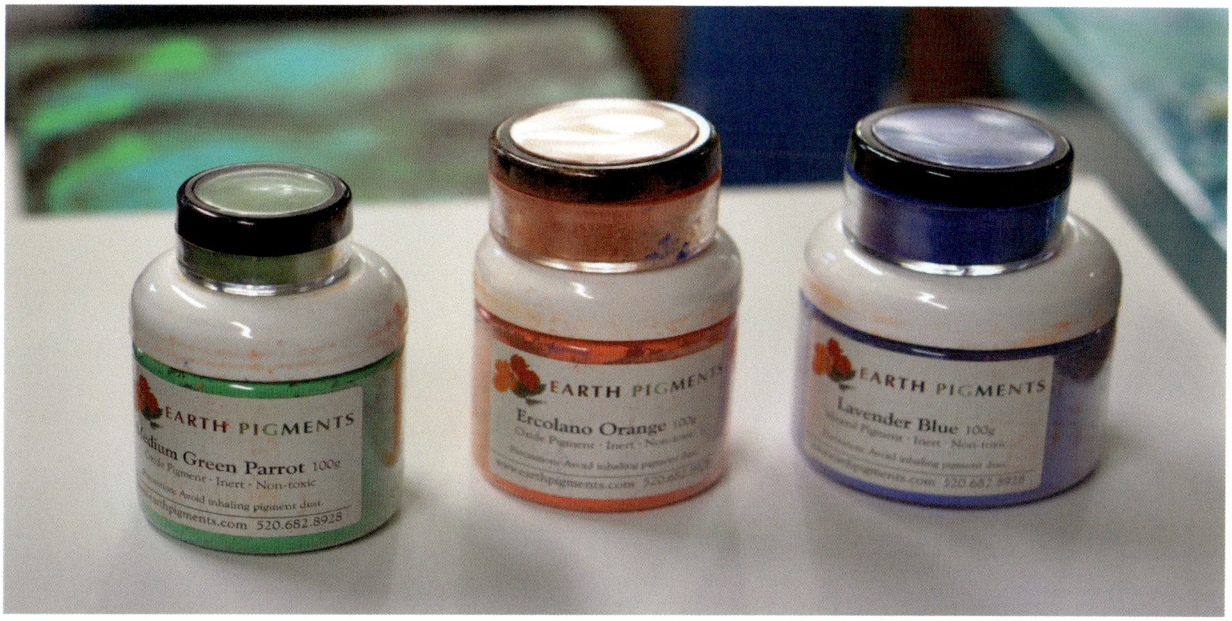

Artist Pigments, Primary Elements Pigments, Pearl Ex Powder

With any art medium it's important to consider the archival needs of your work. Archival means lasting. It means that your color image will not fade or your painting will not crack or peel within a short amount of time. The term archival can be used to describe any medium or technique that is used in art to extend the life of the art. Simply put, it is any effort to preserve a piece of art from the damaging elements of environmental factors. At the very least, that means keeping artwork out of the sun. It should also include sealing your artwork, and allowing mediums to cure properly. While resin is a sealant, it is still important to consider all elements of the art, including the colorants, when deciding on the archival needs of artwork. Painting archivally is necessary for placing art in a gallery.

Artist grade pigments and artist grade paints are archival. Many mica powders are archival. Some are not. Mustard powder and cocoa powder are some of the oldest forms of artist colorants and are probably archival. They may not be accepted by a gallery as archival in modern times. There is much debate on whether or not alcohol inks are archival. Commercial alcohol inks contain acetate and ethanol making them more likely to fade over time. My thoughts are that any color will fade if placed in the sun or in a sunny location. While acids break down pigments overtime, each of the manufacturers of alcohol inks claim they are acid free. Acetate may be the thing that breaks down the pigments in alcohol inks. If you keep all art of out the sun, it is much less likely to fade. It is important to keep all artwork out of the sun, even if you use a resin that has UV stabilizers to resist yellowing.

Craft paints are less archival than artist grade acrylic paints. Hair dye and nail polish are not likely to be archival but will give interesting effects in resin. Glow in the dark paints and pigments will eventually lose their ability to glow. Some last longer than others. Art 'N Glow has great pigments that are very bright and have worked very well for me. Because glow powders and paints lose their ability to glow after about 10 to 20 years (depending on the powder) I want to think about the archival needs of the art. Consider working in acrylic paint or non-glow pigments into the resin glow art, so that when the glow fades the art itself will not fade. I like to use paint or pigment in this kind of art anyway so that the piece is art during the day as well as night.

SECTION 6
EPOXY RESIN

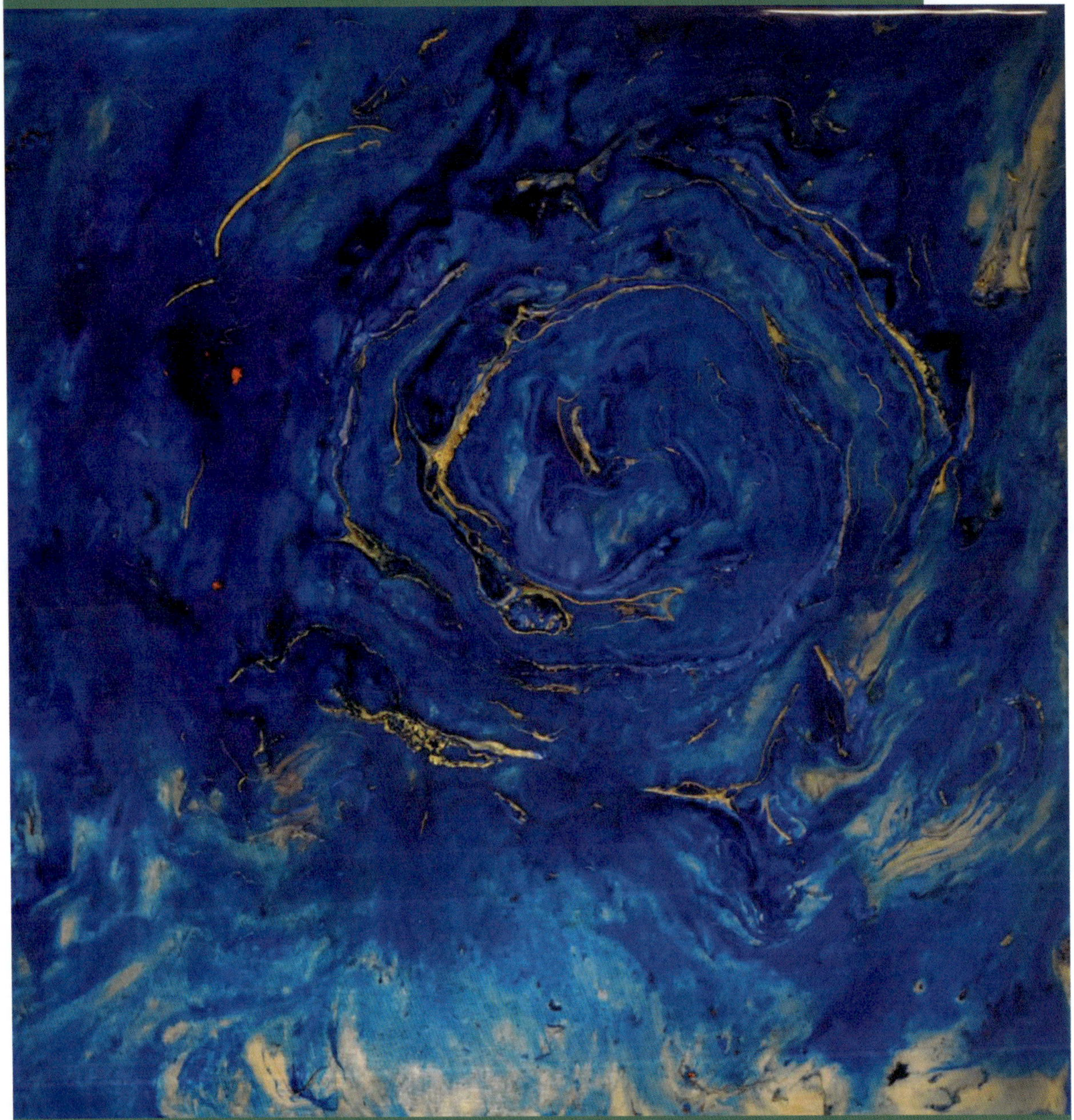

OCEAN WAVE
Resin, Pigments, Ink on Cradled Wood Panel
10"x10" (25cmx25cm)

As more and more artists join the world of resin art, there are more brands of epoxy resin entering the market. I have used many of them in my work. They each have unique properties and characteristics. Some are thin and some are thick. Some yellow and some don't. The ones that resist yellowing claim to have UV stabilizers. This is important when using resin over a white or light background or making light colored resin art. Some cure within 15 minutes of mixing, and some have a work time of 45 minutes. Some are heat resistant to 110 degrees and some claim, a heat resistance of 500 plus degrees.

If you have a specific art project in mind and need to consider the properties of the resin you are using, it's helpful to have a list of questions related to the resin you are considering. Do some research. If needed, contact suppliers with your questions. Be willing to describe the project in order to get help in determining the best resin for the work you are planning.

There are a few things to consider when choosing an epoxy resin. Perhaps the most important is VOCs, or volatile organic compounds. This is for your health and safety. This is about vapor pressure and molecules entering the air at a specific boiling or heat point. Choose a low, or preferably, no VOC epoxy resin. You will be torching and heating. Even though you will wear a mask, the less organic molecules in the air you breathe the better for your health. Do everything you can to ensure the safety of your health. Next is UV stabilizers. A resin that states it has UV or ultra violet stabilization will resist yellowing.

When choosing a resin for painting on canvas, or creating art, it's important to consider the work time. Work time in resin terms is the amount of time that the resin moves and flows before setting up. The time is calculated from mixing to setting up. From the moment the resin and hardener are stirred together, the curing clock begins. This is the beginning of work time. The resin will become sticky and stringy when it is setting up, or curing. The work time is at an end at this stage. When the resin is sticky and stringy it is difficult to work with. Unless the plan is to use the sticky stage for the art. It no longer moves and flows. It sticks to everything it touches. If it is used at this stage, work quickly. It will be unworkable in minutes. The work time of resin varies from brand to brand. Have a clock or timer nearby to help you to stay on track with the project. It is during the work time that the resin is used to create abstract movement on the canvas. The work time is important to consider when removing tape from the canvas. Even though the resin is sticky, it will ooze down the sides of the canvas. Leave the tape on the sides of a canvas if a stiff edge is desired. Remove the tape after the resin has begun to set up if rounded edges are desired.

The brand of resin used will determine the depth of the pour that can be achieved with the resin. When pouring onto a canvas that allows the resin to fall off the sides, the resin will self-level and depth is not a problem. However, if you are taping the sides and creating a dam, be aware of how deep the resin can be poured on the surface of the canvas. The deeper the pour, the more likely the resin is to heat up and cure fast. This can create problems with the surface. The resin can shrink and crack in areas. Check the information data sheet that comes with the resin or contact the manufacture to find out if there are limits to the depth that can be poured. When pouring deep, layers may be required. Keep a single layer no more than a 1/4 inch in depth between layers. Small layers done in many pours will provide depth without compromising surface strength. Another layer can be poured 5 to 8 hours after the first pour. Or let it cure completely and do a light sand before pouring the second layer.

The resin part of epoxy resin has a higher viscosity than the hardener. That means that it is thicker than the hardener. This is important as it pertains to mixing. If the package directions state that mixing should happen by weight rather than by volume, it will be important to stick to that. I have always mixed by volume. I use epoxy resins that have a 1to1 by volume mixing ratio. You may also weigh your resin for 1to1 mixing, but I find that mixing by volume is much easier. See section on mixing resin for the process I use.

Always store resin and hardener at room temperatures. Avoid storing in cold or freezing temperatures. Doing so can result in crystallization of the resin and yellowing or amberization of the hardener. Always mix and use resin in 75 degrees Fahrenheit, or above, conditions.

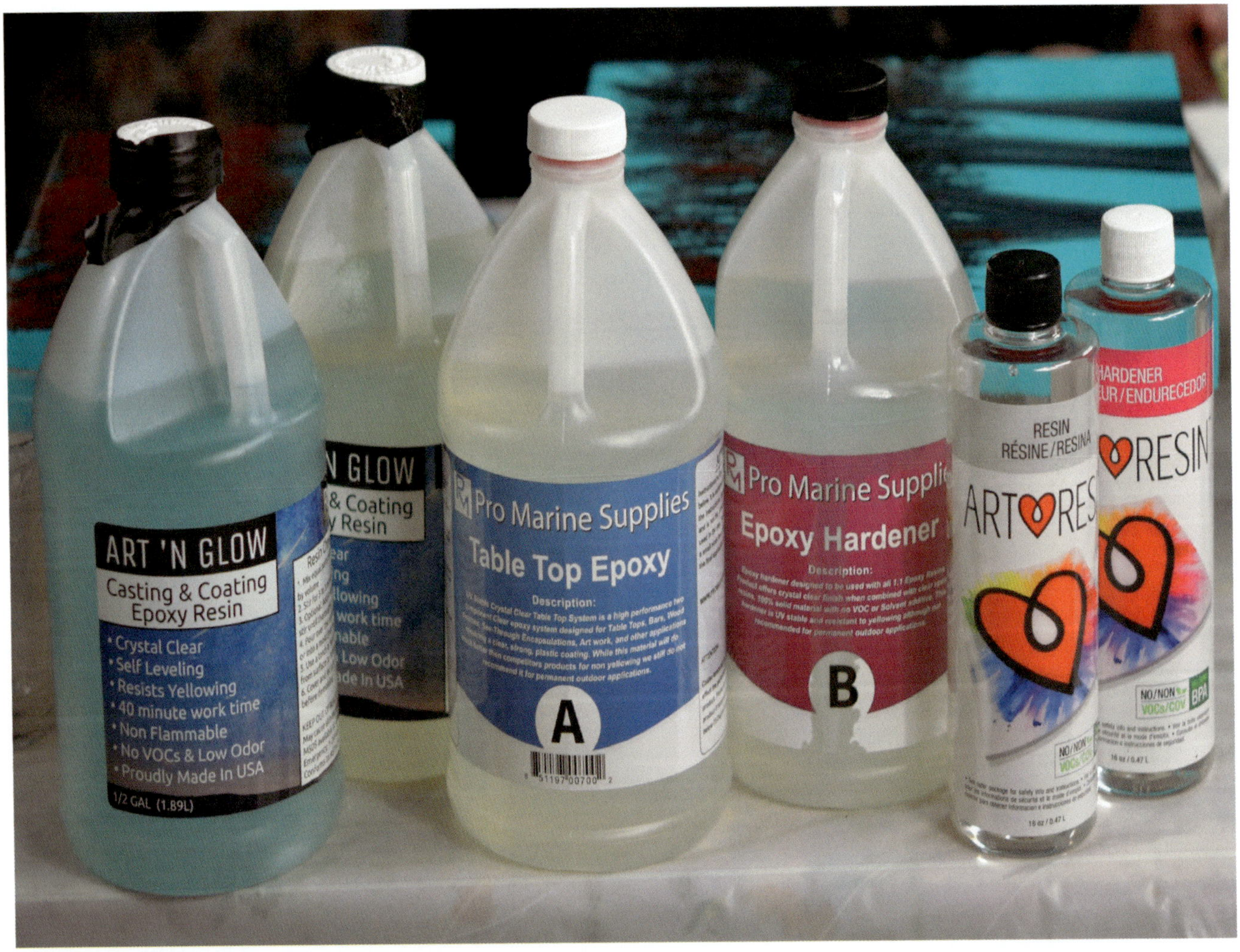

Epoxy Resin
Art 'N Glow, Pro Marine & Art Resin

There are approximately a hundred or more brands of epoxy resin on the market now. The brand chosen depends on the purpose for it and the amount of money to be invested. I will list some of the more popular brands. The number of $ next to the brand denotes the expense of the resin.

Art 'N Glow $$$ 1to1 mixing ratio. Resist Yellowing. VOC free. Heat Resistant to 120*F. Working time is 40 minutes including the 3-4 minutes of mixing time. Cured to the touch in 24 hours. Mix and use in temperatures above 75 degrees Fahrenheit. Mixing and pouring in cooler temps will result in uncured resin. This is an art and casting resin. This is an easy to use resin that has a glass like surface once cured. It is low odor and very few bubbles. I have found it to be non-yellowing. It domes very well. Micro bubbles occur when used in colder temperatures. When used in the correct temperatures there is almost no bubbles.

Art Resin $$$$ 1to1 mixing ratio. Non-yellowing. VOC free. Working time is 45 minutes including the 3 minutes of mixing time. Cured to the touch in 24 hours. Mix and use in temperatures above 75 degrees Fahrenheit. Mixing and pouring in cooler temps will result in uncured resin. It claims to have UV stabilizers. It claims it is safe for direct food contact once cured. It is low odor. I found it to create a lot of bubbles, when stirring, no matter how slow you stir the mix. The bubbles are easily taken care of with a torch. It domes very well. The finish is very clear, like glass.

Eli Chems Mastercast $$$$ 1to1 mixing ratio. Generally, non-yellowing. VOC free. Working time is 15 to 20 minutes including the 3 minutes of mixing time. Cures to the touch in 5-7 hours and fully cured in 24 hours. Mix and use in temperatures above 75 degrees Fahrenheit. Mixing and pouring in cooler temps will result in uncured resin. This is a resin that is very popular among resin users. It cures to a glassy shine. It is also being used for coasters and cheese boards.

Pro Marine $ 1to1 mixing ratio. Generally, non-yellowing. Will yellow if exposed to sunlight. No VOCs. 99% cured after 72 hours. Heat resistance when fully cured is 135*F. Working time is 25 minutes including the 6-8 minutes of mixing time. Mix and use in temperatures above 75 degrees Fahrenheit. Mixing and pouring in cooler temps will result in uncured resin. This is a cost-effective resin that claims to have UV stabilizers. It is used for tabletops and counter tops and has gained huge popularity among artists as a painting and casting resin. It is glossy and glassy. It's easy to use and mix. I find that it only takes 3 minutes to mix.

Envirotex Light Pour On $$ 1to1 mixing ratio. VOC free. Heat resistance is 180*F. Tends to yellow. Use with colorant or when you want an aged effect. Working time of 20 to 30 minutes including the 3-4 minutes of mixing time. Cured to touch in 24 hours and fully cured in 7 to 14 days. Mix and use in temperatures above 75 degrees Fahrenheit. Envirotex is a sturdy and easy to use resin that is well worth the savings in cost, because much of what you do in epoxy resin art is with color anyway. The yellowing of the resin tends to happen universally rather than in patches making it a great resin for aged effects. I've used this resin as clear on dark backgrounds and it works great. Because of the yellowing it is not recommended on white or light backgrounds.

East Coast Crystal Clear $ 1to1 mixing ratio. VOC free. Working time of 15 to 20 minutes including the 3-4 minutes mixing time. Cured to the touch in 24 hours and fully cured in 7 to 14 days. Mix and use in temperatures above 75 degrees Fahrenheit. It is a glossy finish, I find this resin to finish flat, meaning it doesn't dome. I prefer a doming resin. I found it to cure flexible and to take well over 2 months to cure to the point of hardness and a non-scratch surface.

My personal favorites in resin are Art 'N Glow and Art Resin. Both are very clear and sturdy resins. Both are consistent from bottle to bottle, which is very important. For the money, Art 'N Glow does everything that I need for a higher end resin. Of all the resin brands I have tried, Art 'N Glow is the only brand that I have found to resist particles in the surface. Other resins seem to attract them. There is something about the way that this resin is made that causes it to attract particles less.

Many artists use Art Resin and it is a great product. Their website is comprehensive and has most everything you need to know about working with their product including a great resin calculator. The resin I keep going back to is Art 'N Glow. It domes beautifully. It has minimal bubbles in the stir which means less torching. For covering completed oil paintings or acrylic art, Art Resin can't be beat. The glass like finish takes any artwork up a notch.

Pro Marine is a great resin to use when saving money is needed. It is non-yellowing as long as it is not exposed to sunlight or bright lights. I found East Coast resin to cure to a flat surface. Envirotex has been around for a very long time. I can buy it at my local Ace hardware store by the gallon. I use it only for projects that I want amber effects in. It is a yellowing resin.

East Coast is prone to be more flexible of a cure. Most resins cure to a very hard surface that is scratch resistant within 7 to 14 days. I found East Coast took over 2 months to get past the flexible stage and cure to a hard surface. During that time, it was easy to scratch. Even after 2 months I could still scratch the surface just not as easily. East Coast would be fine as a first coat on a surface with a layer of another brand of resin as the top coat for stability. A stable and sturdy cure in resin is important. It does cure very glassy and glossy and doesn't yellow.

Eli Chem's Master Cast is a very popular resin among artists. Eli Chem is a UK based company. Master Cast can be purchased on Amazon and eBay. It is perhaps the most expensive resin on the market. It works well for all your project needs.

Two other epoxy resins of note are Countertop Epoxy and Stone Coat epoxy. Both of these companies sell resins for counter top and flooring, but artists are using them on canvas. There are so many epoxy resins on the market. When looking to purchase the questions to ask any epoxy company are: Is it VOC free? Does it have UV stabilizers? Is it non-yellowing? Is it low odor? What is the work time? How long before it fully cures?

When I am choosing a resin to use I want to be able to reach out and ask questions. Customer service is important. I want to know I can reach out to customer service if I have issues while doing a large project. I email or call and ask questions before purchasing the resin. Most resin manufacturers will provide ample information about their product if you ask for it.

HOW MUCH RESIN TO USE

There are several resin calculators Online for figuring out how much resin is needed for a project. Visit the site for the brand of resin being used and they will likely have a calculator for measuring how much resin is needed for the canvas or project. To determine how much, is needed; measure the sides of your canvas and enter the numbers into the calculator to get the amount in ounces. I always add just a little more to ensure I have enough. I don't like wasting resin so I also have another canvas or some jewel bezels on hand to use the resin.

As a general calculation for how much resin to mix: it takes a minimum of 3oz of mixed resin per 1sq foot of substrate area. That is a total resin mix, or 1.5oz hardener and 1.5 oz resin. The amount can depend on the brand of resin you are using. Some manufacturers recommend 1oz and others recommend as much as 5oz. I say approximate because I round the number up to fit a specific measuring line on a paint mixing cup that I will be using for my mix. I try to measure just a little more than I will need so that I don't have large waste, but that I have enough to cover the surface of the project without having to mix more mid project.

Here is an example: Measure one of each sides of the canvas. The horizontal side and the vertical side. This will give you a measure of the area of the canvas. If you want to cover a painting that is 48x60 it looks like this:

> 48x60=2880 total square inches divided by 144 for square feet.
> 2880/144=20 square feet.
> 20 square feet x 3 ounces = 60 ounces of resin.
>
> For a 5-ounce measure per square feet
> 20 square feet x 5 ounces=100 ounces.

Let's use 100 ounces of resin. To work that into a measure that works with a paint mixing cup, round the 100 ounces to 104 ounces. This will provide 3 mixes of 32 ounces and 1 mix of 8 ounces. You will need 52 ounces of hardener and 52 ounces of resin. Rounding up will make it easier for reaching your paint mixing cup measure lines. It's better to have more than you need than not have enough. For ease of measuring in your cups you will find mixing lines for the 16oz and 32oz mark and the 4oz and 8oz mark. Use these measurements rather than mixing the whole 104oz at once. For this art piece mix 3 containers of 32oz each and 1 container of 8oz total mix. This gives you a total of 104oz. If you mix too much resin at once it will turn hot and begin to smoke. It may harden in your container.

I have provided a list of the most popular canvas sizes, and the amount of resin needed by size. If you are doing multiple pieces, add the amounts together to determine the total amount needed.

Recommended Amount of Resin by Canvas Size. Based on 5oz of mixed resin per sq. ft.

5x5=1oz	6x6=1oz	5x7=1oz
8x10=3oz	8x24=7oz	10x10=3oz
9x12=4oz	10x20=7oz	12x12=5oz
11x14=5oz	16x20=11oz	12x36=15oz
18x18=11oz	18x24=15oz	18-36=22oz
20x20=14oz	24x24=20oz	30x30=22oz
36x36=45oz	36x48=60oz	36x60=75oz
36x72=90oz	40x60=83oz	48x48=80oz
48x72=120oz	60x60=125oz	60x72=150oz

TIP

More than one person is needed for working on a large canvas. When mixing multiple batches of resin, more than one person is needed for the mixing process to ensure the batch doesn't cure before it gets on the canvas. When pouring on the canvas more than one person is needed to help get the resin on the canvas before it begins to cure.

Helpful Conversions

1 gallon = 128oz
½ gallon = 64oz
¼ gallon = 32oz
1/8 gallon = 1oz

1 quart = 32oz
½ quart = 16oz
¼ quart = 8oz

Metric Conversion Chart

To convert

Inches to Centimeters Multiply by 2.54
Centimeters to Inches Multiply by 0.4
Feet to Centimeters Multiply by 30.5
Centimeters to Feet Multiply by 0.03
Yards to Meters Multiply by 0.9
Meters to Yards Multiply by 1.1
Square Inches to Square Centimeters Multiply by 6.45
Square Centimeters to Square Inches Multiply by 0.16
Square Feet to Square Meters Multiply by 0.09
Square Meters to Square Feet Multiply by 10.8
Square Yards to Square Meters Multiply by 0.8
Square Meters to Square Yards Multiply by 1.2

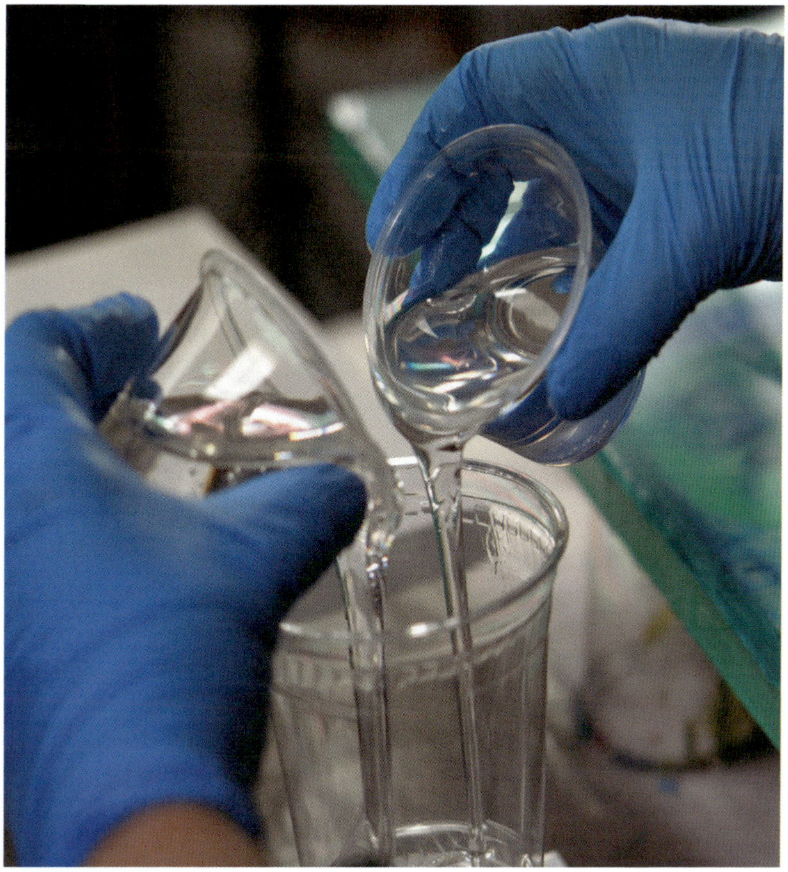

The top picture shows mixing resin by pouring hardener in one cup and resin in another cup and pouring the two cups into a larger cup to stir.

The bottom picture shows a one cup mixing method. I prefer to use a one cup mixing method. Pouring hardener to the first volume line, then pouring resin to the second volume line and mixing in the cup.

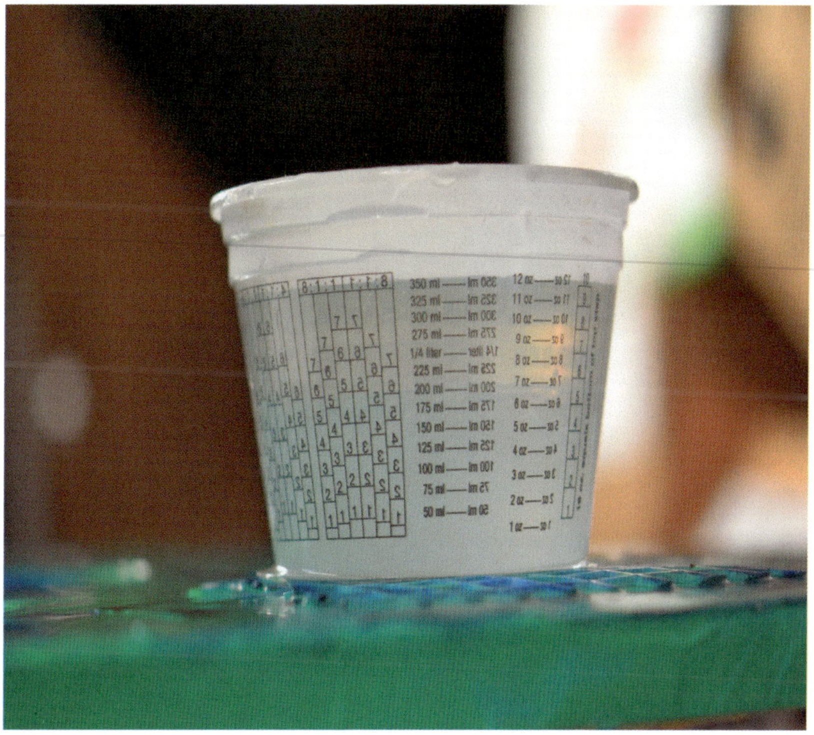

SECTION 7
SETTING UP TO RESIN

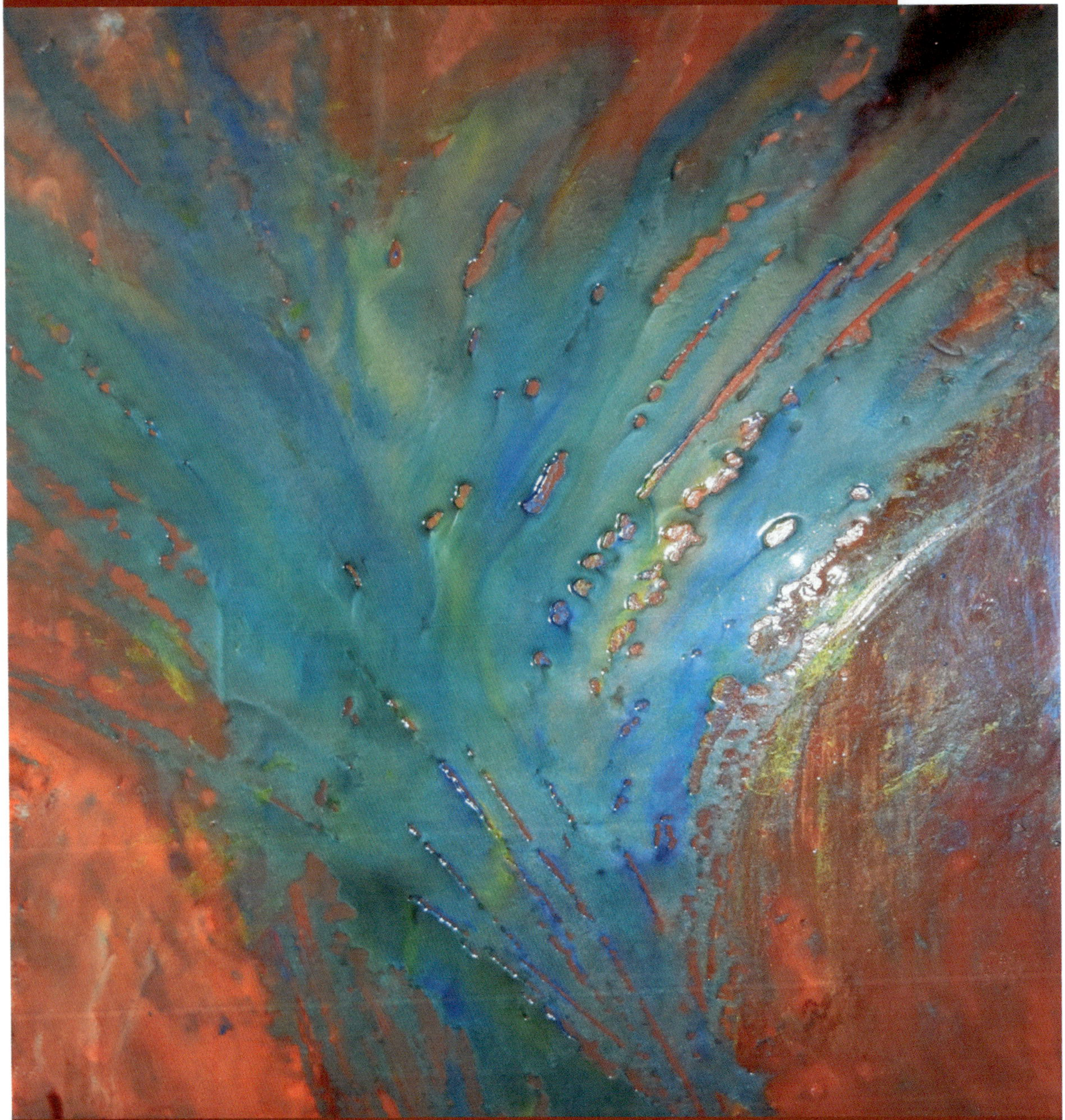

MAJESTIC
Resin Mica & Pigment Powder on Canvas
18"x24" (46cm x 61cm)

Please read the section on safety before continuing.

Setting Up To Paint With Epoxy Resin

Have everything ready before starting the resin project. The resin table or work area should be set up and covered in plastic. Set out the canvas and colorants to be used in the project. Having everything laid out, set up, and ready before mixing the resin will prevent a batch curing in the cup before getting on the canvas.

Elevate the substrate being poured on. This is important because the resin will be allowed to flow over the sides rather than the substrate resting in a pool of resin on the table. I use plastic cups turned upside down to place my canvas for resin pouring. Anything can be used that allows the canvas to be level and the resin to run off the sides. Place the cups towards the middle/center of the canvas. If placed on the edges of the canvas, the resin will run down the cups and cure the canvas to the cups.

Set out the number of cups to be used for colored resin in the project. Small silicone cups work very well for coloring resin and are reusable with cleaning, but disposable plastic cups also work.

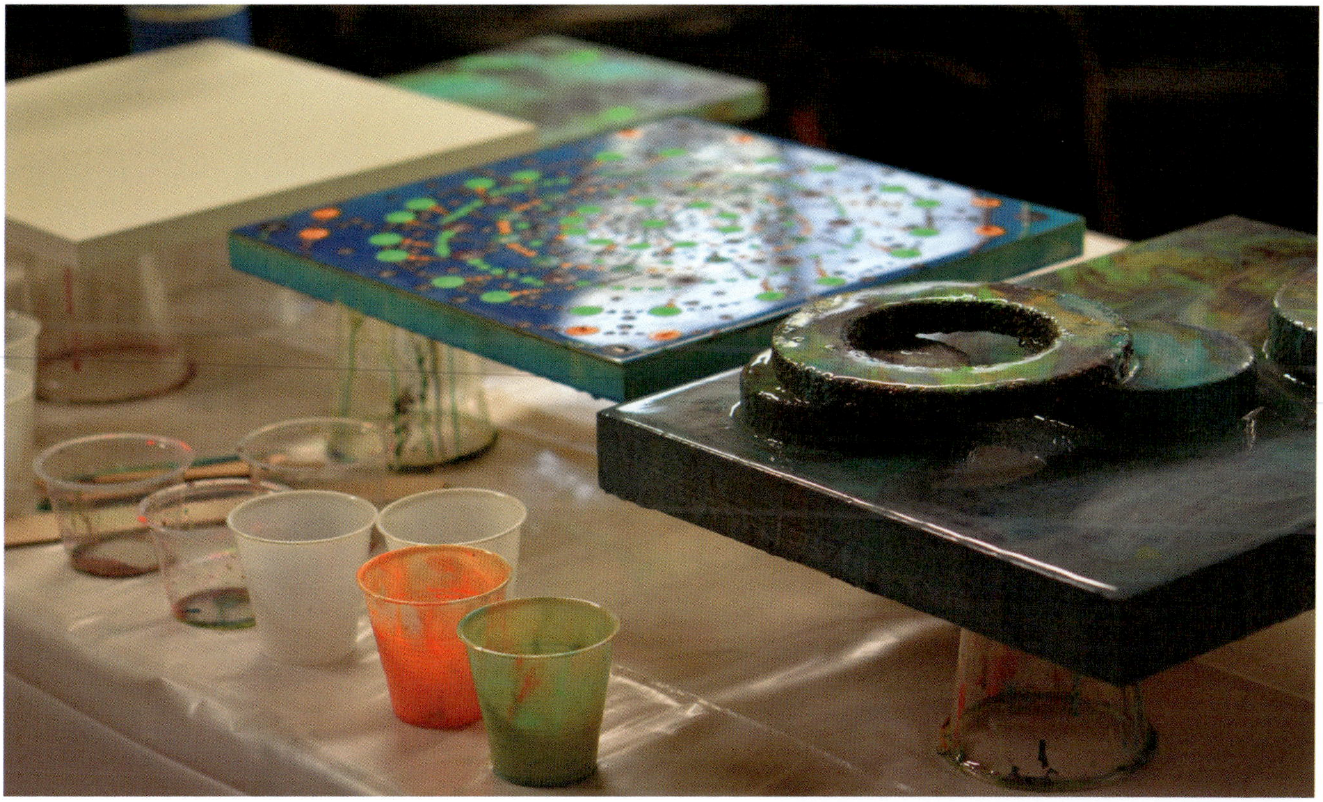

Table Set Up.

It's helpful to have a large cardboard box or plastic storage bin ready to cover the art when finished, and while it goes through the curing process. Boxes and bins in varying sizes can come in handy for this purpose. But if you have a bin that fits over the table just right, then only one is needed. Another idea is to place objects on the table that are taller than the canvas, place a piece of cardboard on top and drape plastic sheeting or a drop cloth over the table. The purpose is to keep dust and hair out of the art while it cures. This way you don't have to sit with the piece for hours picking out anything that might land on it.

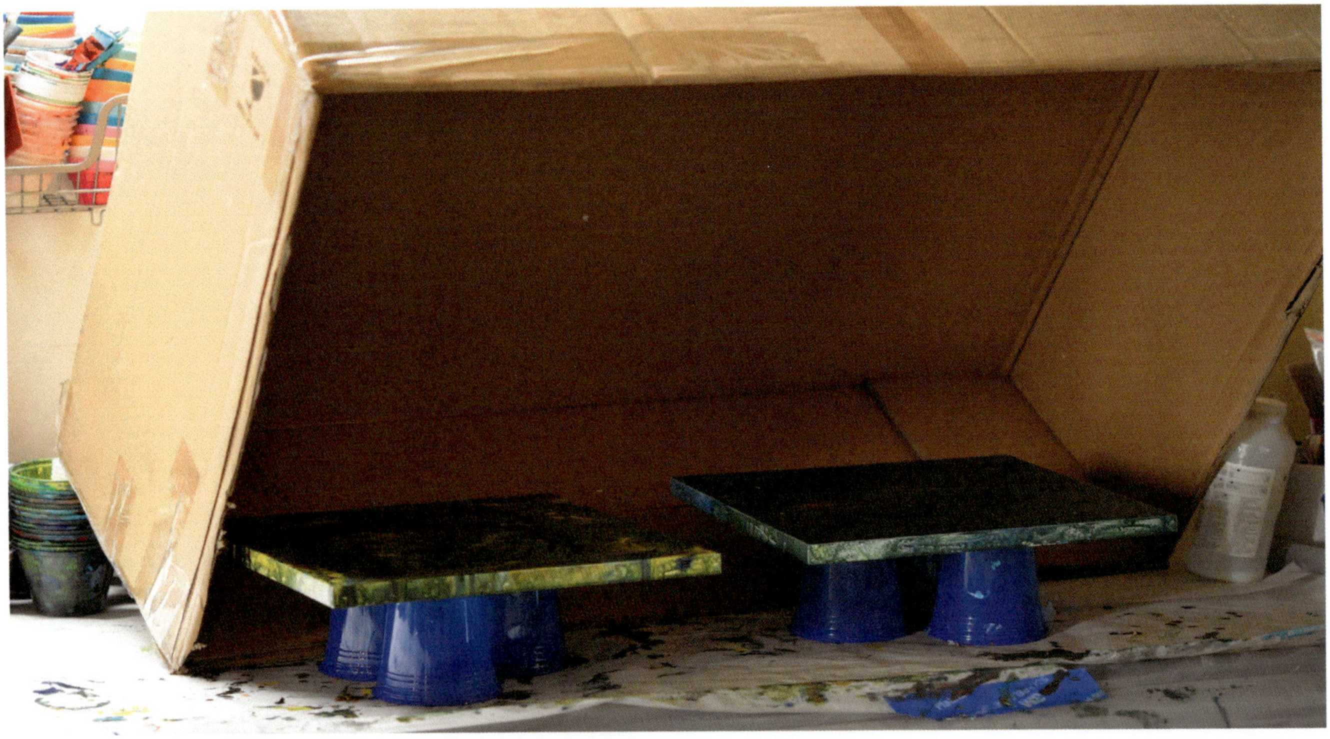

1: A large shipping box used as a dust cover. 2: A large enough box can cover the whole table. 3: When not in use, it is stored above the resin table on a rack.

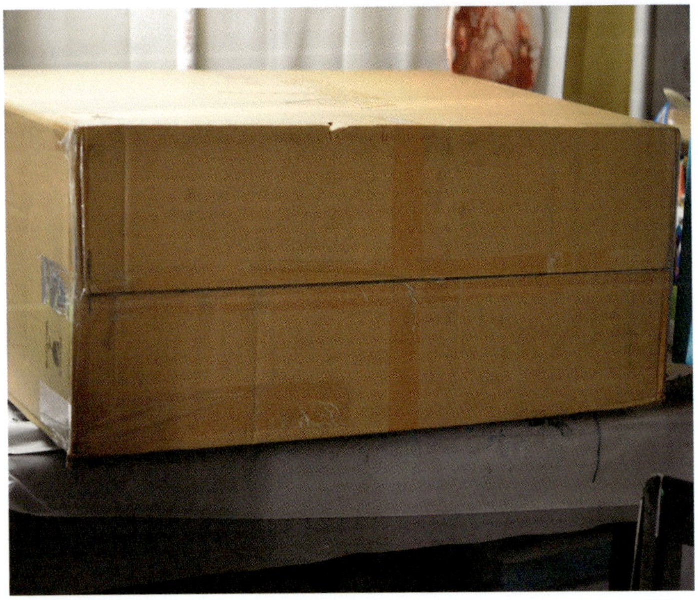

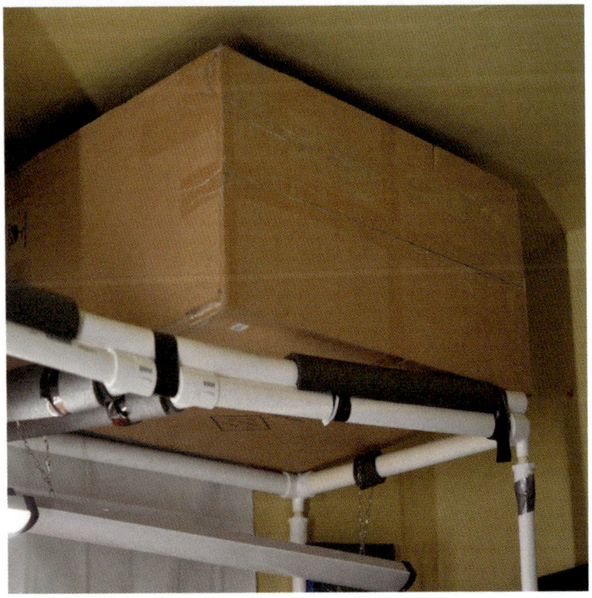

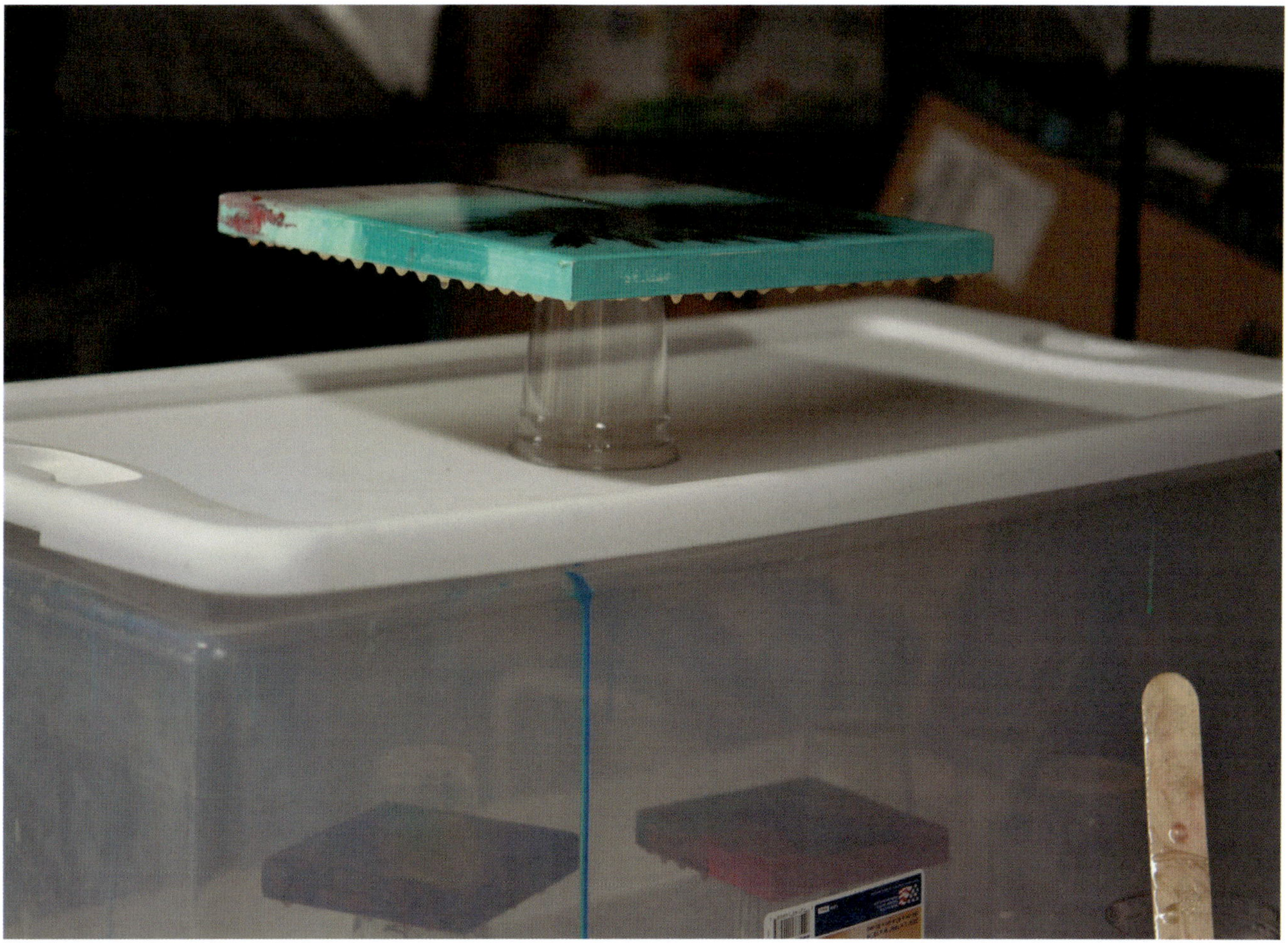

A large plastic storage bin used as a dust cover. Use the top to do more resin work by using the lid as a surface. When finished, use a smaller plastic storage bin to cover the art.

Set aside at least 4 hours of time for the project. If you maintain a resin studio, already set up with a resin table covered with plastic, then you don't need to allow for the extra time setting up the space. If you are in a position of tearing down the table and setting up each time you resin, allow another hour or so for set-up. If the project is a large one, allow 6 hours of time. Prepping and setting up the canvas can take about 15 to 30 minutes depending on how you prep it. Mixing resin takes 3-4 minutes (or longer depending on the brand) and the work time is 20 to 45 minutes (depending on the brand). Adding color to resin takes 5 to 15 minutes. Completing the painting can take no longer than the work time of the resin (20 to 45 minutes). Picking out hair and dust and removing bubbles happens during the work time. Covering the art after completion takes just a few minutes if you have prepared the items you will use. I suggest checking in on the art for the first 2 to 3 hours. Look for hair or dust particles, or for resin that has fallen too much off the canvas. There may still be time to work with a design that has changed in a way you don't like, even though the resin has gone sticky and stiff. After 2 to 5 hours, the tape can be removed from the sides, if used. Remove the tape to avoid a stiff edge.

SECTION 8
PREPARING THE CANVAS

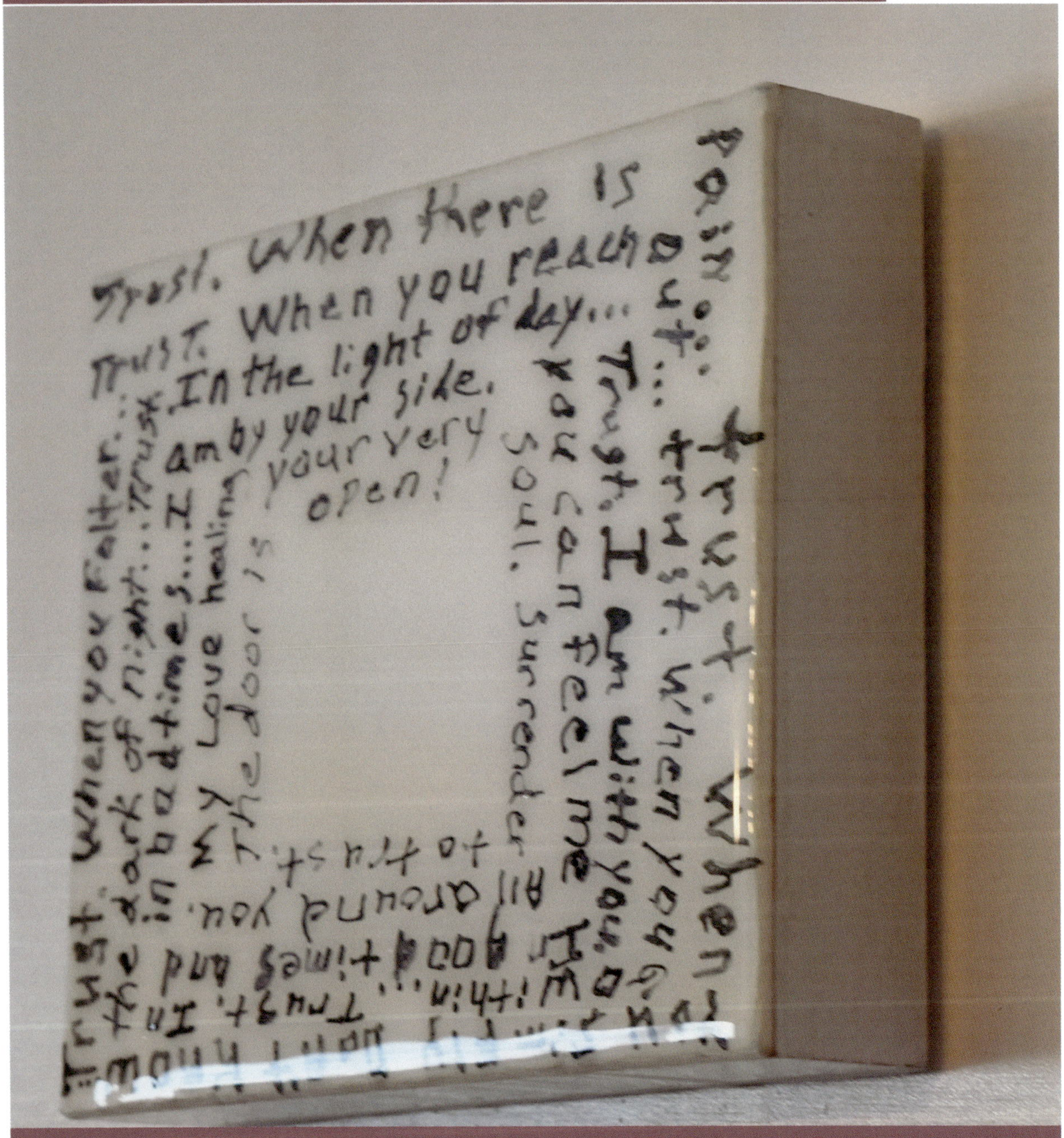

TRUST
Encaustic, Resin on Cradled Wood Panel
9"x9" (23cmx23cm

Throughout the book I will be referring to surfaces used to pour resin on. A substrate is simply a surface that something happens on. I will be using the word substrate and canvas interchangeably. I will be using the word substrate and wood panel interchangeably.

Cotton or linen canvas will require something placed at the back to keep it from sagging in the middle. I use cardboard. It is easy to find. I cut pieces to size from shipping boxes. Place it so that it fills the back of the canvas. Styrofoam or other types of foam cut to size of the canvas may be used instead of cardboard. If resin is poured on a fabric canvas with no middle support the result will be a thick cure of resin in the middle of the canvas and pitting on the outer edge of the canvas.

For wood panel, decide if you need to prime before applying resin. A bare wood canvas can create excessive bubbles. When priming a bare wood canvas, allow it to dry completely before pouring resin. I use Kilz primer from the hardware store. It comes in spray and brush on. I also use Gesso. Painting with acrylic paint or even house paint works for a prime coating. Just allow it to dry completely. Another method for priming is to pour on a thin coat of mixed resin and allow it to cure for a few hours before completing the resin art.

Decide if you want to tape the sides and back. Taping the back of your canvas prevents cleanup of excessive cured resin drips and edges later. I happen to like the look of the drips at the back and sides of the canvas so I usually don't tape mine, unless I get a commission for it to be done that way, or a piece calls for it.

I use HVAC tape. This is an aluminum tape usually used for heating and cooling installations. HVAC tape can be found in the heating and cooling section of the hardware store. It works better than masking tape. It has sharp edges and will cut worse than a paper cut so watch your fingers. If I am doing a pour with taped sides where I plan to remove the tape within an hour or two I will roll a piece of the tape over the glue side of itself so it's easy for me to grab and pull off the painting.

It is important to choose a tape that gives a good seal to the edges of the canvas, as resin can seep through the tape otherwise. HVAC tape or Tuck tape are great options. Tuck tape is house sheathing tape. It may also be called Tyvec tape. Regular painters tape or masking tape does not provide a solid enough seal to prevent the resin from seeping through.

Tip

Remove the tape after 2 to 4 hours (depending on the resin) if you want round or domed edges. Hard edges will result from tape being left on for the duration of the cure. If the tape is removed after the resin begins to cure but is still in the sticky stage, the resin will fall over the sides just enough to prevent hard edges and allow a round or domed edge to the piece. Hard edges can be sanded off with a Dremel tool or with sand paper if the tape is left on.

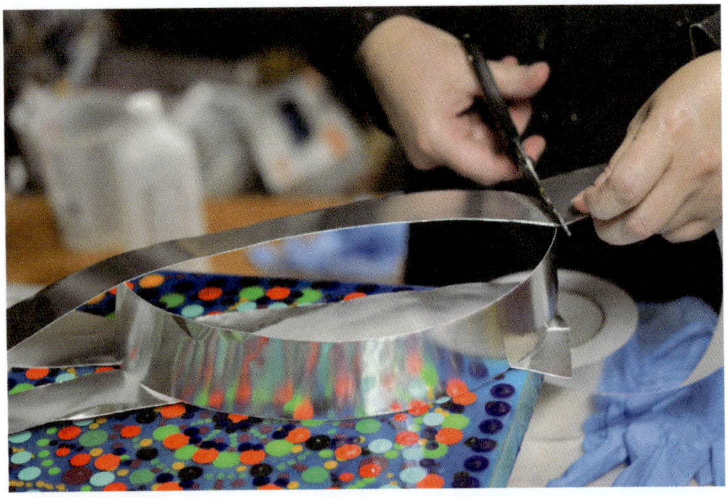

Cut pieces of HVAC tape to the size of the canvas.

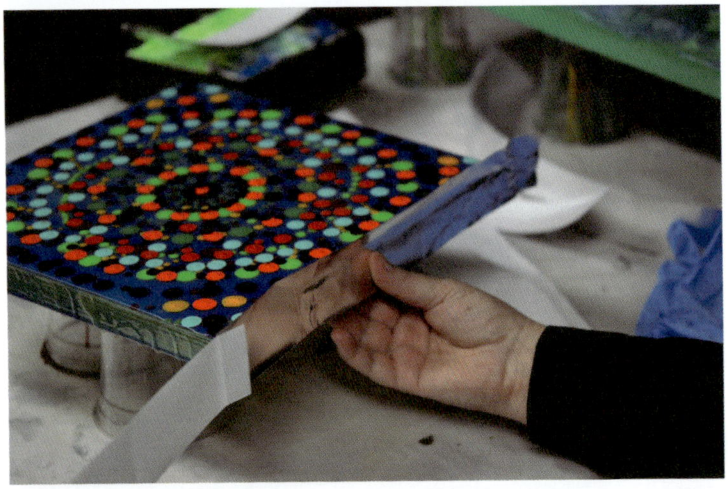

Peel the paper backing off of the tape and apply the sticky side to the canvas above the rim to make a dam for pouring the resin.

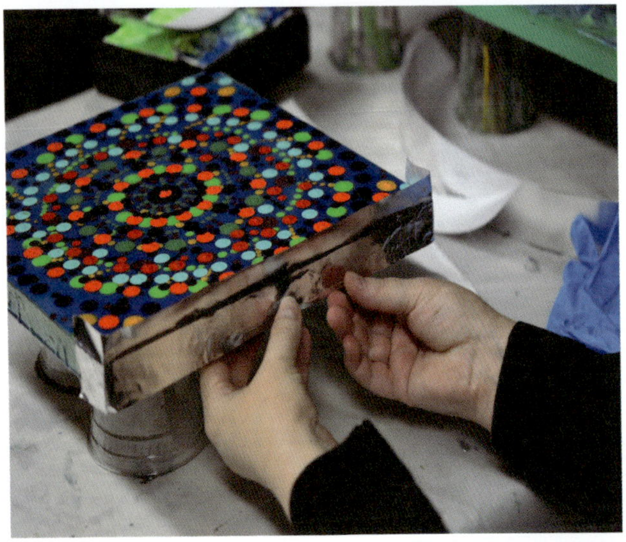

Press the tape into the side. Go over the entire section of tape, pressing it into the canvas. Press firmly to create a seal with the canvas and to keep the resin from seeping through.

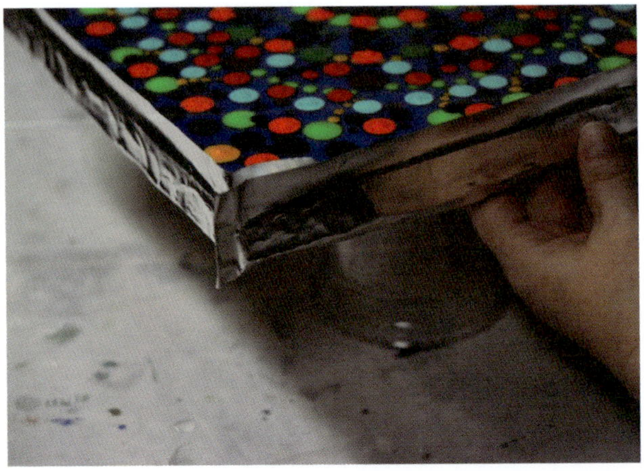

Make a corner edge, by folding a piece of tape back in on itself. This creates a handle for grabbing the tape, and makes it easier to remove the tape later.

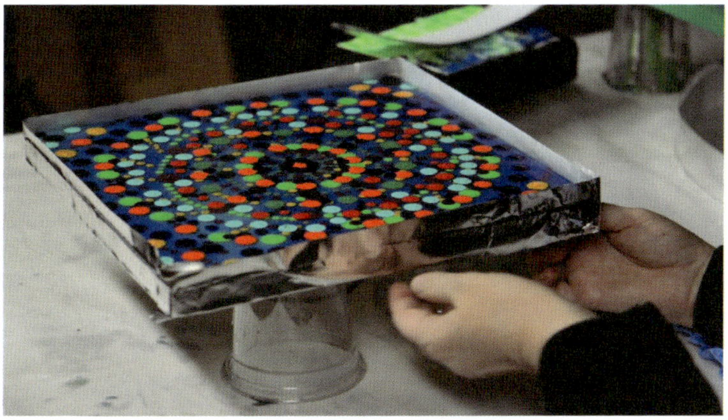

Cover all sides of the canvas. Press in on all sides of the canvas to create a good seal. Fold the tape over the bottom of the canvas on all sides.

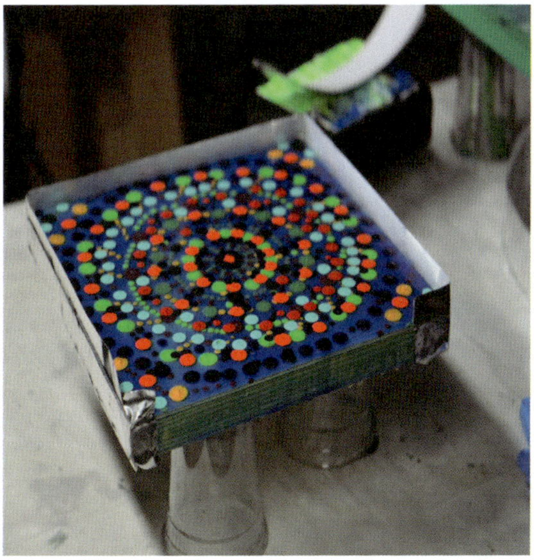

Place the canvas on 2 to 4 overturned plastic cups. Place the cups towards the middle of the canvas and away from the edges. Put the cups as far away from the edge as possible and still keep the canvas stable. This will prevent the resin from flowing down onto the cups and adhering the cups to the canvas. It will give a cleaner edge to the painting. Check the canvas to see if it is level. Resin is self-leveling, which means it moves and flows. There is nothing worse than being half way into your painting, only to notice that the resin is flowing to one side.

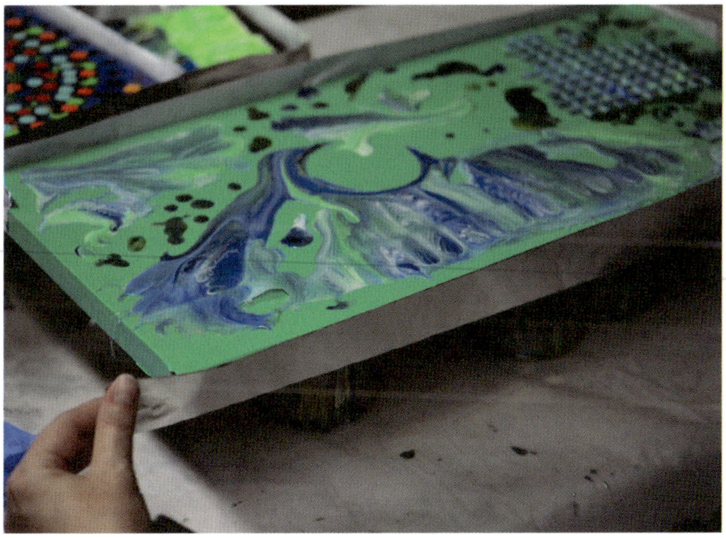

Use 6 cups for a larger size canvas. Place 3 cups on each of the long sides of the canvas.

One small and wide cup is enough for a very small canvas.

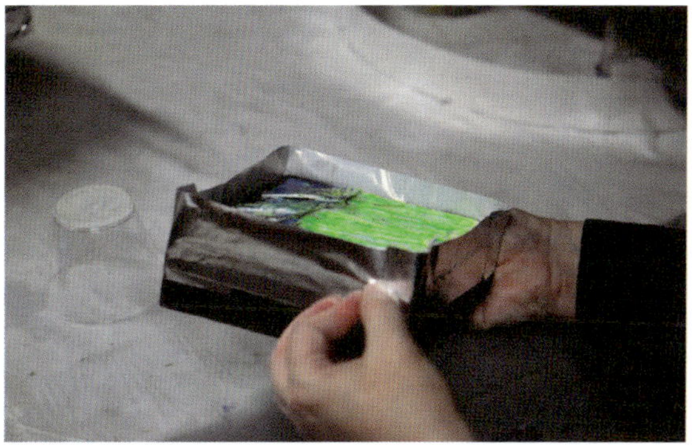

SECTION 9
MIXING RESIN

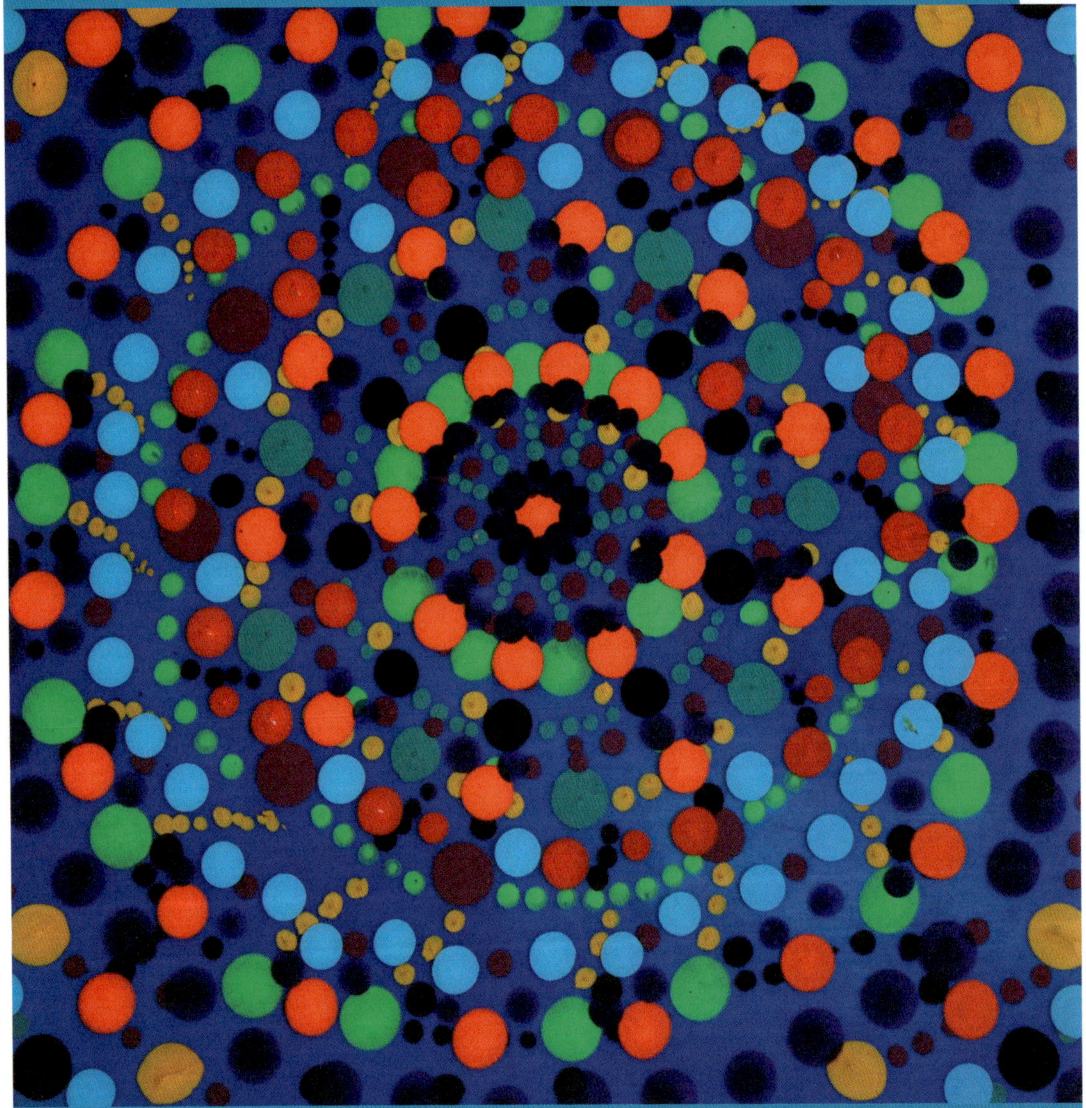

ONCE AROUND
Resin & Acrylic on Wood Panel
12"x12" (31cmx31cm)

Once you have chosen the brand of resin to use, follow the manufacturer's directions precisely for mixing ratios and time. Only mix the amount of resin that you will need in one sitting. Calculate the amount needed for the size of the substrate you are using. If using more than one substrate add the calculations together to determine how much is needed. Have an extra canvas nearby and ready to use any excess resin that is mixed.

All brands of epoxy resin require being mixed at temperatures above 75 degrees Fahrenheit. Trying to mix resin below this temperature will result in uncured resin. The room needs to be 70 degrees Fahrenheit as well. I have mixed and poured in a room that was 65 degrees Fahrenheit and warmed the resin in a warm water bath with success. That said, resin operates much better when used above 75 degrees.

Measuring is the most critical part of mixing resin. The resin and hardener must be measured exact. There are brands of resin that suggest measuring by weight but the majority of them are measured by volume for the mix. Never under any circumstances vary the measurements of the mix. If you look online or on YouTube you will find suggestions of mixing colorants to resin before adding the hardener. Never, ever do this. Always mix the resin first and add colorants to the mixed resin. Adding colorant to resin or hardener, before the mix, changes the volume and will result in a damaged cure. Too much hardener in the mix leads to fast curing and a cracked or warped surface. Too much resin in the mix leads to uncured or sticky resin or very flexible resin.

Mix smaller amounts of resin in a container rather than very large volumes. Most resin manufacturers have a recommended maximum amount of resin that can be mixed in one mixing container. The average recommendation for the maximum amount that can be mixed in one container is 2 quarts. If more than 2 quarts of resin are mixed in a single container it will heat up and cure within 5 minutes. The more you mix the more likely it is to heat up and cure fast. Fast curing times will not allow time to apply the resin to the substrate.

TIP

If you don't have time to stay with your project for a few hours at least, save it for another day. When the painting is finished it still requires monitoring during the curing process for at least an hour or two.

The maximum amount that I recommend for mixing at one time is 32oz or 1 quart. However, 24oz is a better mixing volume. If I am doing a large pour I keep my mix at 32oz or 1 quart in a single container and mix multiple batches for the pour. That may mean I mix up 4 or more containers of resin. I mentioned in the section on resin that it is necessary to have more than one person available to work on a large canvas. With 4 or more containers being mixed for 3-4 minutes it's easy to see why you need at least 2 and maybe 3 or 4 people on hand for doing this kind of pour.

Heat is a consideration when determining the depth of the pour. When taping the sides of a canvas or project, be mindful of how much resin is being poured onto the surface. Most resin brands have a depth of use when liquid. If too much resin is poured at once it will overheat and cure within 5 minutes. Too deep a pour on the substrate can cause cracking or warping in the cured surface. This goes for pouring into molds as well. For very deep molds, be aware that you will need to get the resin into the mold quickly and that it will set quickly. This may affect the integrity of your mold for future use. Consider layering pours for deep molds or deep pours. Each layer can be allowed to run off the canvas, or if a dam is used, pour no more than ¼ inch thick. Some resin brands can go as much as an inch thick. Check the data sheet or with the manufacture on the brand being used.

Most resins have a 1to1 mixing ratio and a 3 to 4 minutes mixing time. That means you add equal parts resin and hardener and mix for a minimum of 3 minutes for the ingredients to activate. There is a small variation of mixing times from brand to brand. Read the instructions on the brand you will be using. Some brands have a 2to1 mixing ratio. That means you use 2 parts of resin and 1 part of hardener. Always read the instructions when purchasing a new brand of resin.

The process of mixing resin is really simple. Mix resin and hardener in equal parts by volume. Or if using a 2to1 ratio, mix double the amount of resin to hardener. When mixing in one cup, and the hardener first and the resin second. As soon as you stir the two parts together the mixture will turn cloudy. Continue to mix until the mixture is free of streaks. With many brands of resin this means the resin will be clear and see through when thoroughly mixed. Some resin brands are slightly milky when thoroughly mixed and not completely clear. With these brands it is important to stir until all swirls or streaks are gone.

It is possible to over-mix resin. Too much mixing can speed up the curing process. Over-mixing creates excess bubbles in the mix. If the instructions say mix for 3 minutes, the maximum mix time should be 5 minutes. Really, 3 minutes is all you need for the mix time but if you are still seeing a streak in the mix go ahead and mix for another minute or so.

There is a recommended method to add hardener to one cup and resin to another cup and then pour the two cups into a third cup and mix, scraping the sides of the mixing cup several times during the mixing process. Mix for 2 minutes. Then pour the mixture into another cup and get a new stir stick and mix for another minute. This is a perfectly fine way to mix the resin and will result in a great mix. That is a lot of cups. That is a lot of wasted cups that go into the trash bin. I have used the same mixing process across many resin brands and for many years and it has never failed me. I use a one cup mixing process.

I use plastic paint mixing cups from the hardware store. The reason I use plastic paint mixing cups from the hardware store is that it has measurement marks right on the cup. It's more likely to be precise because these cups are made for mixing solvents and paints. These cups are made of a plastic that resin won't cure to. After the resin dries, it can be peeled right off. The cup can then be used for another resin mixing.

Resin does not stick to silicone. This makes silicone measuring cups ideal to use. Check them ahead of time to ensure they are the right measurements on the cup. I once purchased silicone measuring cups and used them only to notice the resin and hardener levels in the cup didn't look right. I poured the batch in a paint mixing cup to check it and it was off. I cleaned the cup and checked it by adding cups of water to the lines and sure enough it was incorrect. If you purchase silicone measuring cups that are made for kitchen use, check them ahead of time to ensure the measurement markings are correct.

A few things to know about mixing before we get into the mixing process. Always use a clean mixing cup and clean stir stick. You can reuse mixing cups and stir sticks as long as they are clean and free of debris. I'll show you how to get dried resin out of the cup later. Put on a pair of nitrile gloves before mixing resin. Wipe down the outside of the resin bottles to ensure no debris or dust falls into your mix. When mixing resin, use a stir stick that allows for scraping the sides and bottom of the cup. A jumbo craft stick or plastic ruler works great. A through mix is what ensures a proper cure. If there are unmixed bits on the sides or bottom of the cup, you don't have a thorough mix. Scrape the stick a few times on the side of the cup so that you mix in the resin from the stick. Use a mixing cup that is about 25% larger than the amount being mixed. This way you won't spill the resin on the sides of the cup as you stir.

When pouring the hardener and resin, always open the bottles and pour one at a time. Do not mix up the caps from the bottles. Doing so can result in the cap sealing on the bottles, and requiring pliers to remove. Remove the cap from the hardener bottle and pour the amount needed. Replace the cap immediately when done pouring. Repeat with resin. Replace the cap immediately. This will help avoid getting the caps mixed up.

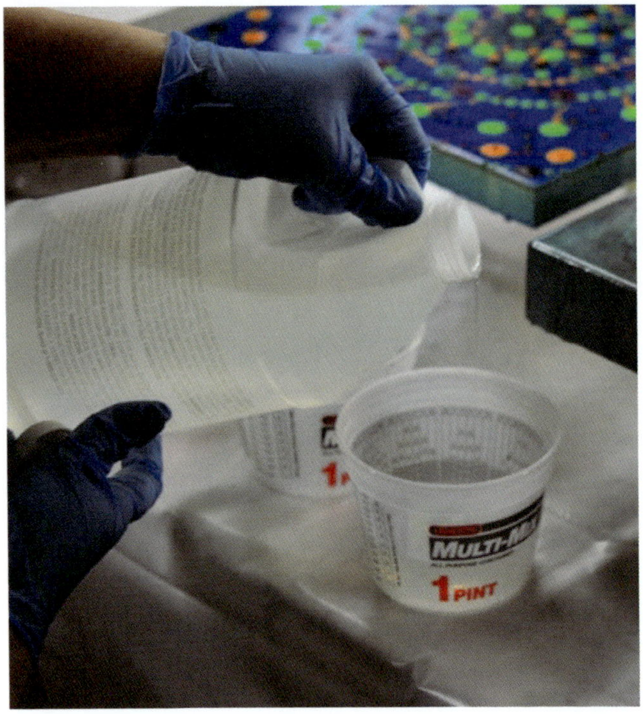

Paint mixing cups work great for mixing resin.

Add the hardener to the cup first. Add the resin to the cup second. Resin has a higher viscosity (thickness) than hardener. Because the hardener is thinner than the resin, the mixture of hardener will be more exact by adding it first. It is easier to stir thick down into thin, than to stir thin down into thick. In addition, it is hardener that lines the cup rather than resin. Hardener is easier to scrape from the cup and stir into the resin.

Use larger wooden craft sticks and reuse them several times. I also use silicone spatulas for stirring resin. The wooden craft stick is bare wood and creates some bubbles in resin. This is why I reuse them several times. The first use seals the wood with resin. Some resin artists leave the craft sticks in the cup to make it easier to pull out dried resin. I don't do this. Instead I put them on top of the cup to dry so I can reuse them several times. Once the craft stick is dried with a little coat of resin it will create less bubbles in your next mixing batch. The dried resin pulls out just fine, using your fingers.

Silicone spatulas do not create bubbles but require wiping down with alcohol and baby wipes while the resin is still wet. I have allowed the resin to cure on the silicone spatula and peeled it off after. This works OK but leaves little bits of resin that take a lot of alcohol and baby wipes to clean up. I have recently found that plastic rulers work great for mixing resin. The cured resin peels off the ruler.

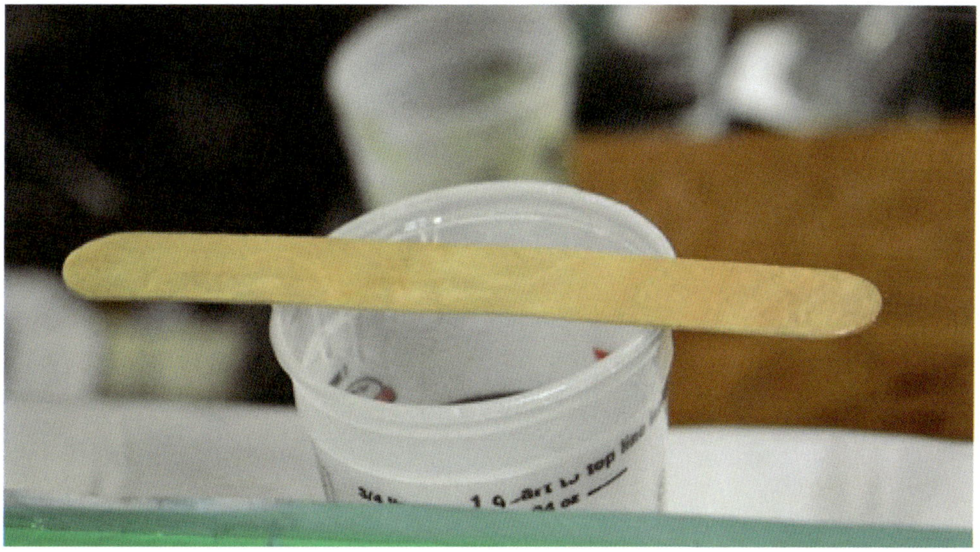

Craft stick placed on top of resin mixing cup to dry.

MY MIXING PROCESS

To paint mixing cup

Add hardener to mixing line A
Add resin to mixing line B
Stir slowly for 3 to 4 minutes; scraping the sides and the bottom of the container several times.
Scrape the stir stick on the side of the cup a few times.
Resin is ready when it goes from cloudy to clear. Continue to stir for the recommended amount of time, even if it clears before the recommended amount of time. Do not over-mix.

Stirring slowly ensures fewer bubbles in the mix. Scraping the sides and bottom of the cup several times and scraping the stir stick on the side of the cup ensures a thorough mix.

For example: If I want 12oz of resin
6oz+6oz=12oz
Add hardener to 6oz line (Be precise. Do not go over or under the line.)
Add resin to 12oz line (Be precise. Do not go over or under the line.)

Add Hardener to 6oz line.

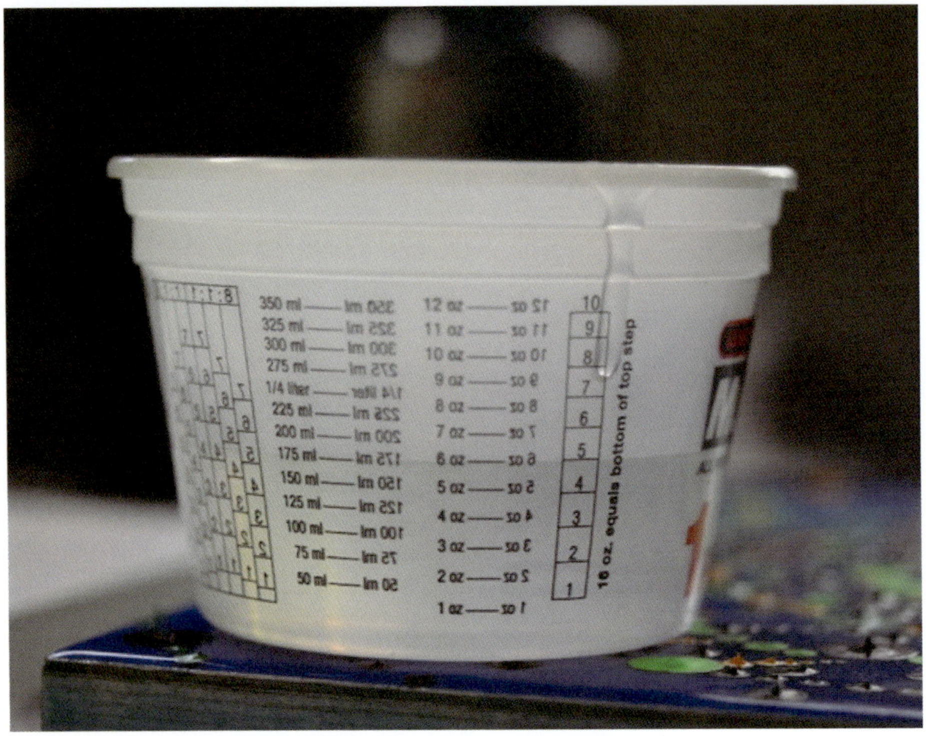

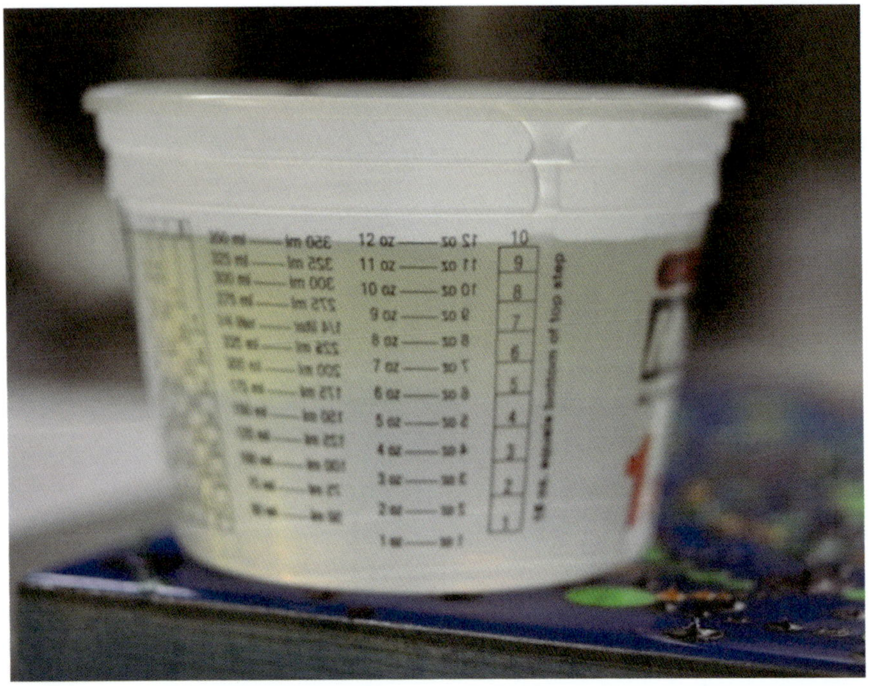

Add Resin to 12oz line.

This method requires a bit of math but it really is the most precise method, as long as the lines on the cup are precise. I once had a cup that caused the resin mix to harden instantly in the cup. The measurement lines were mis-marked, causing too much hardener to be added to the mix. I had purchased a few of these cups online. I checked the other cups to see if the mixing lines were off. I measured using water, and sure enough the lines were off. I have used these cups for years and only had it happen once. I bought them online to try a cheaper resource.

Slowly mix the resin. Scrape the sides and bottom of the cup several times. Make sure the stir stick makes good contact with all sides of the cup & with the bottom.

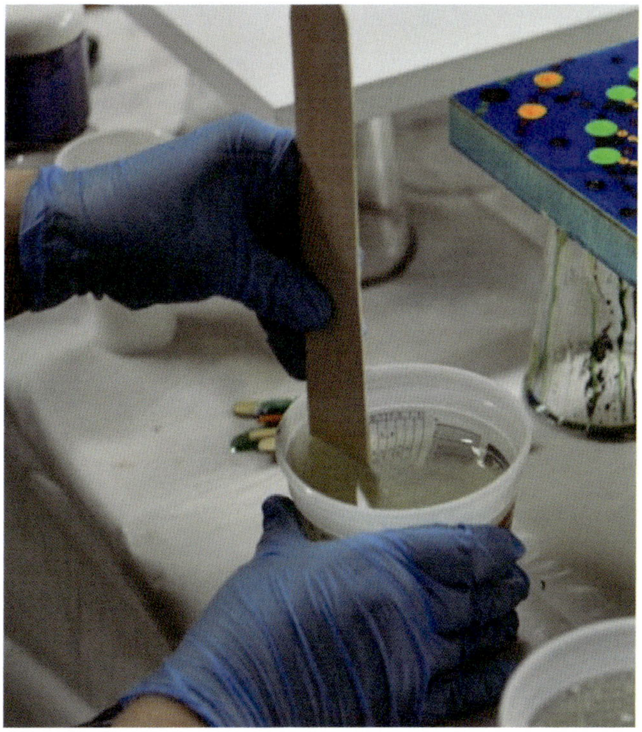

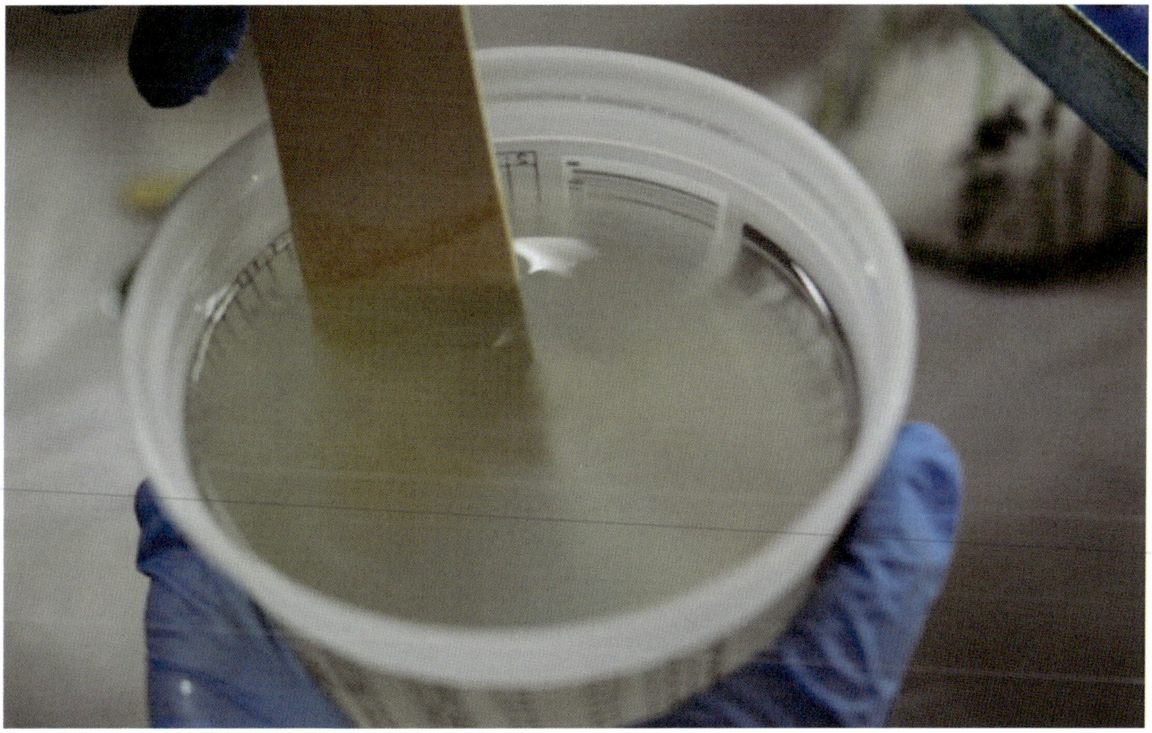

As soon as the resin and hardener are stirred together the mix turns cloudy. Scrape the sides and bottom of the container several times during the mix. Scrape the stir stick on the side of the container at least once during the stir. The mix will turn cloudy as soon as you stir the two parts together. Stir until the mixture becomes clear. This takes about 3 or 4 minutes. Always stir for the amount of time recommended on the resin manufacturer's packaging or included information sheet.

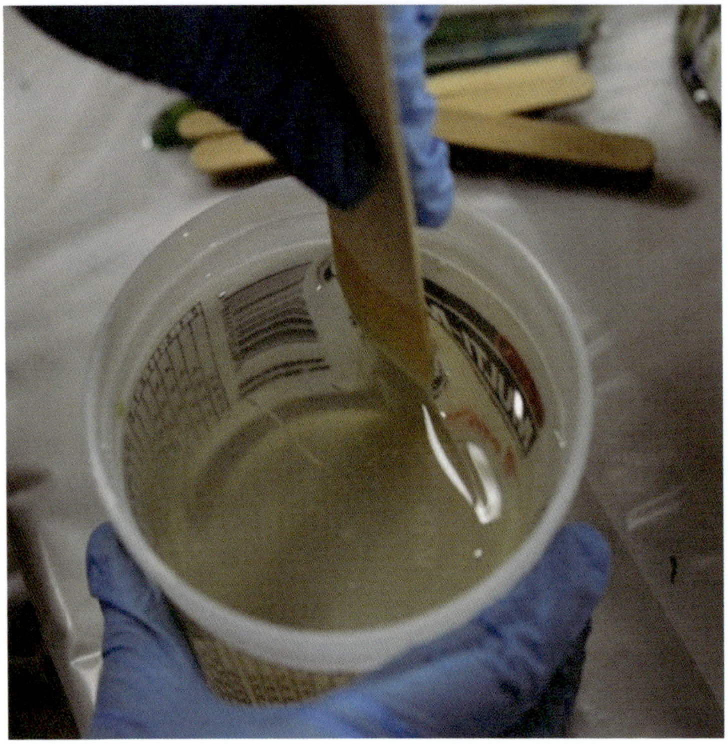

Crystallized stream in the last stage of mixing.

Continue to stir if you see crystallized streams or swirls in the mix. It may look clear but you still have to stir a little more.

The resin mix is ready to use when it is clear in the cup
.

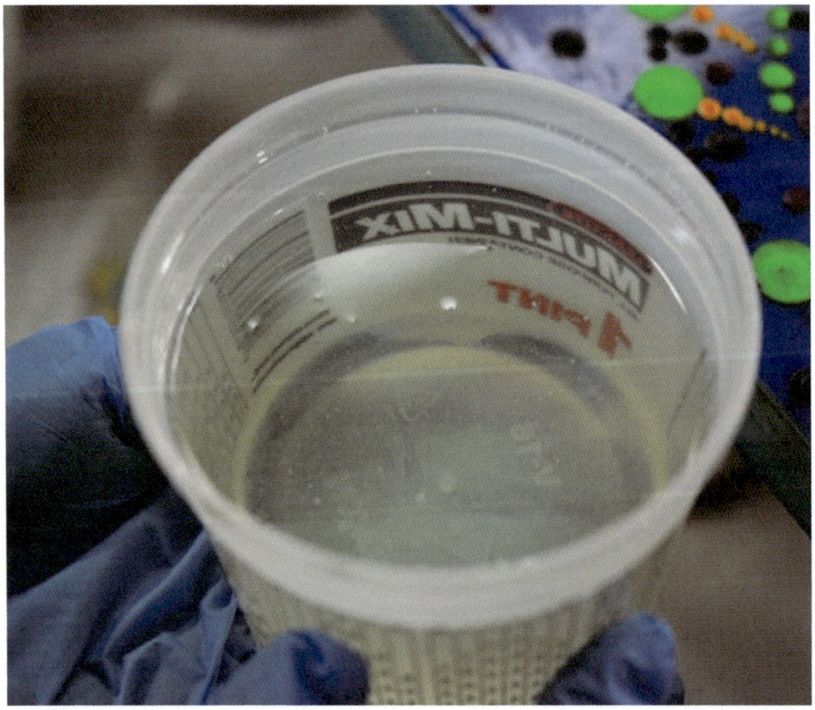

When the mixture is clear and no longer cloudy, crystallized, or swirly it is ready to use.

Once the resin is mixed there will be bubbles. Don't worry about them at this stage. You can take care of them when the resin is on the canvas.

Always read the package directions on the resin being used. Some resin mixtures are thicker than others and it is difficult to see the mix go clear as you are stirring. For these reasons, stir for the stated time in the package insert. Scrape the sides and bottom as you do.

Let's go through this one more time, and with a different resin and a larger mix.

Mixing 16ounces of Resin

Measure the hardener to the 8oz mixing line.
Add the resin to the 16oz mixing line.

Stir for the 3-4 minutes as directed by the manufacturer. Here I am mixing a different brand of resin. Not all resin brands go completely clear when mixed. Even though they are not fully clear, they will still cure to a glass finish. This resin does not go completely clear once stirred. I stir for 4 minutes. The resin I am using here has a 40 minutes work time. This gives me plenty of time to complete my design.

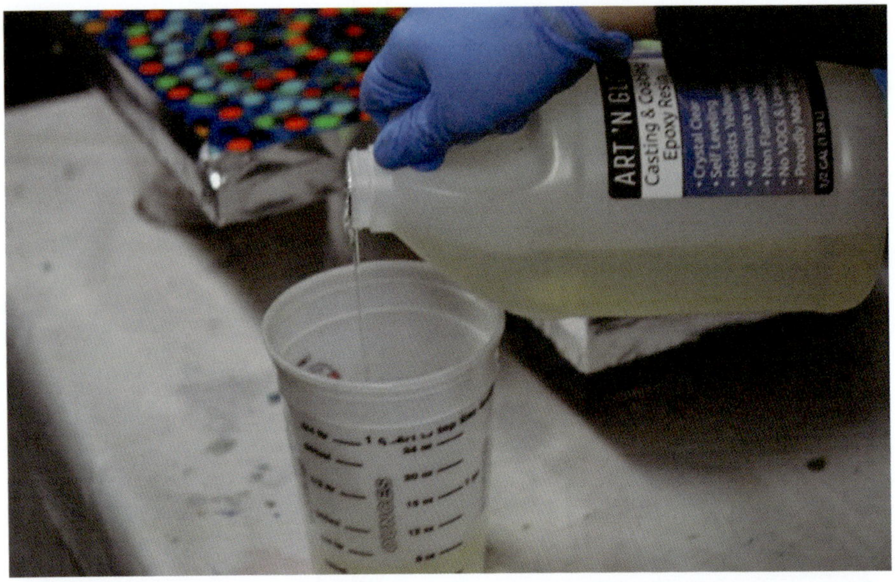

Pour hardener to 8oz line.

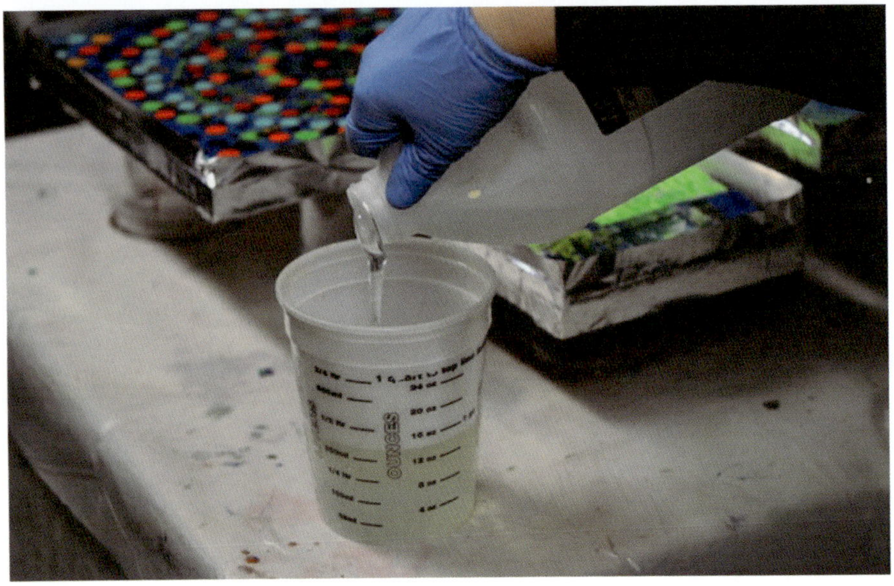

Pour resin to 16oz line. Almost there.

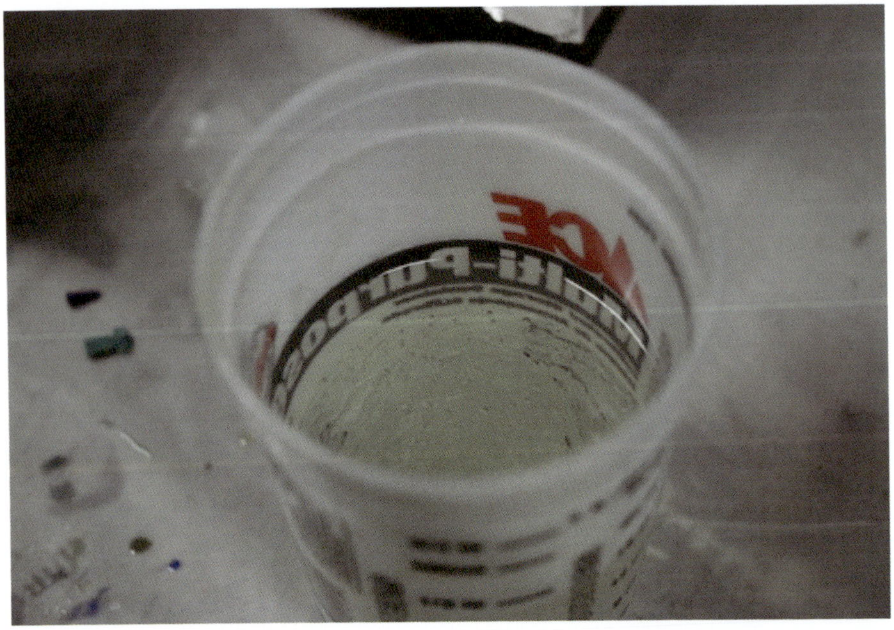

Ready to stir.

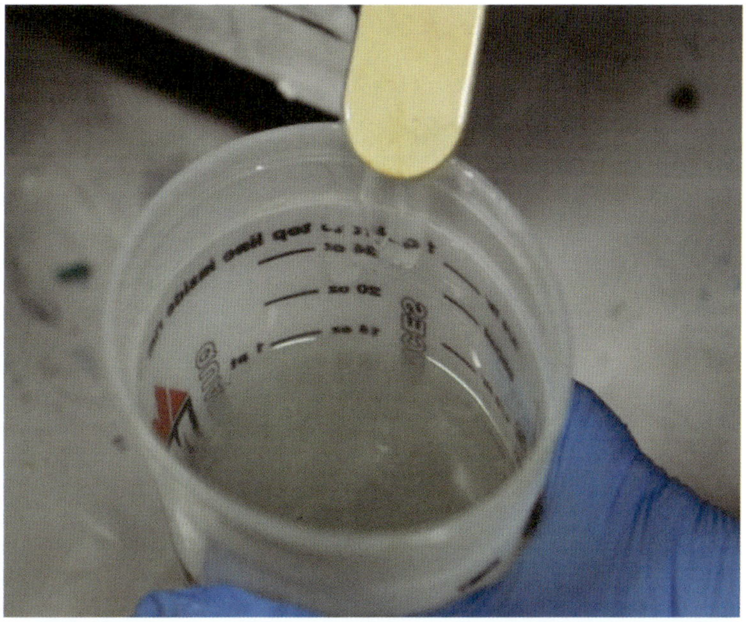

Stir until the resin and hardener mix. Scrape all sides and bottom of the cup. Scrape both sides of the stir stick on the side of the cup. Then continue mixing.

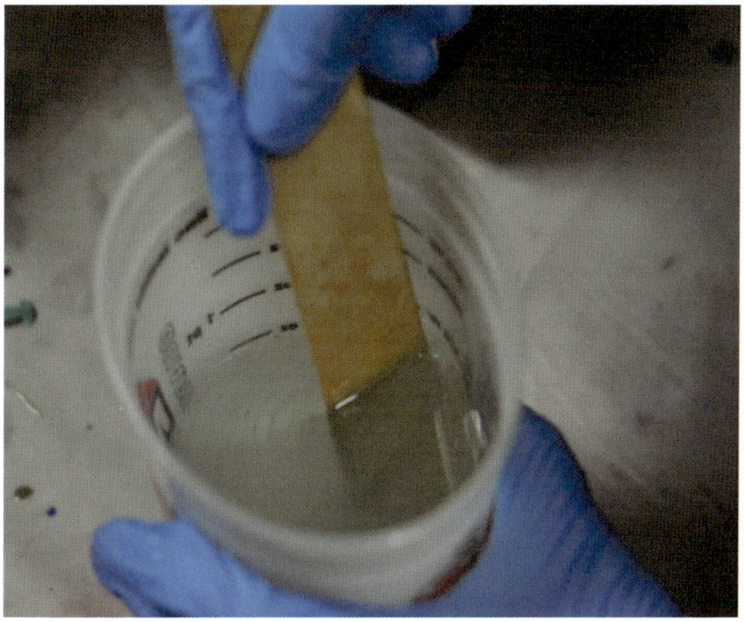

About 3 minutes of stirring and it's still not ready. Even though this resin isn't as clear I can still see swirls or crystal streams. The circle patterns in the resin are an indication it needs more stirring.

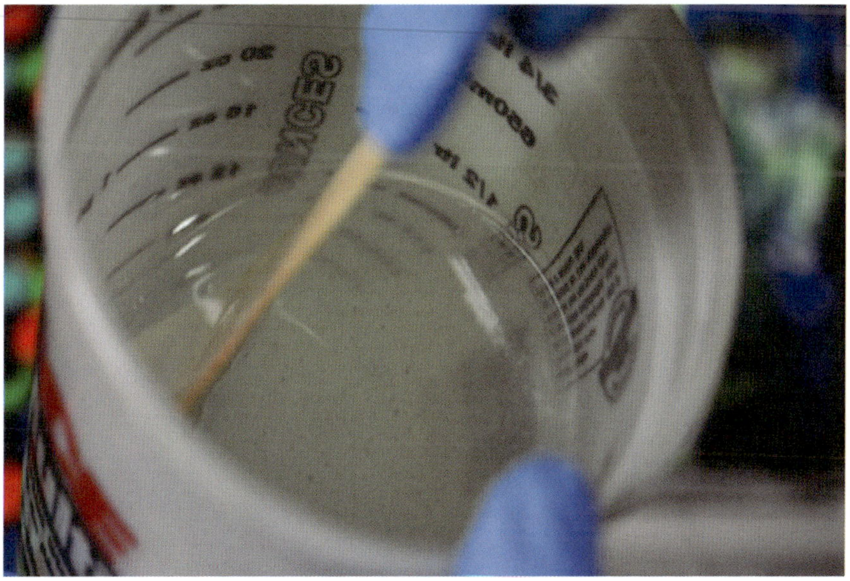

Ready to use, but not crystal clear. There are no swirls or crystal streams when I move the stick around. Even though it is slightly milky in color, it cures to a beautiful glass finish.

SECTION 10
ADDING COLOR TO RESIN

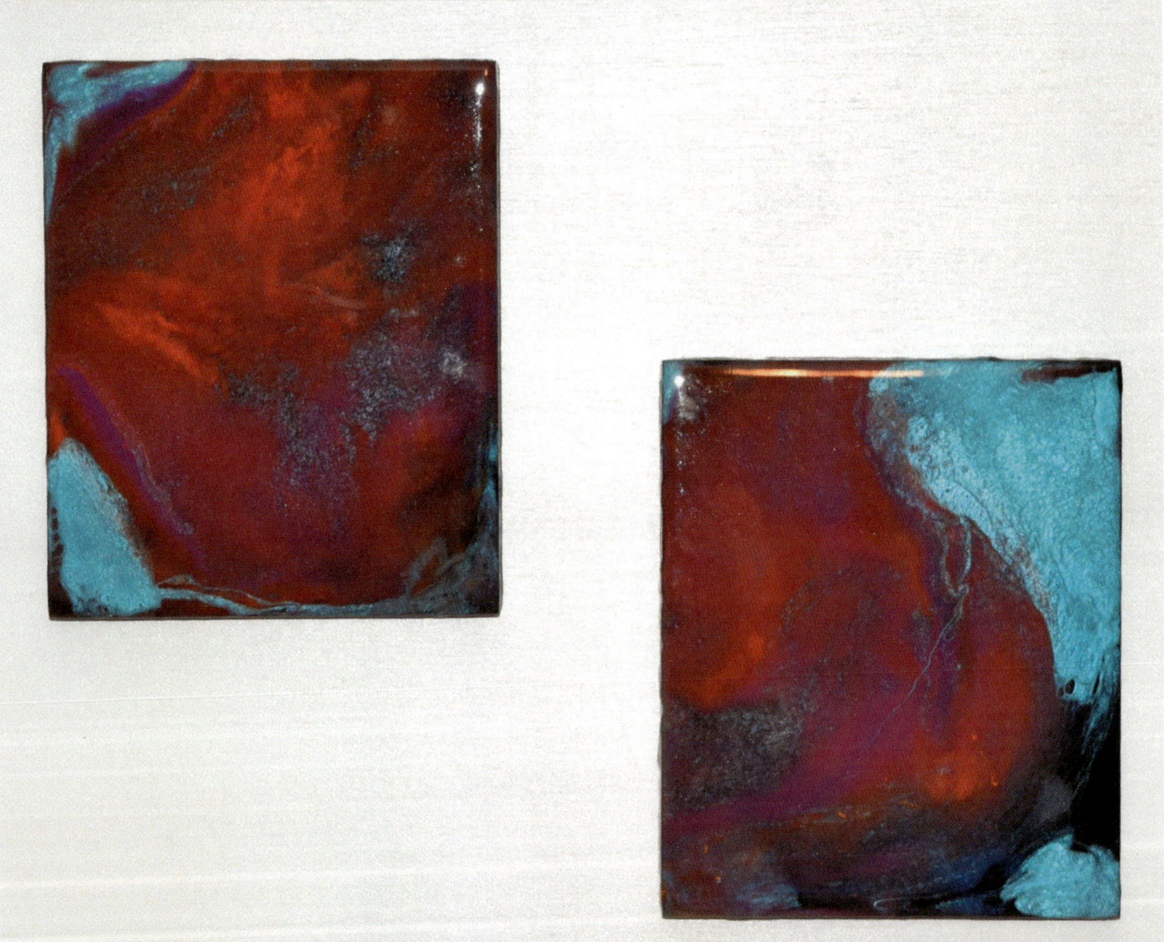

EYE OF THE BEHOLDER
Resin, Pigments Diptych on Cradled Wood Panel
8"X8" (20cmx20cm)

In this section, there is information on the best ways that I have found for adding color to resin. I'll give some tips for mixing color into resin. From here on out whenever resin is mentioned I will be talking about mixed resin. This means resin and hardener mixed together and ready for a pour. Regardless of the colorant being used, it is important to add no more than 10% color to 90% resin.

I will be talking about colorants that create cells and lacing in resin painting. Cells are circle patterns that form as a result of chemical reactions that occur in mixed resin and colorants. Lacing is a pattern that forms as a result of chemical reactions that occur in mixed resin and colorants. Colorants create the chemical reaction that cause cells and lacing. This occurs when the density of one color is different than the density of another color. Adding oil or alcohol changes the density of the colorants and creates cells and lacing. Using oil paints in resin art naturally creates cells and lacing because the density of oil and mixed resin is different. Mixed resin is one density and oil paints are another density. If one or more of the added colors are also different densities, cells and/or lacing occurs. Even though it sounds like using oil, alcohol and resin would not work together to create a proper cure, they do. As long as you don't use too much of any one thing to mixed resin. Once mixed together, resin is always trying to cure. As long as the basic ingredients of the hardener and resin are not overpowered with other ingredients a proper cure will be the end result.

TIP

It only takes a tiny amount of acrylic paint to tint resin to the color of glass or crystal. Touch the end of a toothpick or craft stick to the cap of a tube of paint and mix into resin for slightly tinted resin.

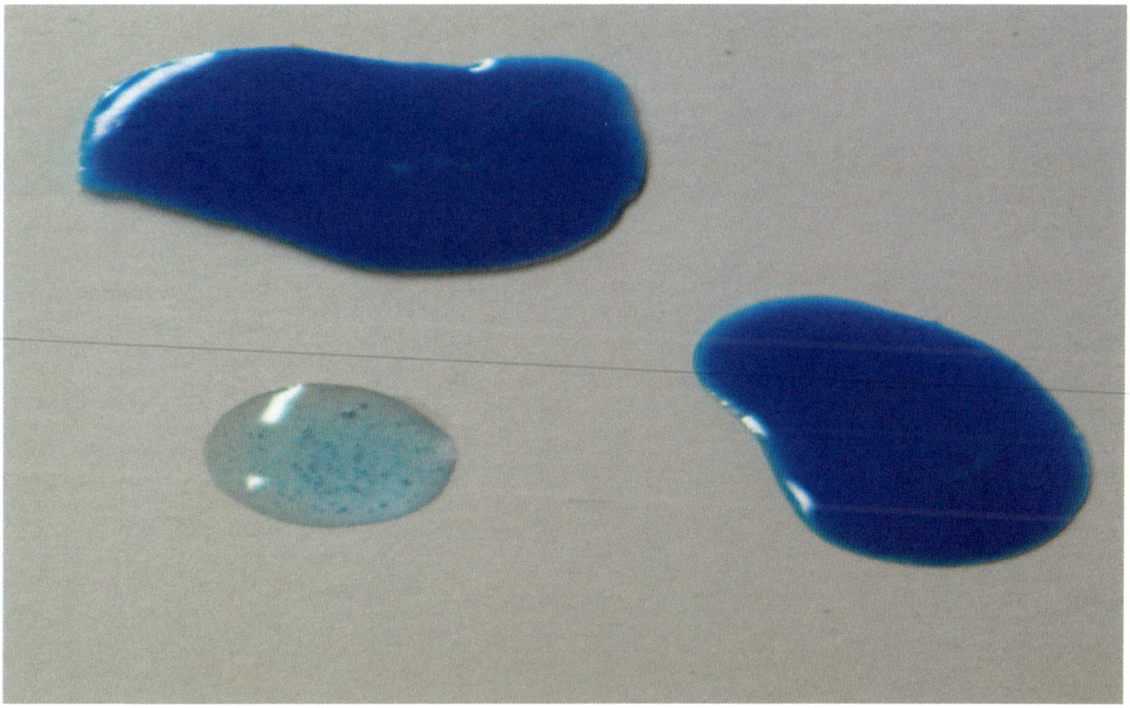

The lighter resin piece has the smallest amount of blue acrylic paint. The two darker pieces have more of the same color.

ACRYLIC PAINTS

When coloring resin with acrylic paint, use no more than 10% paint with 90% mixed resin. Acrylic paint has water and other additives that can cause mixed resin to destabilize and remain sticky or flexible after curing. If too much acrylic paint is used, the resin will be flimsy and flexible after the cure. A finger placed on the cured resin will leave a fingerprint. Many resin artists prefer not to use acrylic paint for this reason. It is possible to use it. It works well in resin applications. As long as no more than 10% paint is used in the mixed resin.

The main reason acrylic paint is chosen by some resin artist is that it's easy to mix into resin. No preparation is required. Simply add a small amount and mix. If more color is desired, add a little more. Try to add the least amount possible to color the mixed resin.

Acrylic paint works great for creating crystal coloring effects in resin, or colored glass effects. If acrylic paint is used for this, only use a very tiny amount. To use this method, stick the very tip of a toothpick in the cap, or just inside the tube of a chosen paint color, and swirl it into the resin. A craft stick dabbed on the open tube of the paint will provide enough paint to color the resin for this effect. Completely mix it into the resin.

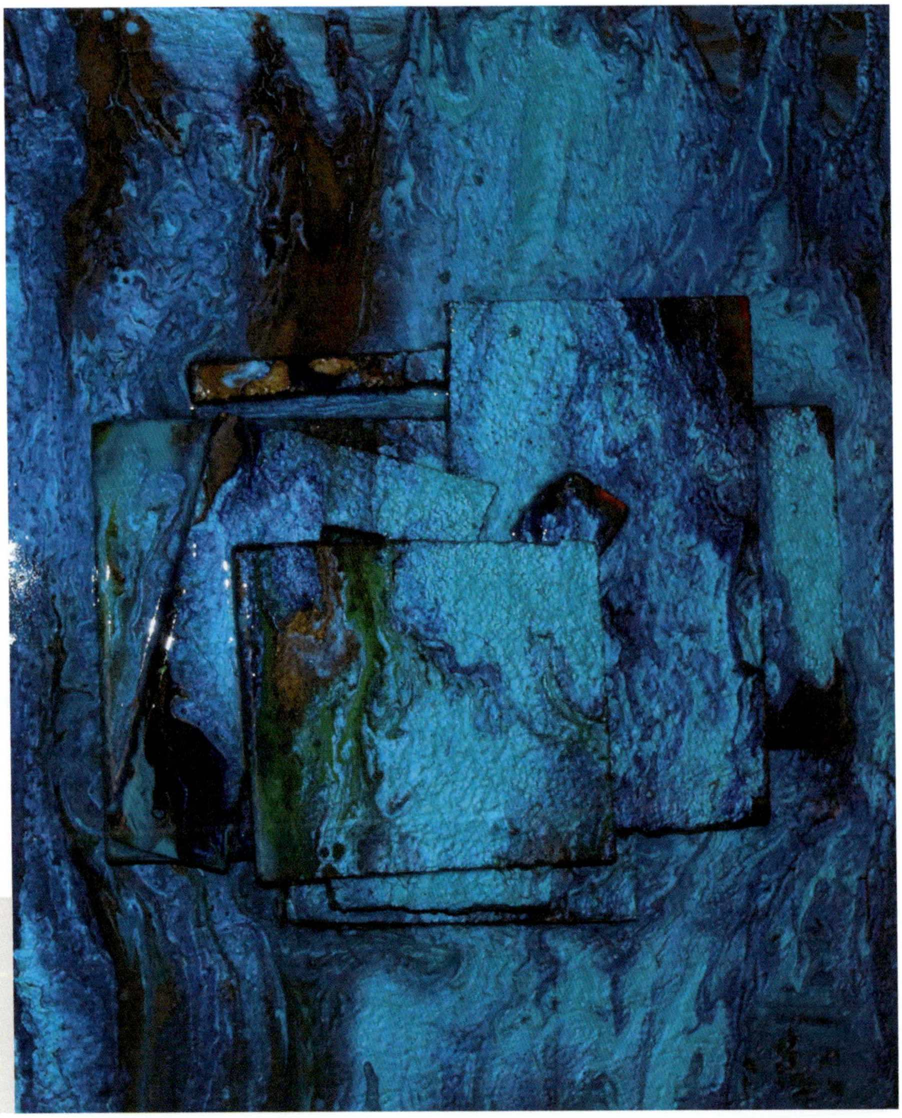

FINDING THE WAY
Resin & Acrylic Paint on
Cradled Wood Panel
16"x20" (41cmx51cm)

POWDER PIGMENTS

When coloring resin with powder or mica you don't have to be as precise with the 10% colorant to mixed resin rule. The stability of the resin doesn't change with powder pigments. I wouldn't go crazy and add 40% or 50% but you don't have to measure precisely either.

The more pigment powder used the more it will speed up the work time. Resin work time is the amount of time the resin is fluid and flowing and before it begins the curing process. Using 10% powder to 90% resin will ensure the work time will not change. If more than 20% powder to 80% mixed resin is used the work time will be cut in half. A little goes a long way with pigment and mica powder. It colors very well. A ¼ teaspoon of pigment powder will provide great color to a full cup of resin. The more powder used the more saturated. It only takes a tiny amount to create a crystal look to resin. A speck of powder on the end of a craft stick is enough to change the color of the resin to look like a crystal.

Many mica powders are less prone to clumping in resin than pigment powder. A few mica powders still clump. When using mica, you may add it right into the resin. Pigment powder, on the other hand, generally always clumps. There are a few methods for adding pigment powder to resin to avoid clumping.

Add pigment powder to a tiny amount of mixed resin and work out the clumps before adding it to the rest of the mixed resin. Use a craft stick and press the pigment powder into the resin on the side of a small plastic or silicone cup. When it is fully mixed, pour in more of the desired amount of resin. This is the method that I use primarily. Try to remove all clumps before adding the full amount of mixed resin. It's easier to press out the clumps when working with a small amount of mixed resin. It's not so easy once the full amount of mixed resin is added to the color mixing cup.

Use parchment paper to premix the pigments with resin. On a piece of parchment paper, use a make-up spatula to smooth and mix together the amount of powder with a little bit of mixed resin. Press and stir together until fully mixed. When fully mixed and all lumps are gone, scrape up the mixture and place in the color mixing cup. Add more resin to the cup until the desired color is reached. Stir well. Using this method, you may mix colors of pigment powder to create a new color, or add glow powder to add glow effects to the resin art.

CAUTION

Some powder pigments are toxic. When inhaled the body absorbs them, creating a health hazard. When mixed with resin, or other liquid components they lose their ability to become airborne. Always use a face respirator or at least a face mask with working with pigments in powder form.

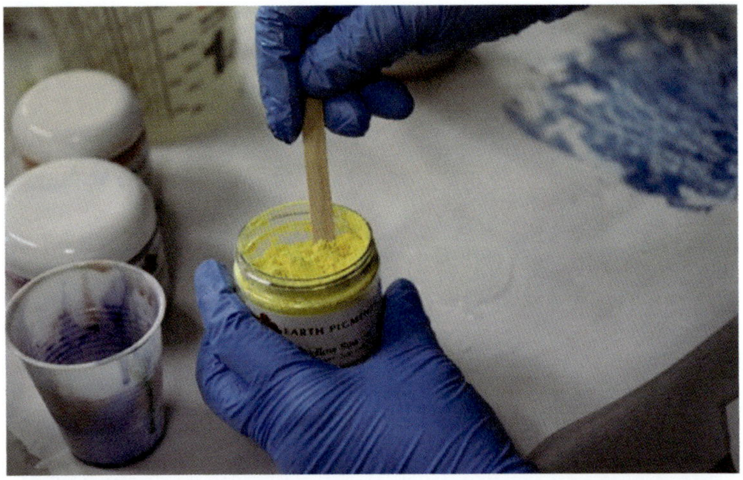

Use a clean dry craft stick to measure pigment powder on parchment paper and mix with resin.

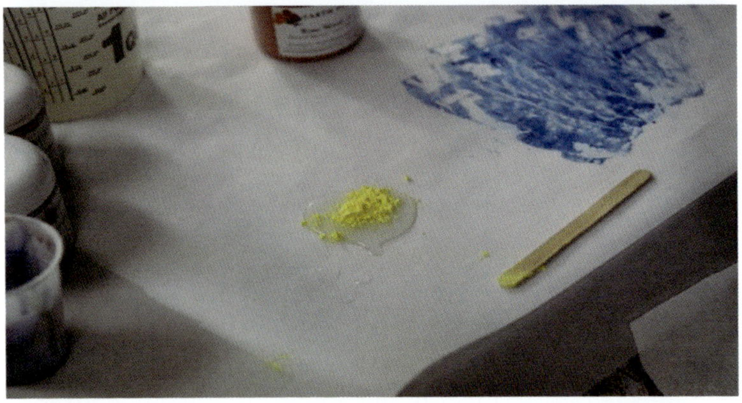

Pigment powder and mixed resin on parchment paper.

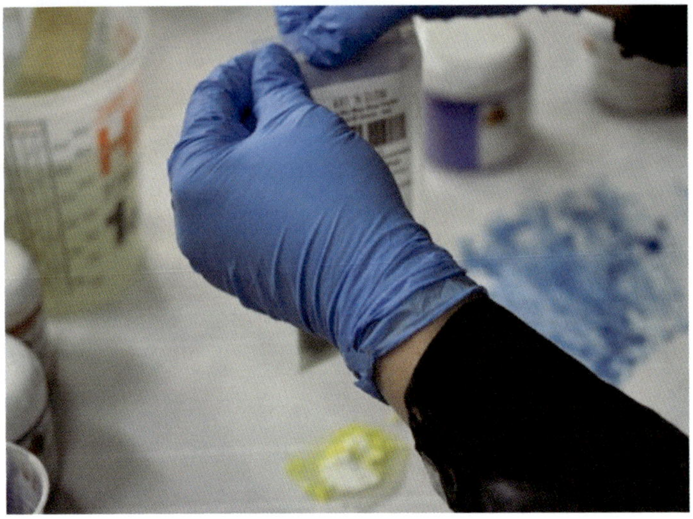

Adding glow powder to pigment powder and mixed resin.

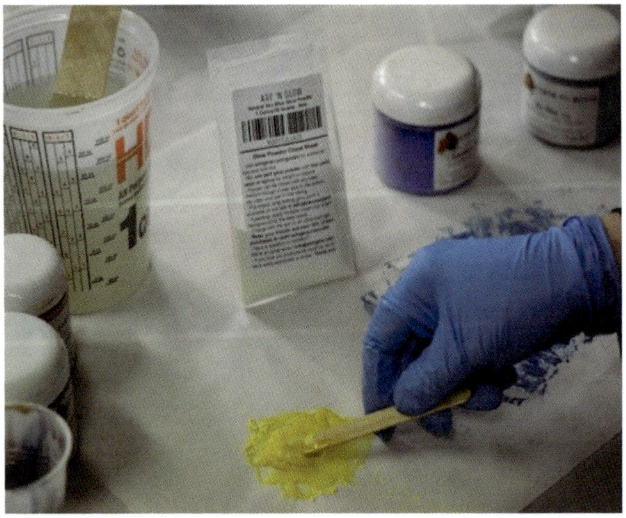

Press the powder into the mixed resin. Stir together until thoroughly mixed.

When thoroughly mixed, scrape back into the cup. I am using a cup from a previous pour. The resin in the cup has been checked to ensure it is fully cured and no loose pieces are going to land in the cup.

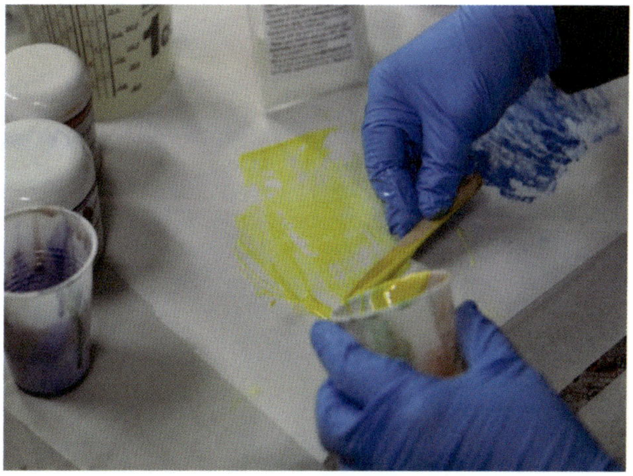

Add more mixed resin to the color mixing cup to reach the desired amount needed.

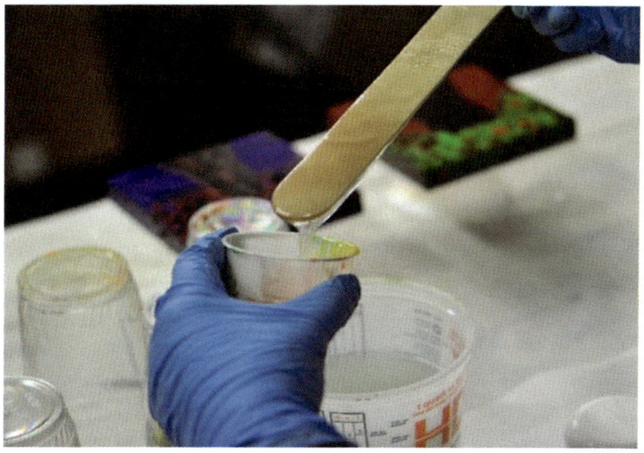

Stir to mix well. It is now ready to use.

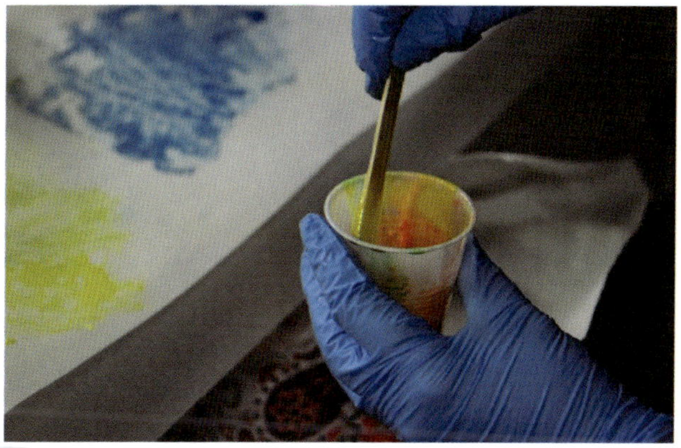

TIP

Titanium dioxide is the pigment powder used to make white acrylic paint and white oil paint. It can be purchased in art stores or online very inexpensively. It is pennies on the dollar compared to the cost of white paint. Using titanium dioxide as the white colorant over acrylic or oil has many benefits. You can control the amount of color pigment. By using the powder, greater color saturation is achieved because there are no additives. Adding titanium dioxide to a drop or 2 of safflower or linseed oil allows you to create your own oil paint. But it also allows you to create a white colorant that creates cells and lacing in your art.

Linseed Oil Method

Mix 1/4 teaspoon pigment powder with 1 to 2 drops of safflower or linseed oil. This is making a kind of oil paint. On a piece of parchment paper, use a make-up spatula or craft stick to work ¼ teaspoon pigment powder and oil together. An art palette knife can be used for this step. Do not use art palette knives in mixed resin as it will ruin the palette knife. Once the powder and oil are thoroughly mixed add to mixed resin. This method will give cells and lacing. Any use of oil in resin painting will give cells and lacing.

Polymer Medium Method

Add 1/4 teaspoon pigment powder to a drop or two of polymer medium, or artists pouring medium before adding it to the resin. This is essentially making a kind of acrylic paint but without the additives that are usually in the paint. To use this method, mix 3 to 4 drops of chosen medium to ¼ teaspoon of pigment powder. Continue adding the medium 1 drop at a time until well blended. Add desired amount to mixed resin. The benefit of using pigments mixed this way, rather than using acrylic paint, is that you can control the amount of polymer or pouring medium mixed to combine the pigments. The result is more pigments in the resin. More pigments equal greater color saturation.

Isopropyl Alcohol Method

Mix ¼ teaspoon pigment powder with a little bit of isopropyl alcohol. To use this method, mix 3 to 4 drops of 91% or 99% isopropyl alcohol to ¼ teaspoon of pigment powder until blended. Keep adding isopropyl alcohol 1 drop at a time until blended and free of clumps. I usually do this in the cup I'm going to add my resin to. I simply mix on the side of the cup with a craft stick. The use of isopropyl alcohol can create cells and lacing in resin. The smaller the amount of isopropyl alcohol you use the less cells and lacing are likely. If cells and lacing are desired, add several more drops of isopropyl alcohol to your mix. Alcohol is flammable and can ignite when torching for bubbles in resin. Use caution.

TIP

Dust pigment powder in the color of choice over the surface of a poured resin painting for special effects. Using metallic mica or pigments gives the most interesting effects.

OIL PAINT

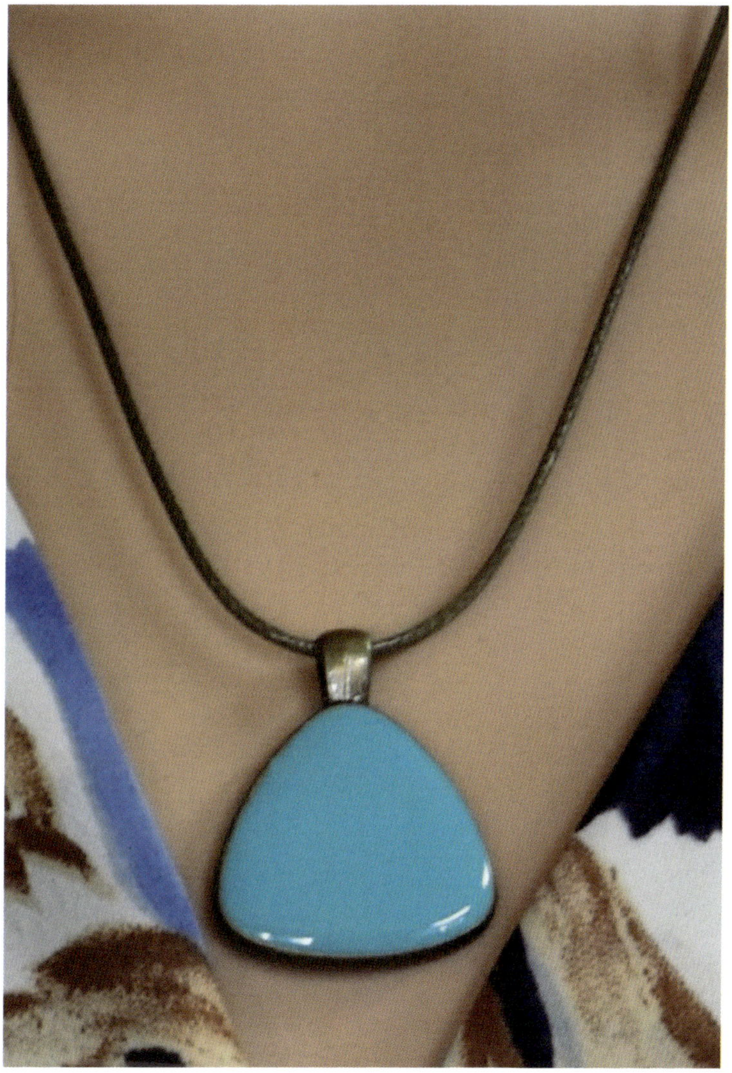

Resin & Oil Paint in Bronze Pendant

Coloring with oil paint is not only possible but wonderful. Other resin artists are often incredulous when I tell them I paint in resin with oil paint. Resin artists say "it's not possible to paint with resin because it destabilizes the resin. The oil paint doesn't cure properly with resin." Not only is it possible to paint with oil paint but it is an ideal medium to work with, when done properly. It actually makes the resin sturdier than resin alone. Oil paint in resin makes beautiful jewelry.

Using oil paint in resin requires preparation. When using oil paint, first mix the paint with walnut oil, safflower oil or linseed oil. Add just enough oil to remove all lumps and smooth out your paint. If the oil paint is already creamy in texture, it may only require working it around with a craft stick before adding it to the resin. I do this in the cup that I am going to be adding my resin in.

Start by adding 2 drops of walnut or linseed oil. Add a small bead of oil paint, to equal ¼ teaspoon. Use a craft stick to work the oil into the oil paint. Mix until the oil and paint are well blended and free of clumps. Then add the paint to mixed resin, keeping to the 10% paint 90% mixed resin rule.

Another method for mixing is to squeeze the oil paint on parchment paper drop on a little mixed resin and mix until all lumps and clumps are smooth. Use a make-up spatula for this. Scrape up the mixture, place it into a color mixing cup and add more resin.

Adding too much oil paint to mixed resin without proper stirring will result in pitting in the surface of the cured resin. This can be a cool effect that can be covered with another layer of resin to seal it in. A finger pressed on the cured surface will pick up uncured oil paint. If this occurs, and you like the art, another layer of clear resin will seal the pits and bits of uncured oil paint. This happens when clumps of oil paint are left in the mix. They sit there on the canvas and the resin moves around them, leaving divots. I believe this is why many resin artists say that oil paint doesn't work with resin. To avoid this, smooth out any clumps before the mixture goes on the canvas. I have found that as long as you properly stir the oil paint with the mixed resin it does not affect the stability of the resin. Even if you add a little too much oil paint to the mixed resin.

Add a little mixed resin to a bead of oil paint.

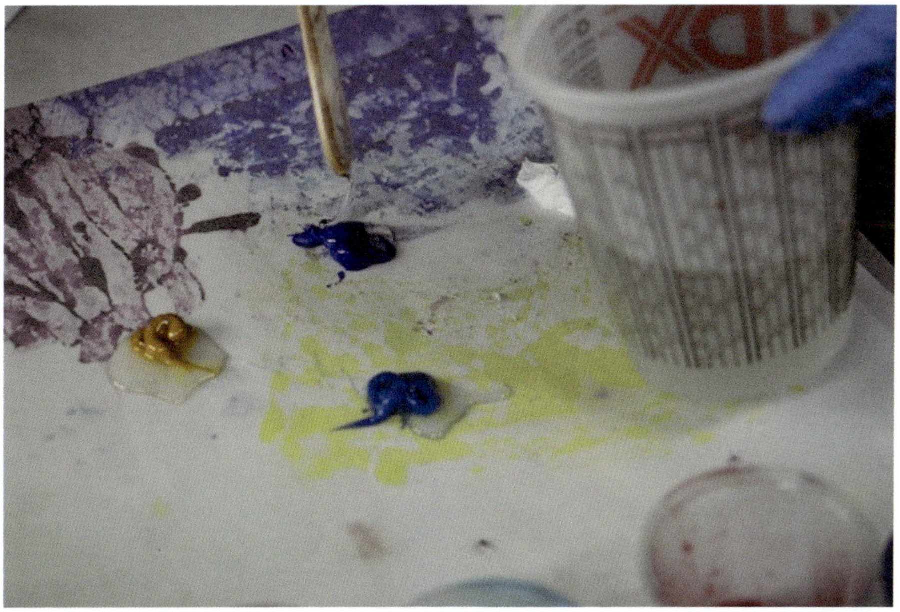

Press the resin and paint together and stir it in.

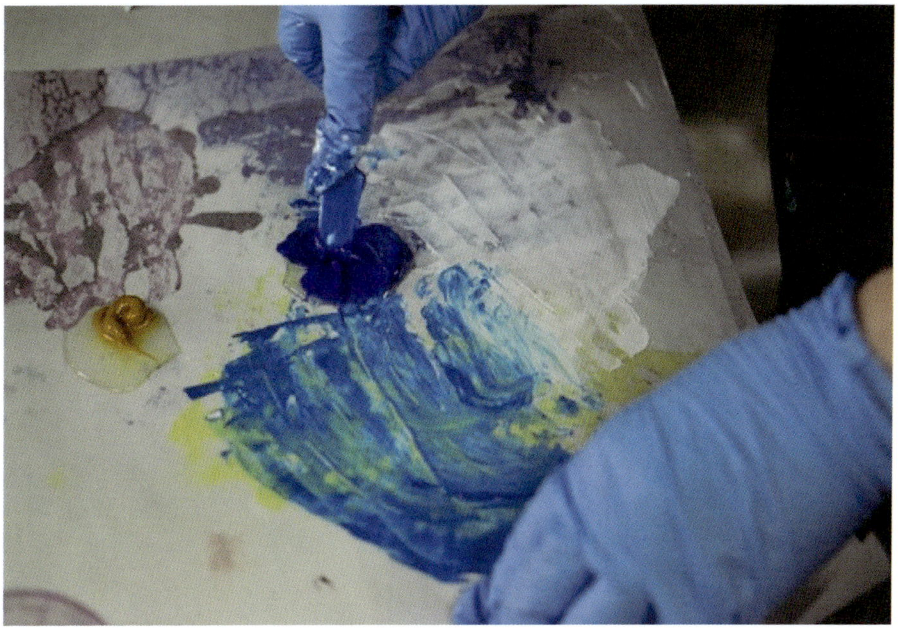

Blend well.

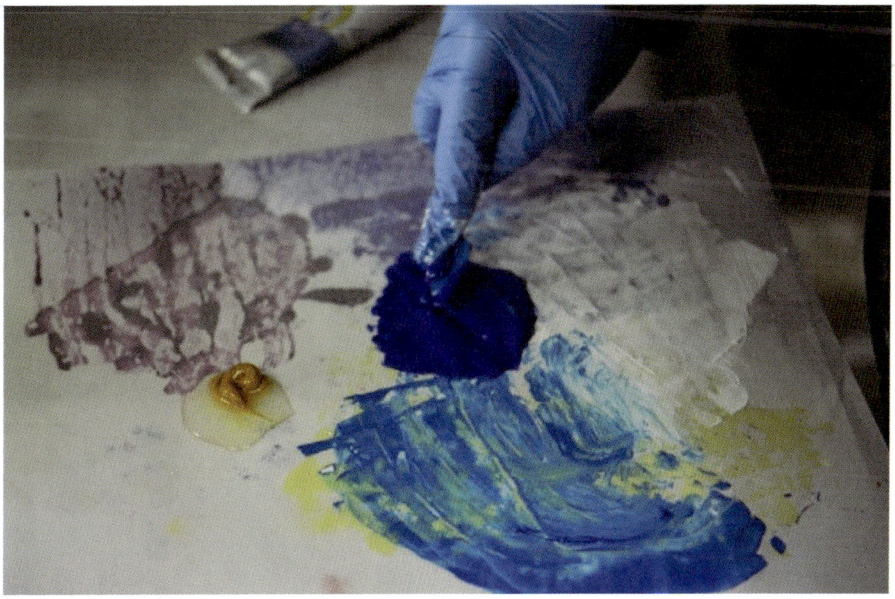

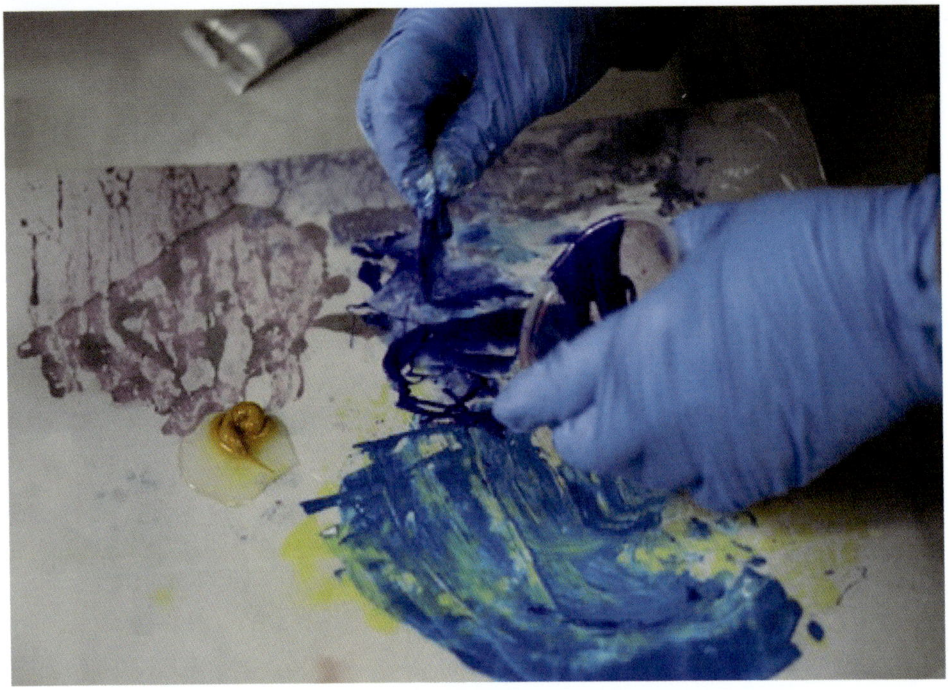

Add the mix to a cup with more mixed resin. Stir well.

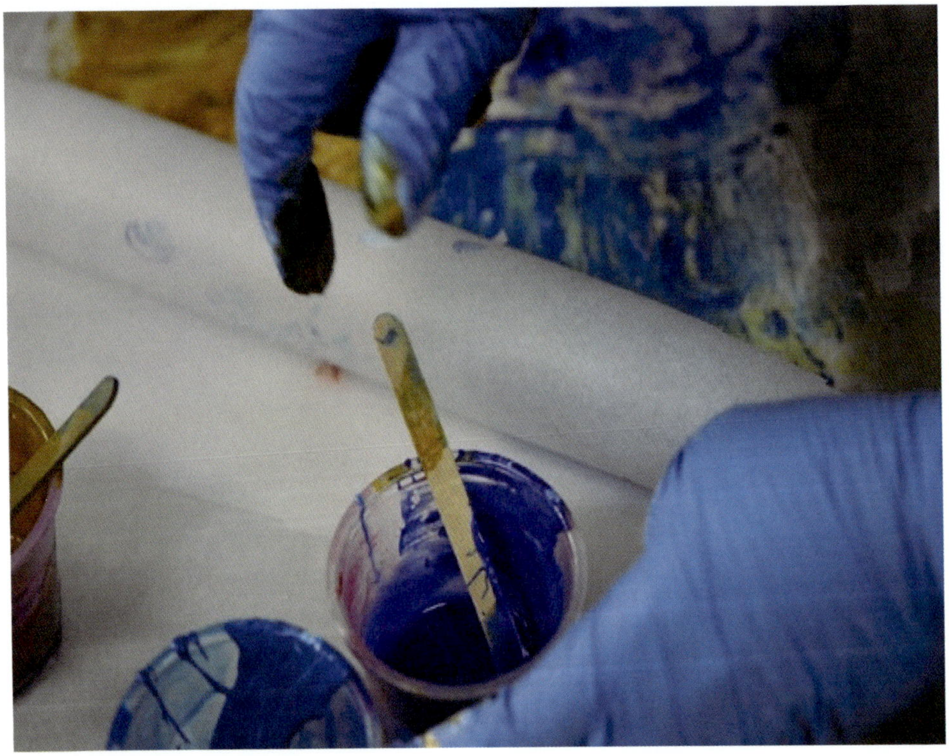

It's ready to use.

Adding oil paint to resin is fun to experiment with. If a very clear painting is desired or you are working with light or white paints choose safflower oil as your mixative over walnut oil. Walnut oil is slightly more yellow than safflower oil. Oil paint gives incredible color saturation, and creates a sturdy painting. The added oil will create cells and lacing. Oil paint provides incredible color, lacing and cells. Oil paint in resin makes stunning paintings.

When using inks to color resin, stir them directly into the resin. Drop them directly from the bottle on top of clear or colored resin for affect. Mixing ink with paint or pigments gives really interesting effects. Acrylic inks and alcohol inks can be dropped into or mixed with acrylic paint, and then mixed with resin. To mix inks of any kind in resin, use a drop at a time until you get the color you want. To use them on the surface, drop them on and let them spread, or swirl them with a toothpick. For an interesting effect layer drops of clear resin between drops of inks.

TIP

Try layering colors of alcohol inks on the surface of resin. Pour a flood coat of resin. Drop a color of your choice. Choose a complimentary or contrasting color to drop on top of the first color. Continue layering the colors until you have the effects you desire. Clear mixed resin can be poured in the center of the ink for even greater effects.

Tints or resin tints are manufactured by companies that sell resin and are made for coloring resin. Follow the instructions for using them. Start with a little bit of color. Less is usually better with resin tints. Resin dyes are made and sold by epoxy resin companies for coloring resin. They are not the same as craft or fabric dyes. Follow the instructions for using them. Start with a little bit of color. Less is usually better.

TIP

You can make alcohol ink by adding pigment powder to isopropyl alcohol. Given that commercial alcohol inks are said to be non-archival due to using acetate which can break down pigments overtime, it is worth it to make your own. Alcohol inks can be made by soaking permanent marker inserts in 91% isopropyl alcohol. Use pliers to break apart the marker. Remove the liner that contains the ink. Place it in a bottle with alcohol. Allow it to sit and absorb the ink. It's messy but you can do it.

Craft or fabric dyes are usually liquid or water based and should be used sparingly in resin. Use a drop or 2 at a time until you get the color you want. Never use more than you need, as it may weaken the resin. If too much dye is used in the resin, pits and rivers will result in the cured resin. This can be an interesting effect that can be strengthened with a pour of clear mixed resin over the top.

You are ready to let your **creativity** *flow!*

SECTION 11
PAINTING WITHRESIN

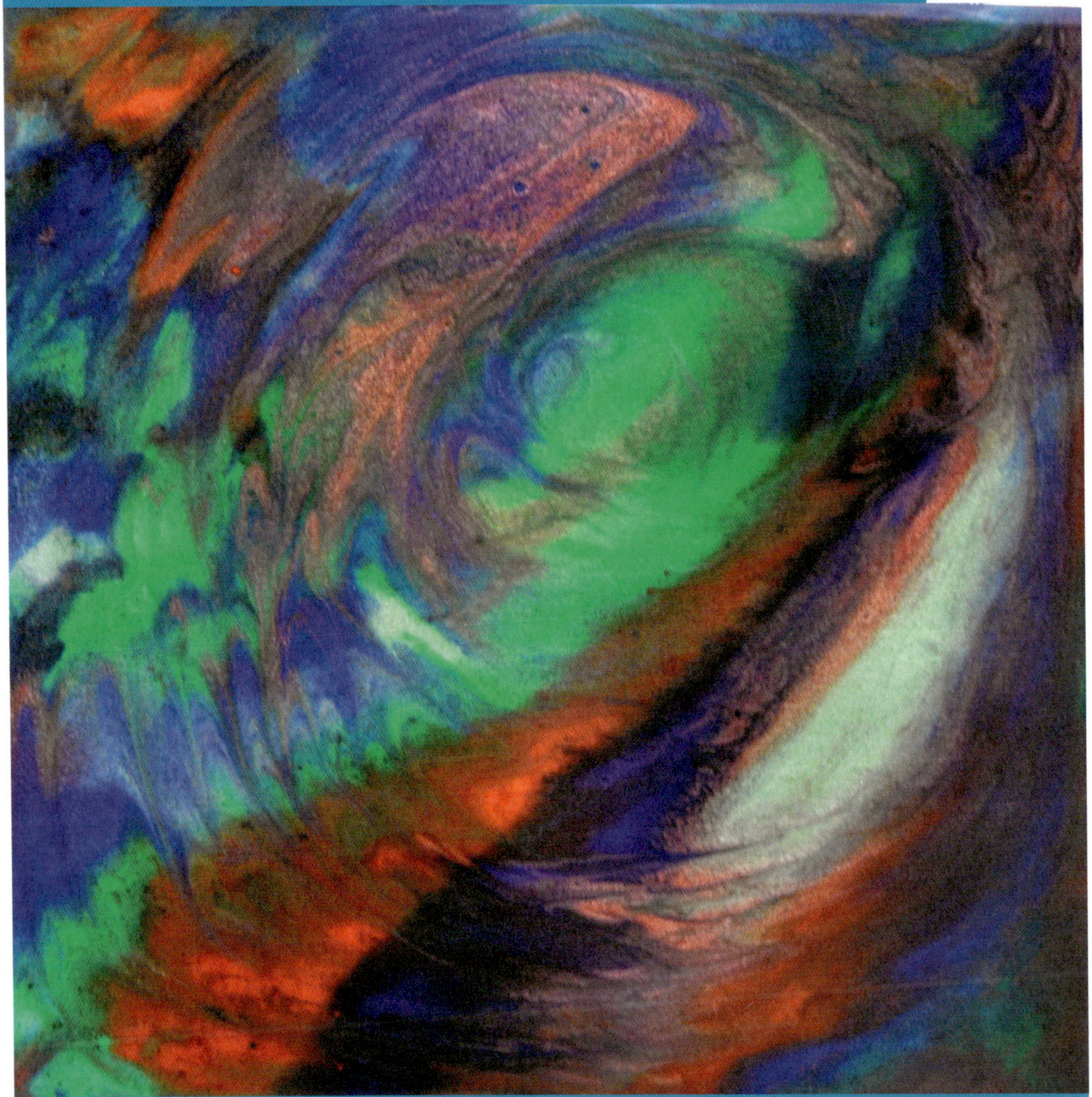

ANGEL WINGS
Resin, Pigments, Mica on Cradled Wood Panel

12"x12" (31cmx31cm)

Let's paint with resin.

NEXT STEP

Once the resin is mixed, divide it into smaller mixing cups and add in the colorant of choice. Small plastic or silicone cups are great for this step. It's helpful to keep some clear resin aside for adding on top, or using as a base coat.

TIP

Layer 3 to 4 pairs of gloves on your hands before beginning a complicated resin project. That way you can take off a pair of gloves and have a fresh pair to work with already on your hands. This also helps for when you need to torch but still need to work on the art piece.

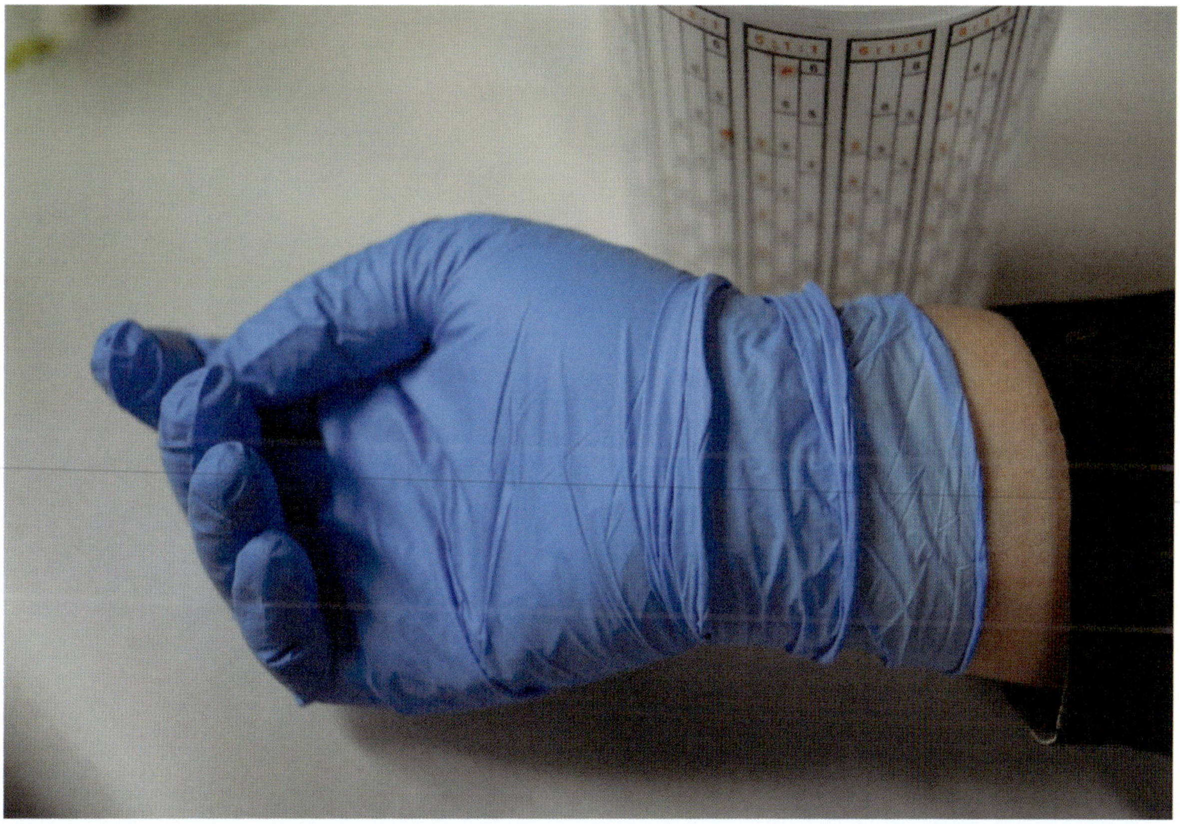

Three pairs of gloves. Layered for ease of pulling off.

PIGMENT POWDERS & RESIN

I am using pigment powder stirred straight into the mixed resin for this project. I am not premixing it with the resin or any other additive.

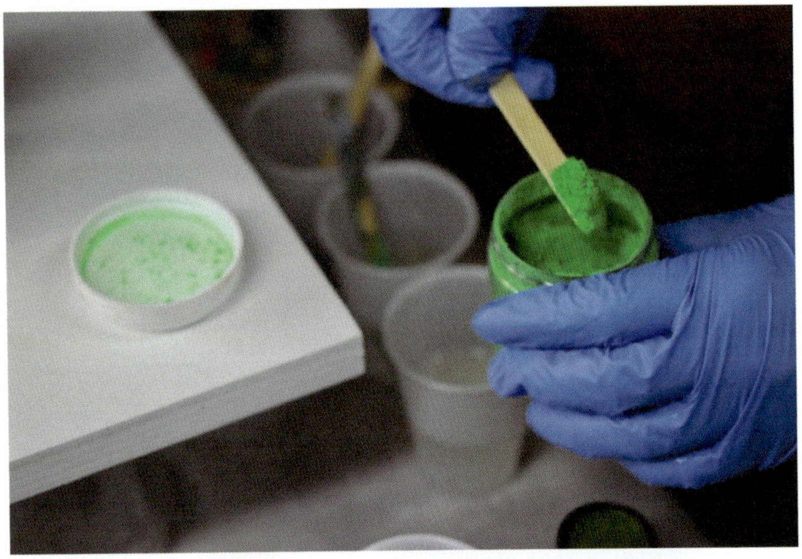

Adding pigment powder to resin.

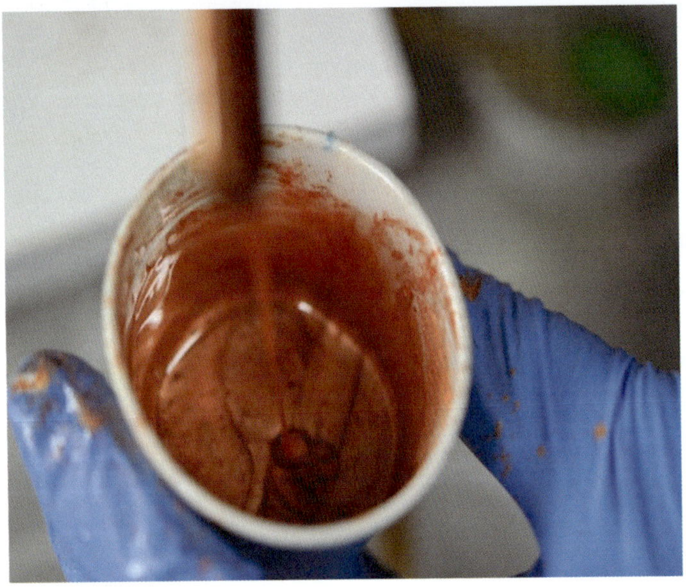

Mixing copper mica into resin.

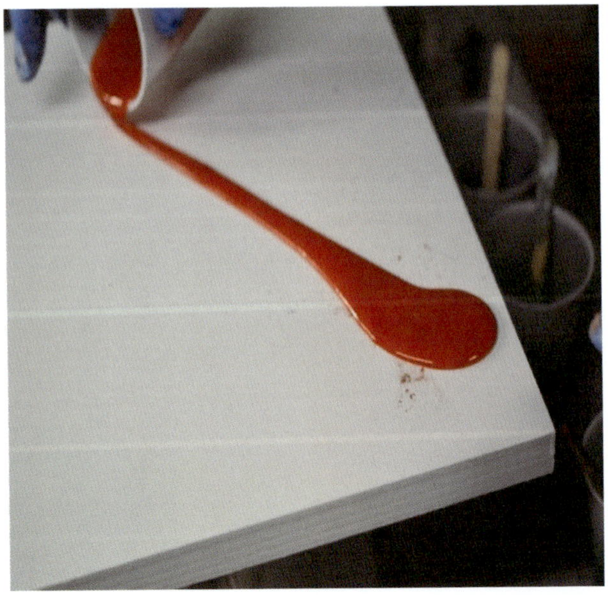

Mix up all chosen resin colors. Decide on the type of resin pour you want to do. I keep clear resin and colored resin cups lined up next to the canvas.

TIP

When the resin begins to warm to the touch it is curing. It will thicken and slow down it's ability to move around the canvas. Work quickly you only have a couple of minutes before it becomes stringy.

Turn the cups upside down on the canvas to let the last bit of paint land on the canvas.

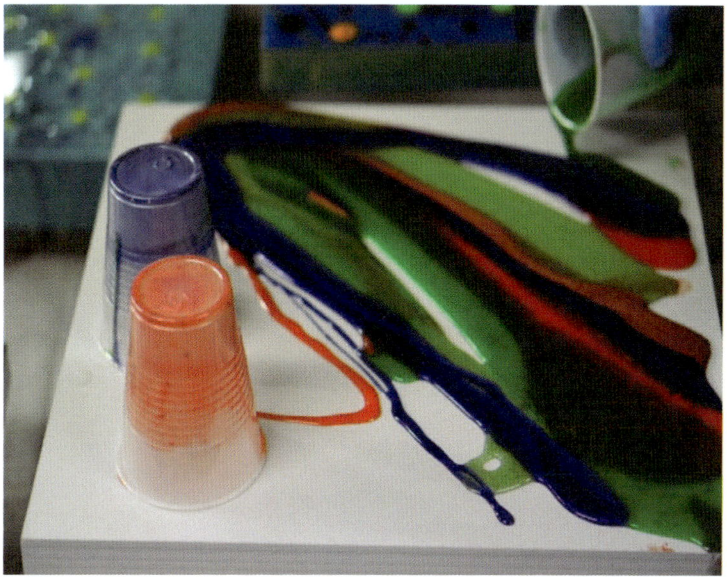

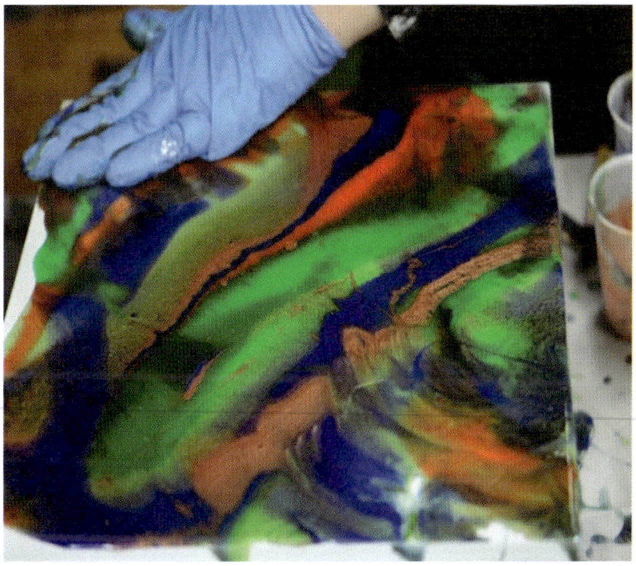

Cover the entire surface with mixed resin and colorant. Spread it around using anything you choose. A brush will need to be tossed after resin. A silicone spatula is great for spreading. I prefer to use my gloved hand.

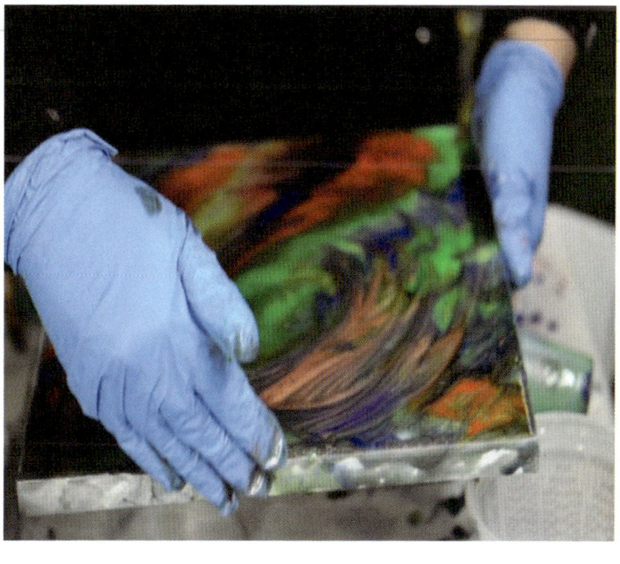

Spread the resin onto the sides of the canvas, unless you have taped them off for clean sides. Move the resin to the edge of the painting and allow it to fall over the sides. By covering all sides in resin, you are priming it so that the resin will fall off uniformly. When the resin falls over the sides, spread it out to fully cover the surface area.

I often start with a pour of clear resin to prime the canvas. Then pour on the resin & color. Put enough resin on the surface to completely cover the canvas. I could brush off that excess copper pigment but I know that the added copper powder will create some lacing in the resin.

Swirl in a design if you choose.

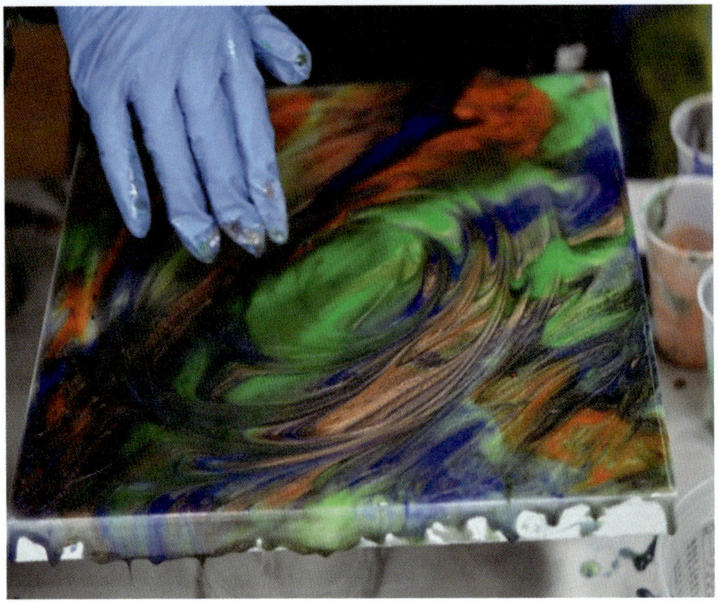

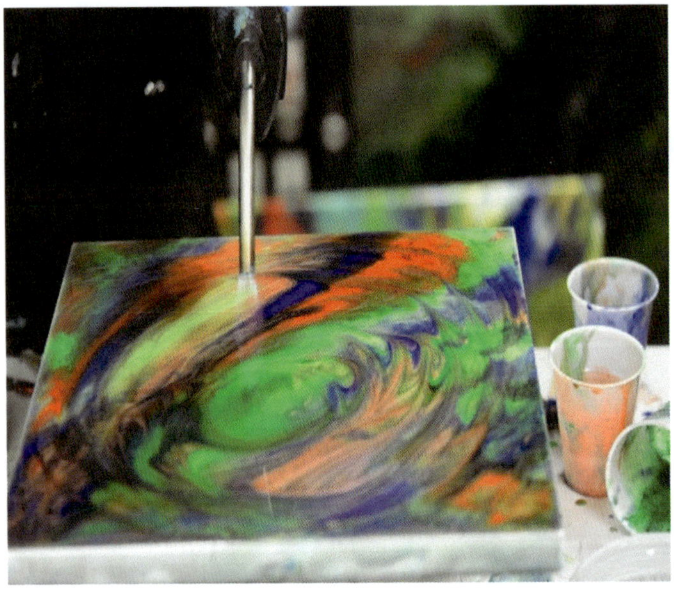

Torching for bubbles. Go over the canvas lightly with the torch. The torch should not touch the resin.

Using a small screwdriver to remove a particle of dust from the resin.

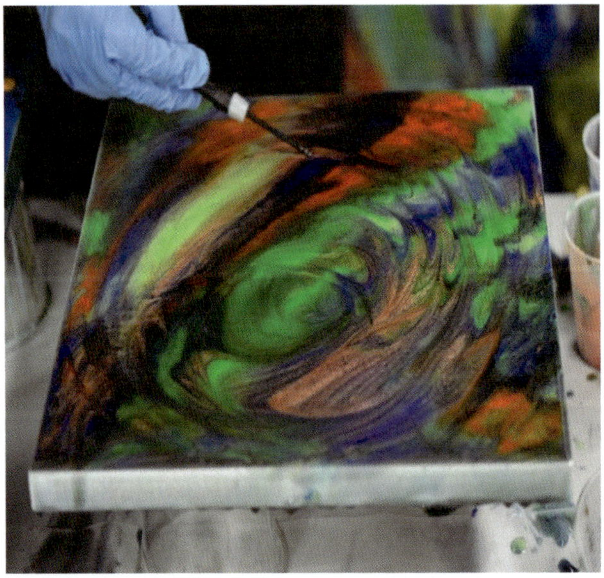

Use a propane or butane torch to remove bubbles from the surface of the poured resin. A torch gives greater control. A heat gun blows air and will move the resin around, which will change the image in the resin on the substrate. I use a propane torch from the hardware store. I also have a smaller butane torch that I keep as a back-up.

Lightly run the torch over the surface to remove bubbles. The torch should not touch the resin. Keep the torch about an inch above the surface of the resin. The carbon dioxide and a little heat is what pops the bubbles. Be careful not to burn the resin or overheat it. Don't stay in one area to long. A light once over is all it takes. Don't over torch. Over torching can cause the resin to cure in spots and create waves in the painting. Remember, a light once over is all it takes. Look the painting over. Check it for bubbles. If you see any, torch again. It should only take 2 to 3 times of torching to remove bubbles. Any more than that can risk burning the resin. Give yourself a maximum of 4 times of torching during the work time. Don't stay in one area too long.

Long tweezers are best for removing any bits of hair or dust particles from the resin. If you don't have tweezers use a small skewer, screwdriver, or any item you can lift with. In 10 minutes, torch again. Look for particles and remove if you see them. Come back in 10 or 15 minutes and check for bubbles and particles. Torch again if needed. Remember, a light once over is all that is needed. Keep checking the painting for dust and bubbles for the next hour.

When you are happy with the outcome, it's time to cover the art. Use a clean plastic bin or cardboard box. Another method is to place cups or items taller than your art around the perimeter of the table then place a large flat piece of cardboard on top of them. Make sure the cardboard does not touch the art. Finally, drape the cardboard in plastic sheeting or drop cloth. I keep a large shipping box above the resin table that is easy to take down and cover the art. It covers the entire table. I used a box knife to cut out one complete side of the box for a perfect fit over the table. I have a large plastic storage bin that I use to place over pieces. Sometimes, I want to continue working on another piece. I place the lid of the box on top and continue on another piece. I have varying sizes of plastic storage bins that I use to place over smaller pieces. I can use a smaller storage bin to stack on the larger one when needed.

When using tape, I find it best to remove the tape from the substrate before it fully cures. I usually remove the tape after 2 hours, but if you really want a clean side you can wait 5 hours. Removing the tape before it fully cures helps the resin to fall over the sides and prevents hard edges. After removing the tape, replace the cover because dust and hair can still stick to the art at this point.

FLOOD COAT

A flood coat is mixed resin, without colorant, poured over a surface. It can be used to coat a completed painting or as a second coat on a colored resin project.

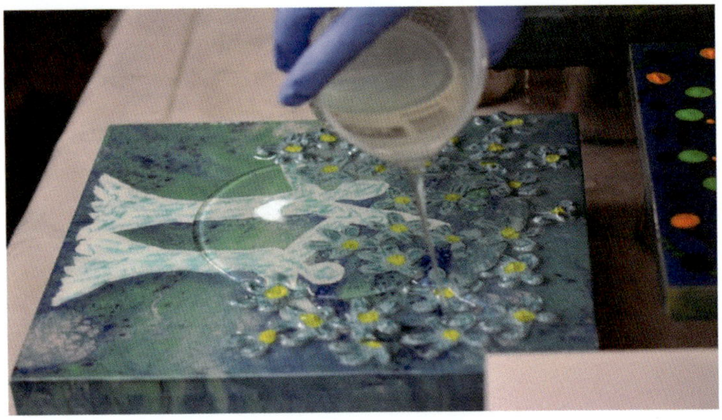

When clear coating an already finished painting with resin, pour clear resin right onto the surface. A thin layer is all that is needed. This is a second layer of resin on this piece.

Mix the resin according to directions. When pouring on a dimensional painting, start with the highest points first. Allow the resin to spread onto the base from the highest levels. Finish pouring resin where needed to cover the entire piece.

Clear resin flood coat on dimensional art. This is a second layer on a sanded surface.

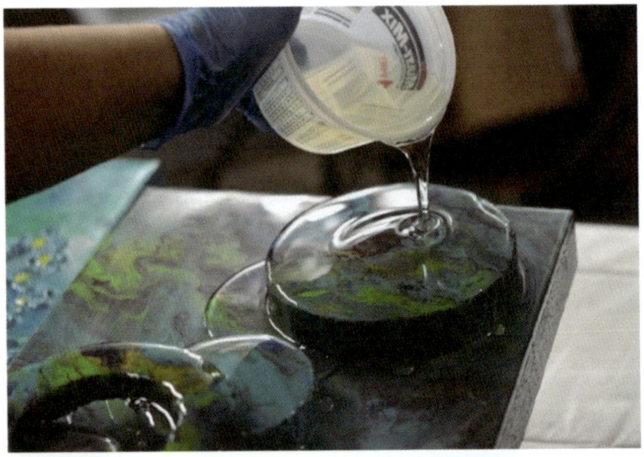

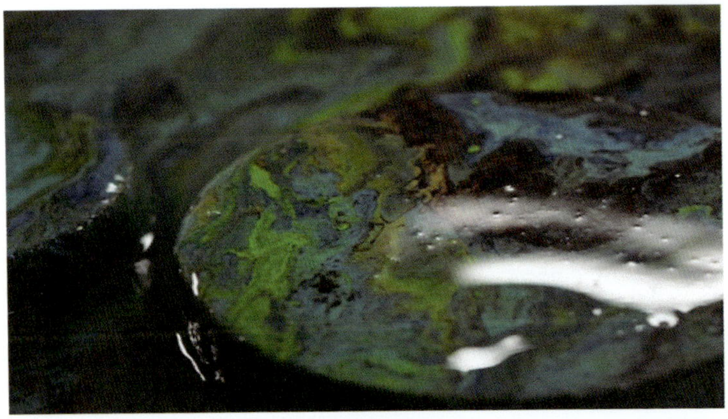

Bubbles on the surface. A light torching removes them.

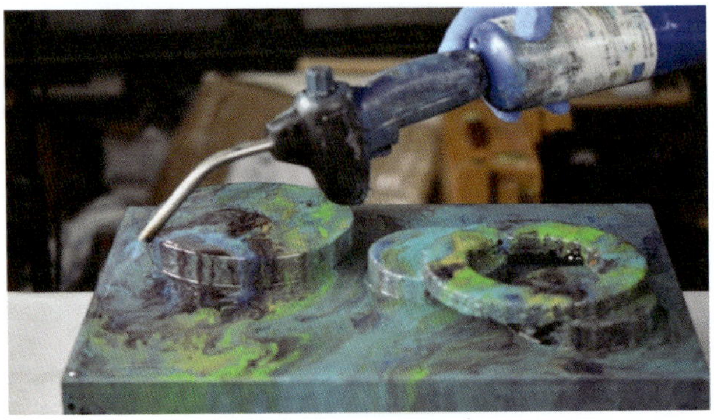

Take care of the bubbles with a propane or butane torch, or with a heat gun.

RESIN MIXED MEDIA ART

Now let's do some resin in resin art, or resin mixed media art. I'm using leftover resin from another painting and using it to make a new painting. The pieces of cured resin are pieces from the table that fell on to the plastic sheeting. I peeled them off and cut them down to size. The grid was from a jewelry silicone mat that I use. I'm using mixed liquid resin as the glue to hold the pieces in place and then pouring more resin on top. I painted the wood gesso board with a base of acrylic paint in emerald green.

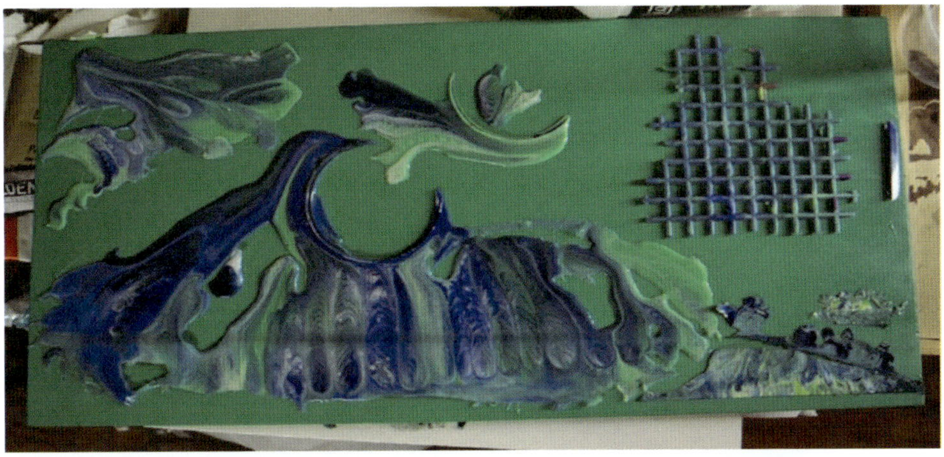

Pieces of Resin Ready for Mixed Media Art.

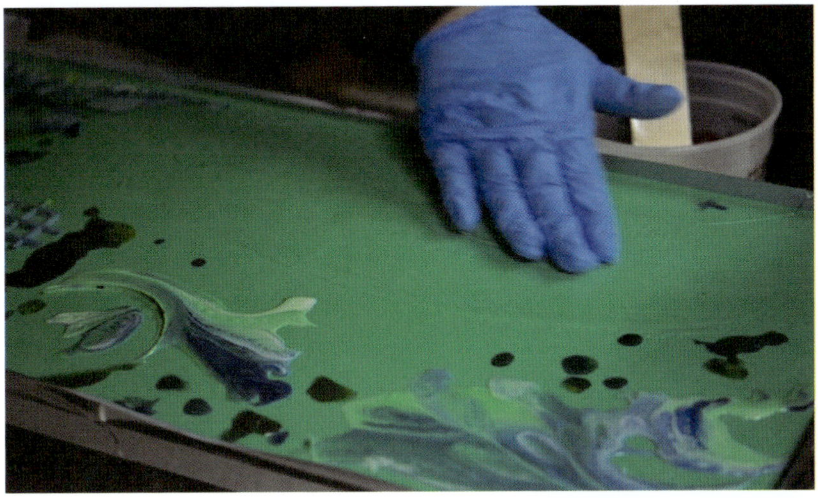

Lay down liquid mixed resin in the area to receive the mixed media pieces.

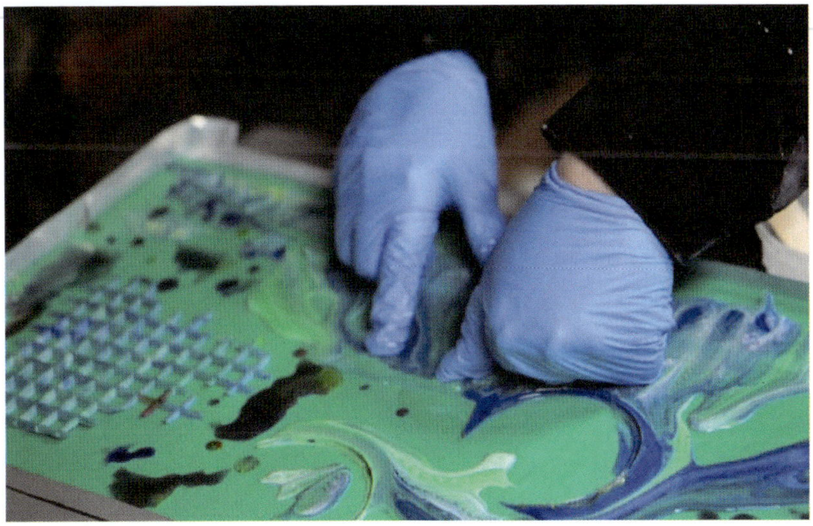

Place the mixed media piece into the wet resin and press down to seal.

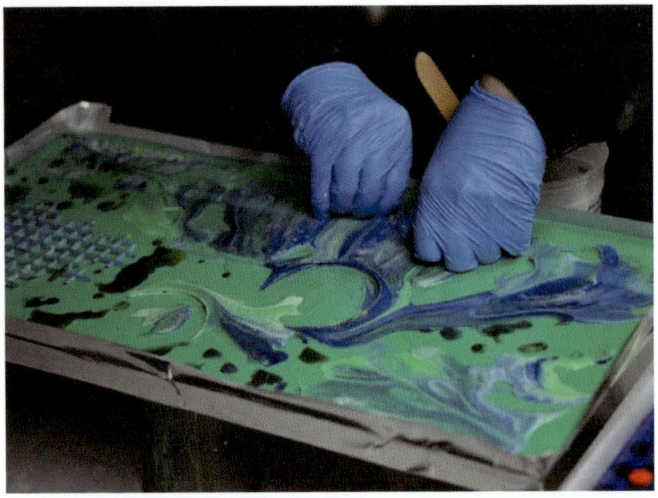

Continue to press and smooth the mixed media piece into place.

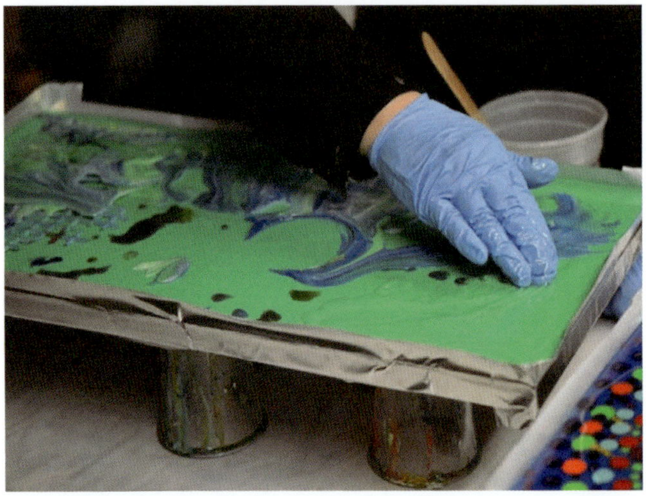

Repeat the process until all the mixed media pieces are glued in place.

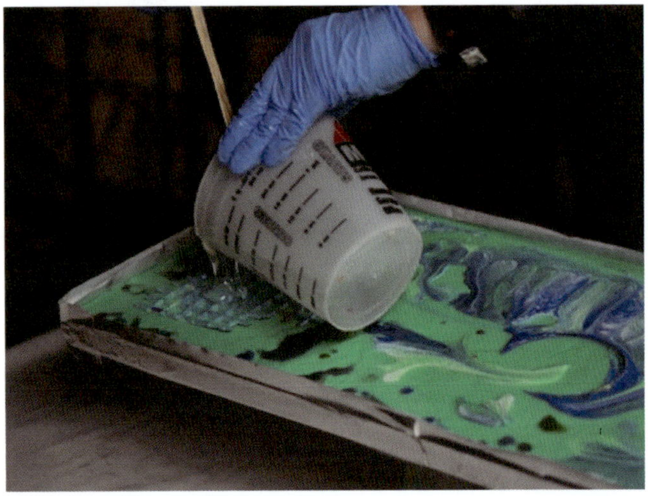

Cover the whole surface with a flood coat of mixed resin.

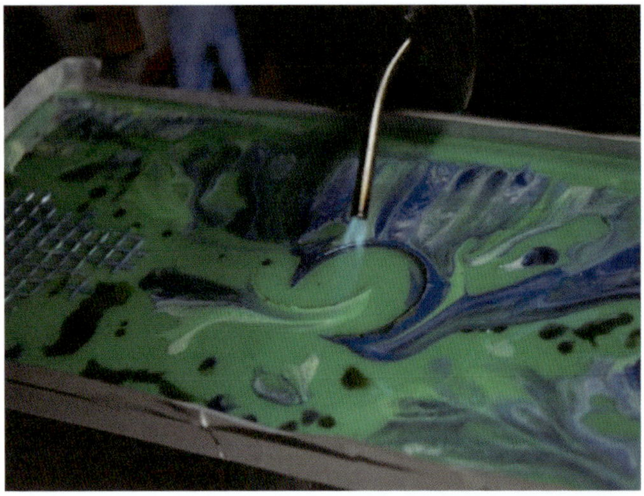

Torch. Move the torch lightly over the surface.

TIP

As long as the plastic sheeting on the table is clean and free of debris the resin that falls from the substrate on to the sheeting can be used. It can be scooped up and placed on another canvas, or used to make jewelry. Using a gloved hand or plastic spoon, pick up resin that has fallen on to your plastic sheeting and add it to the canvas. It can be scooped up and placed into a cup, if coloring the resin is desired.

TIP

When working with mixed media art, or a busy substrate, tilting doesn't always move the resin where it needs to be. If there is more resin in one area, but you need it in another area, place your gloved hand gently on the heavy area of resin and lift up. Move over to the area you want to place the resin and squeeze your hand closed.

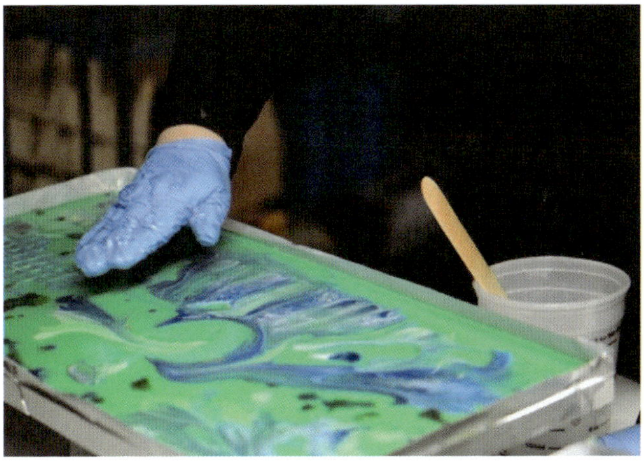

Place a gloved hand down into the area to pick up resin.

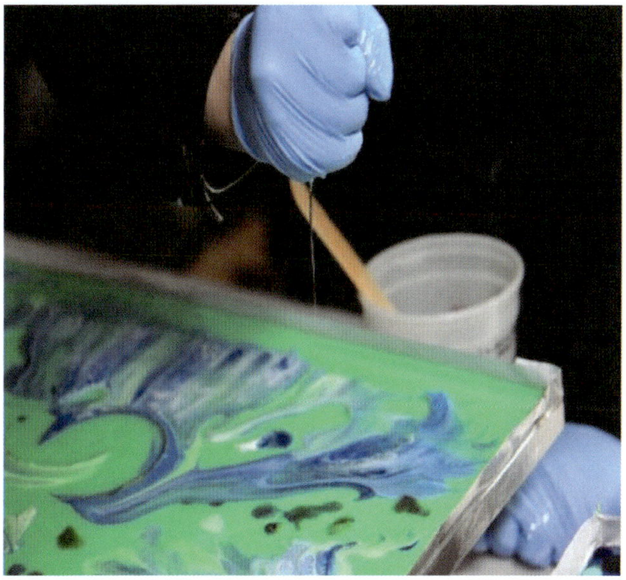

Squeeze resin from gloved hand on the area you want to place it.

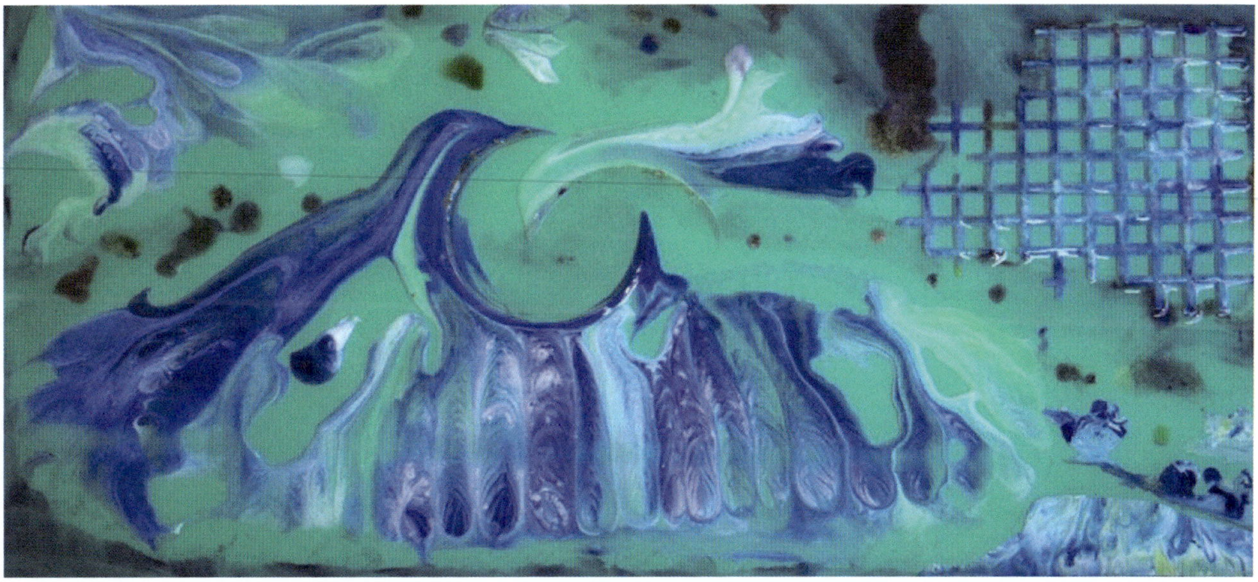

The finished piece.

SIDE BY SIDE: RESIN WITH OIL PAINT & RESIN WITH PIGMENT POWDER

For this painting project I am working on two pieces. I am using the same colors in two paintings. Only I'm using pigment powder in one and oil paint in the other. I mix both the pigment powder and the oil paint with a little resin on a piece of parchment paper. I use a small mixing spatula from the beauty supply store. These spatulas are used for make-up and for spa treatments. When the powder and resin are fully mixed, scraped up the mix and place it in a plastic cup. Add more resin to achieve the desired color. Mix well. Make sure there are no streaks in the mix.

Let's start with pigment powder.

Add pigment powder to a little resin, on top of parchment paper.

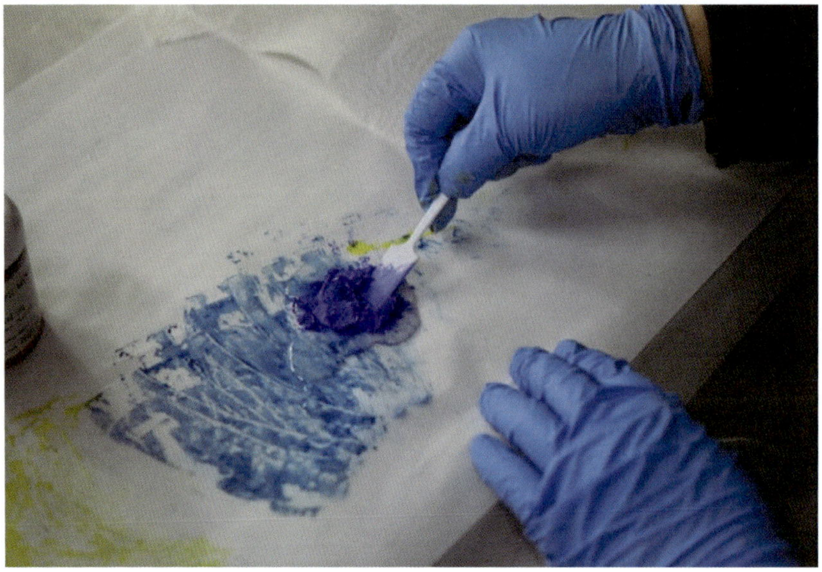

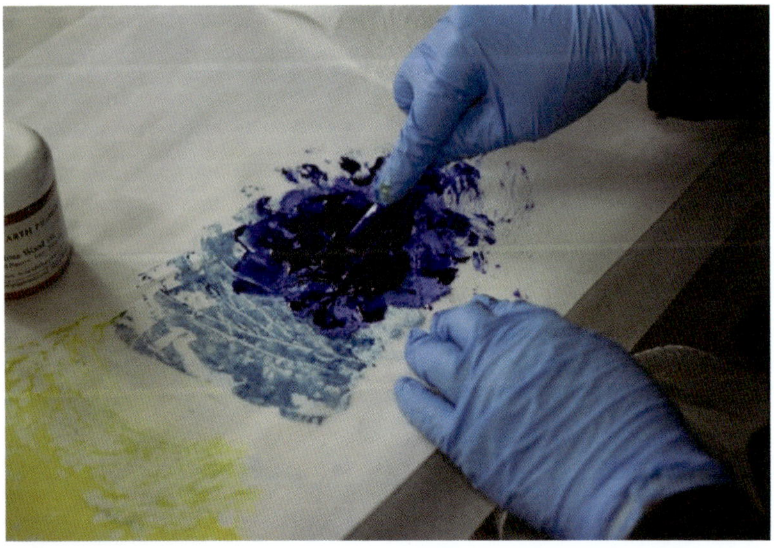

Press the two together until smooth. Mix well.

Scrape the pigment mix into a plastic cup.

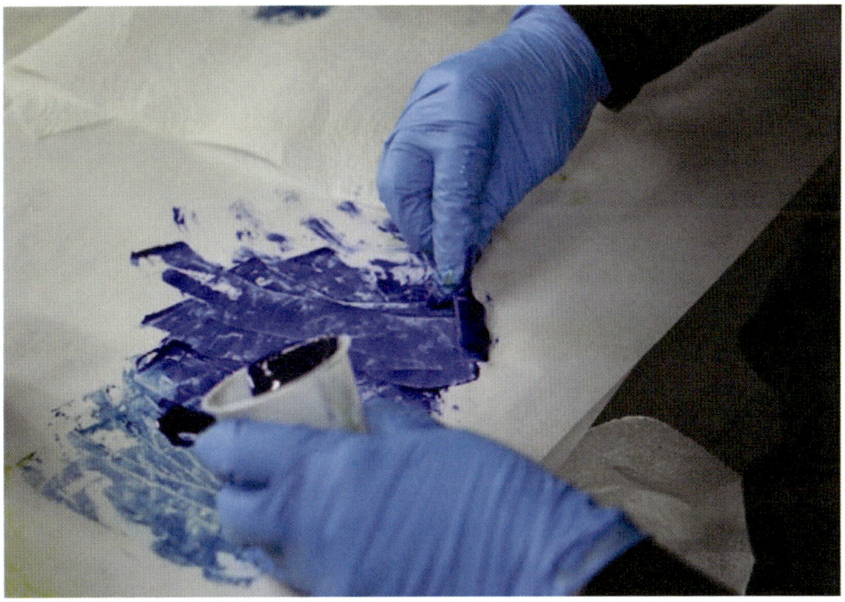

Add more clear mixed resin.

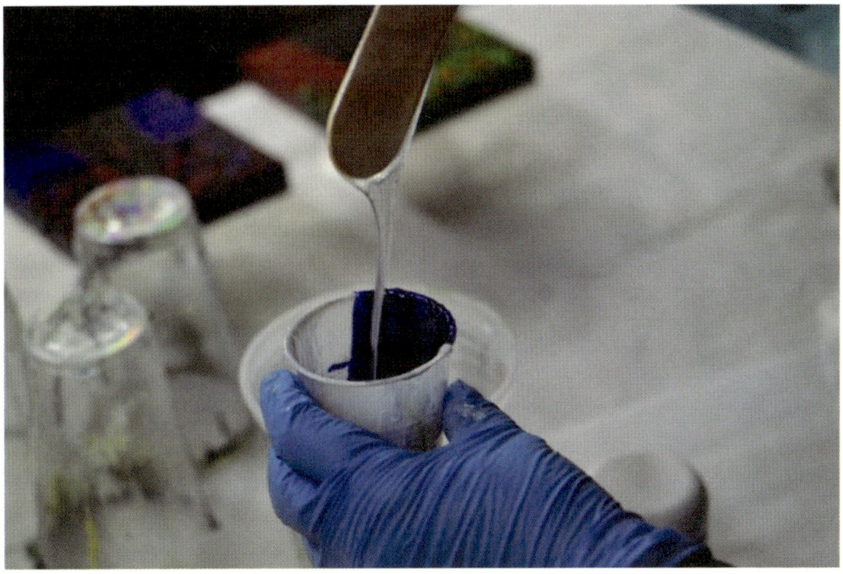

Stir well.

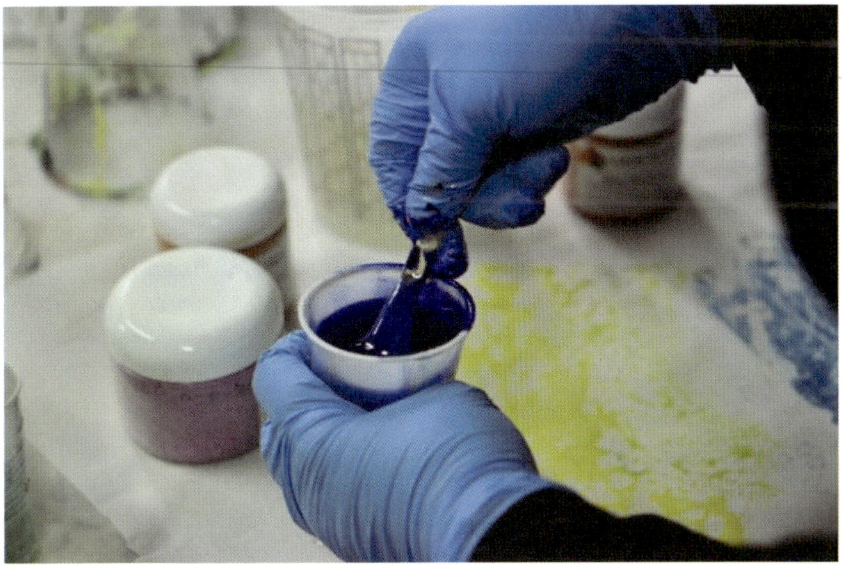

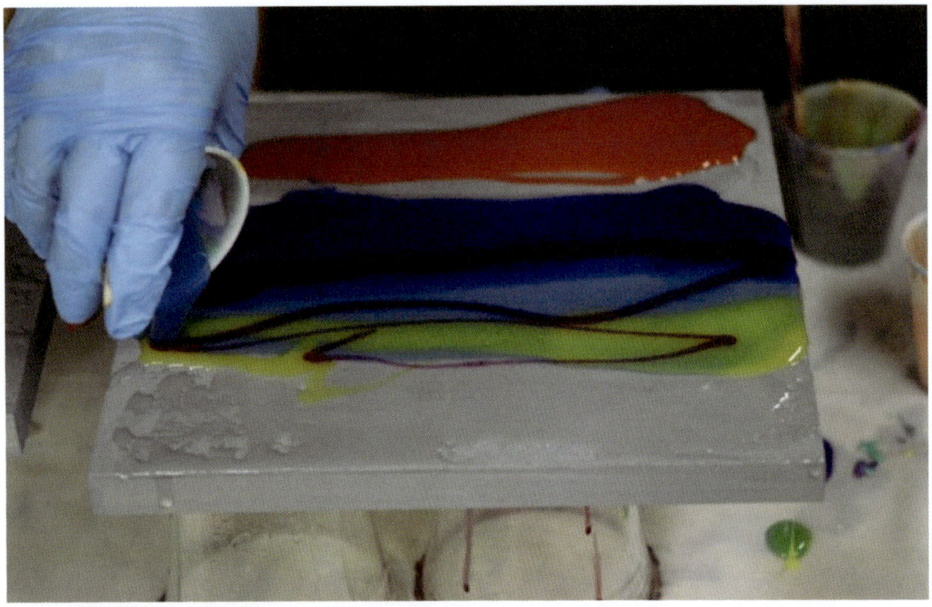

Pour the colors on the canvas.

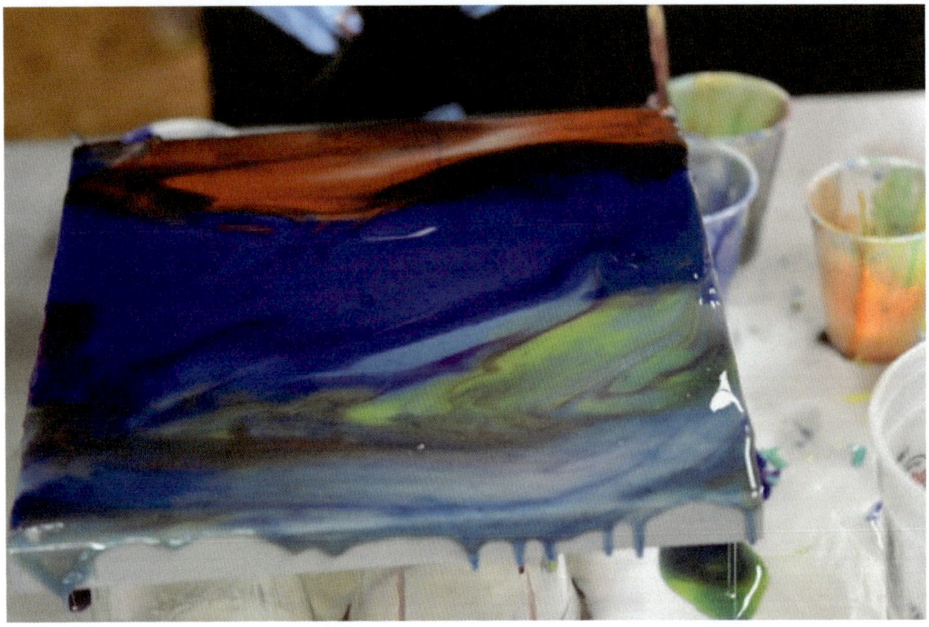

I'm going for a beach scene.

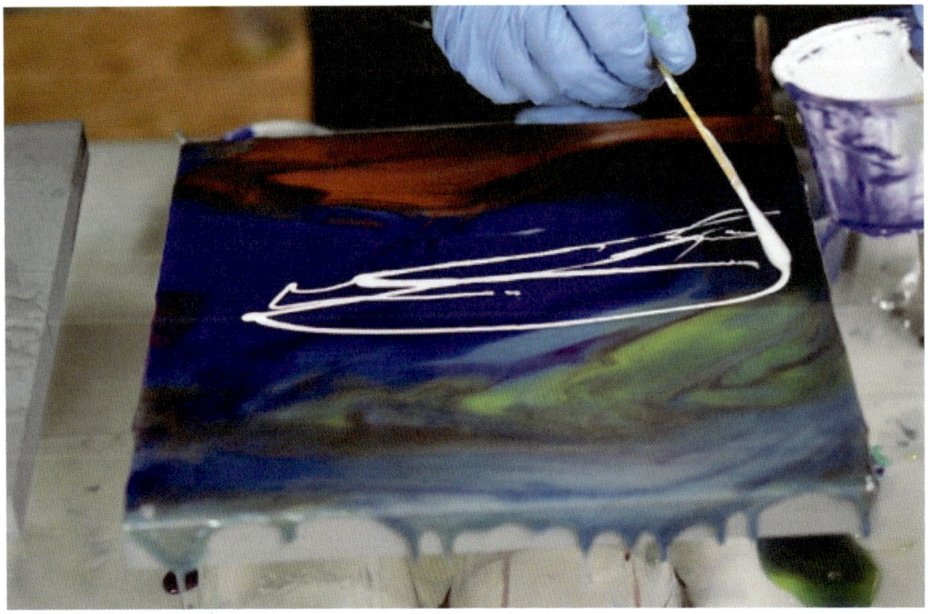

Swirl it in and blow it around for wave effects.

Work on the waves. Blow through a straw or use a hair dryer to move the white around.

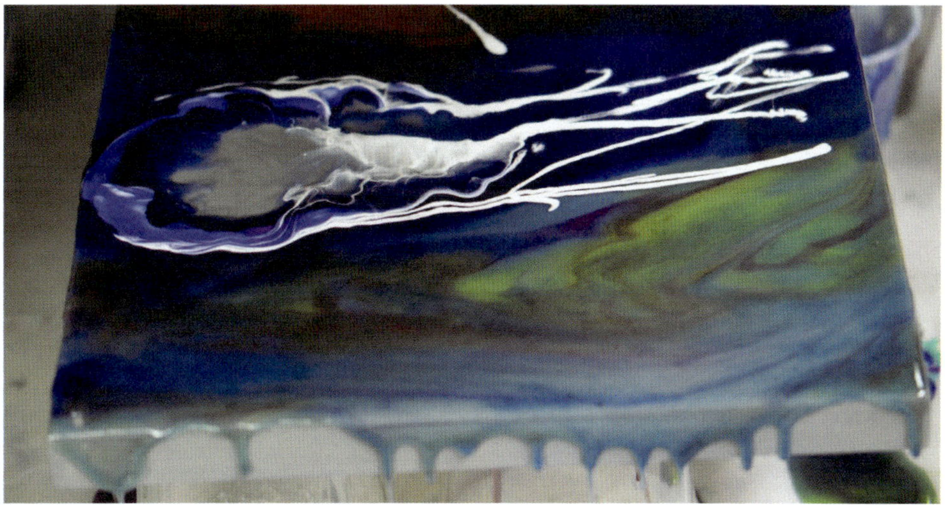

Give it a torch to remove the bubbles.

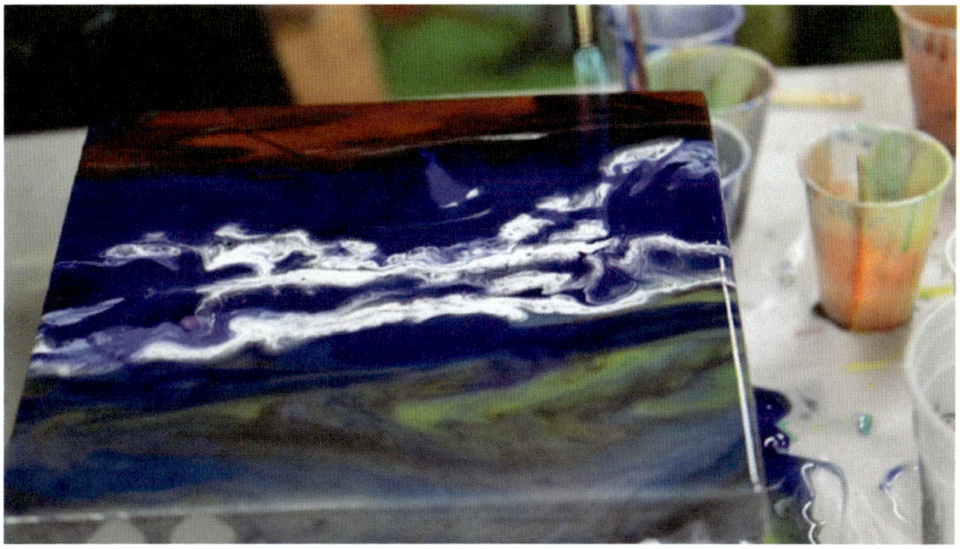

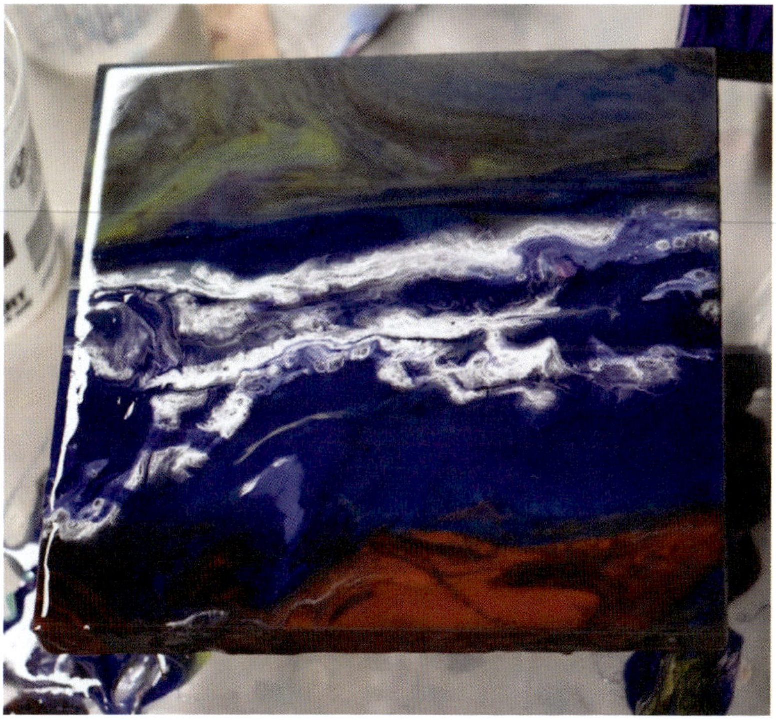

2 hours after completing the pour.

OIL PAINT & RESIN

Mixing

Place the chosen oil paint colors on a piece of parchment paper. Then pour a little bit of mixed resin on top. Work the oil paint into the resin. Scrape it up and put it in to a plastic cup. I am reusing plastic cups that have cured resin in them.

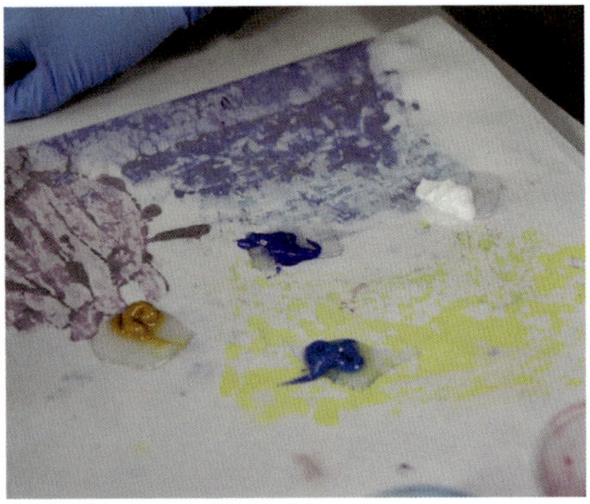

Oil paint and mixed resin on parchment paper. Ready to blend. The parchment is folded over for a clean side. I mixed the pigment powder & resin on the reverse side.

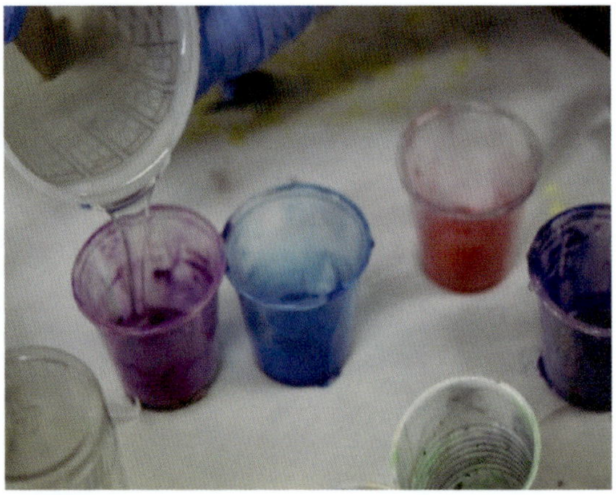

Pour clear resin in the cups that will receive the premixed oil paint.

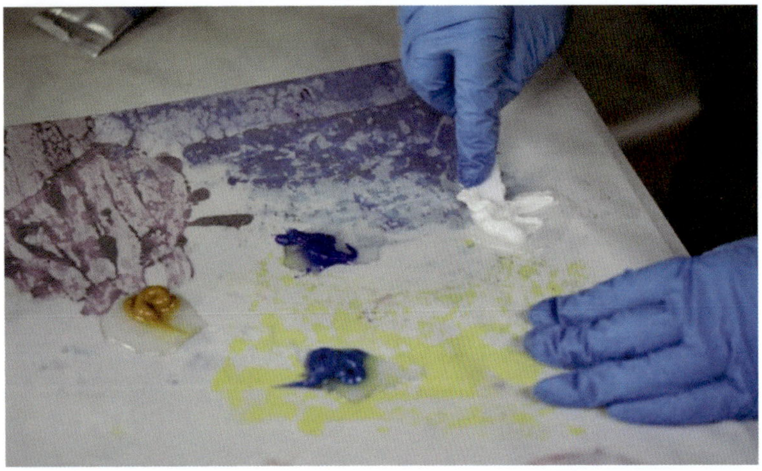

Press and mix until all lumps are gone.

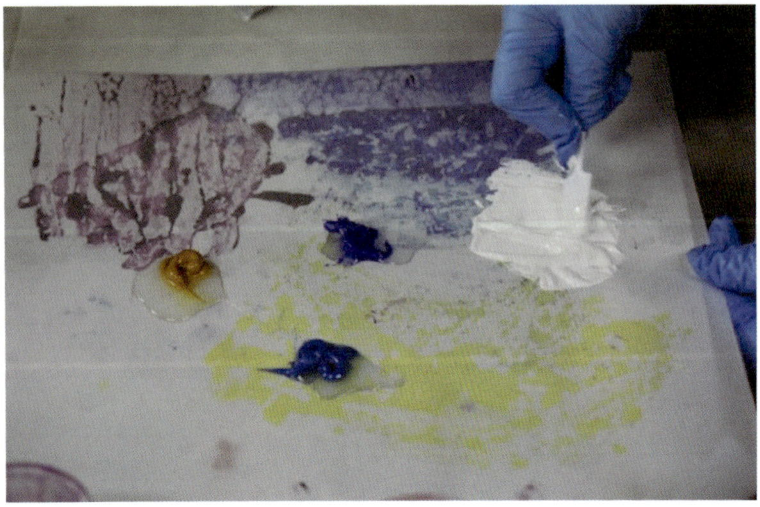

Smooth the mixture of oil paint and resin until all lumps are gone.

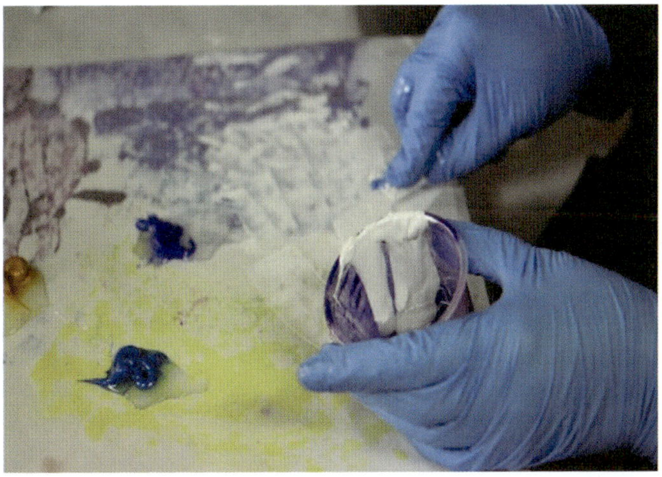

Scrape up and place back into the cup with clear resin. Mix well.

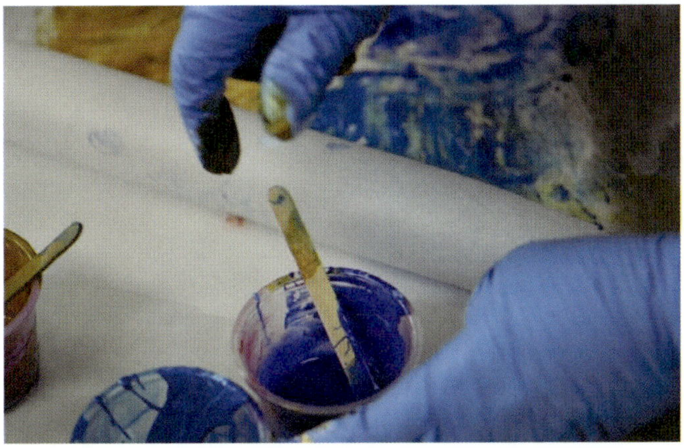

Repeat until all the colors are mixed.

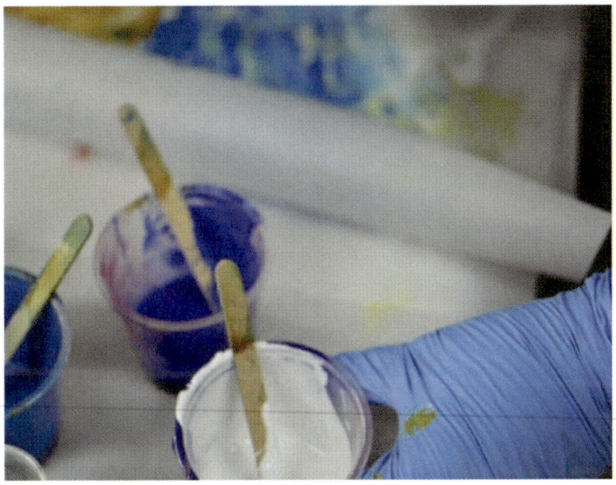

All the cups are mixed and ready to use.

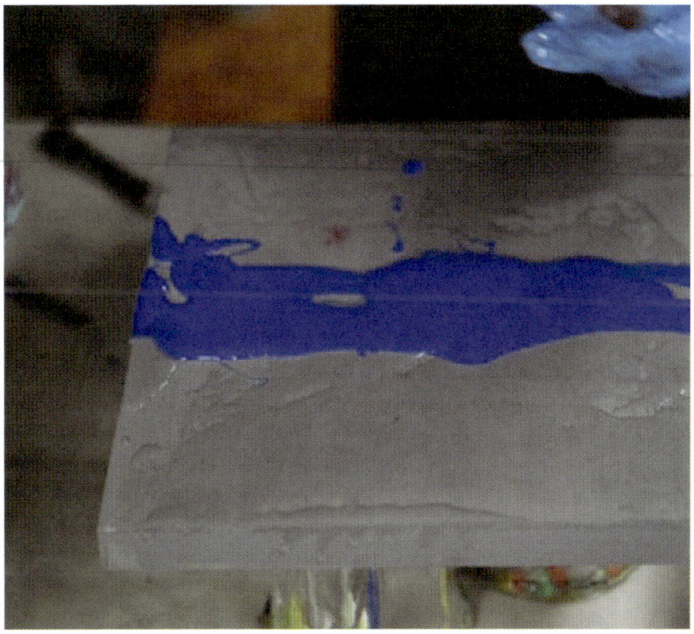

Start placing the colors on the canvas.

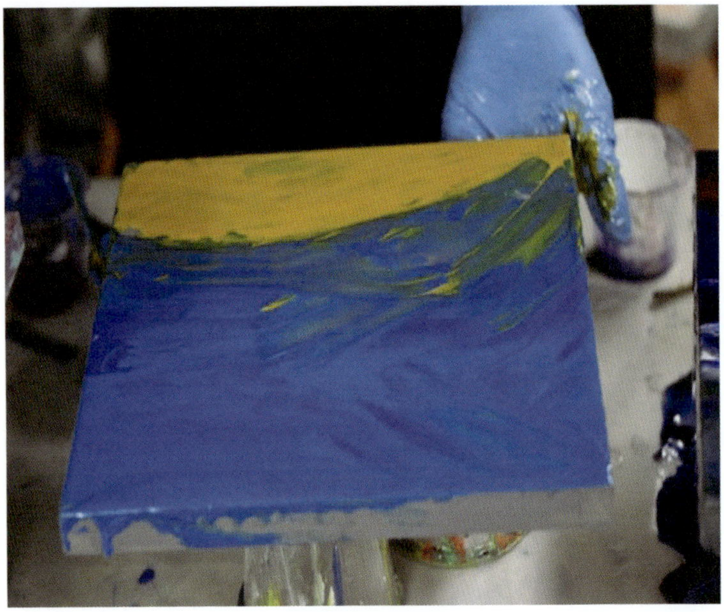

Spread the color on the canvas.

White oil paint does not move easily, blown through a straw or with a hair dryer, when used with other opaque oil paint. The mixes are too dense. It will still spread out and lace on its own. Oil paint naturally laces and cells. To achieve the best cells, layer oil paint & resin mix on top of clear mixed resin.

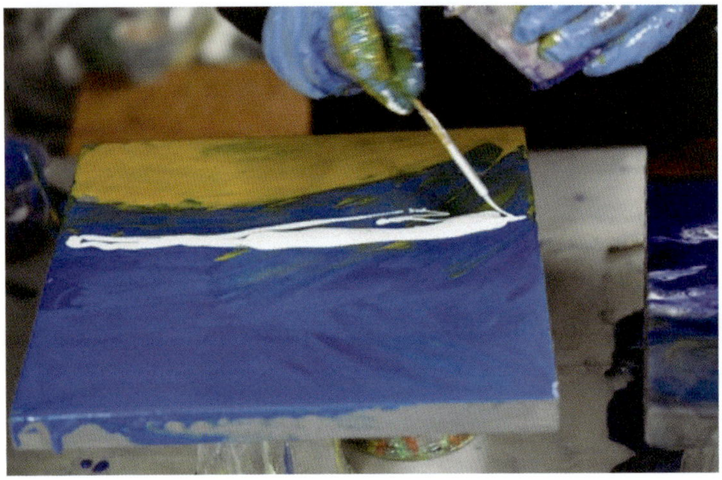

Stream in the white color.

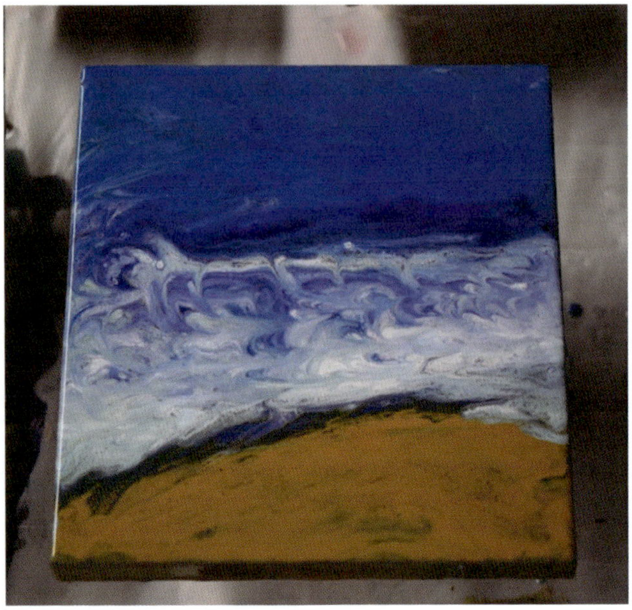

Checking in 2 hours later.

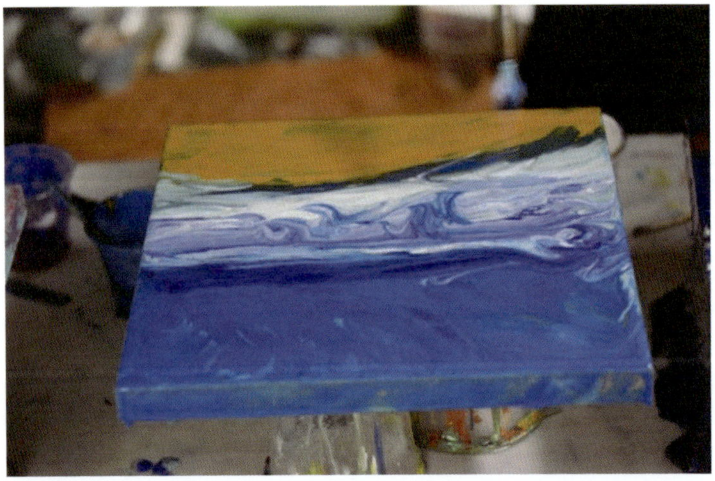

Torch when you are satisfied with the composition.

WORKING WITH CRAFT DYE IN RESIN ART

For this project, I am adding craft dyes straight into cups of mixed resin. When adding any colorant to resin, stir well to ensure a proper mix. Craft dyes can also be used on fabric. This means there are ingredients in them to help them adhere to fabric. Salt and vinegar are common ingredients in fabric dyes. Vinegar will thin out resin. Salt may pit the resin. The more of these dyes added to resin the greater the risk of curing issues in the resin. I am adding a little more than the few drops recommended, because I want to see what the effects will be. I am adhering to no more than 10% colorant and 90% resin.

Orange dye added to mixed resin

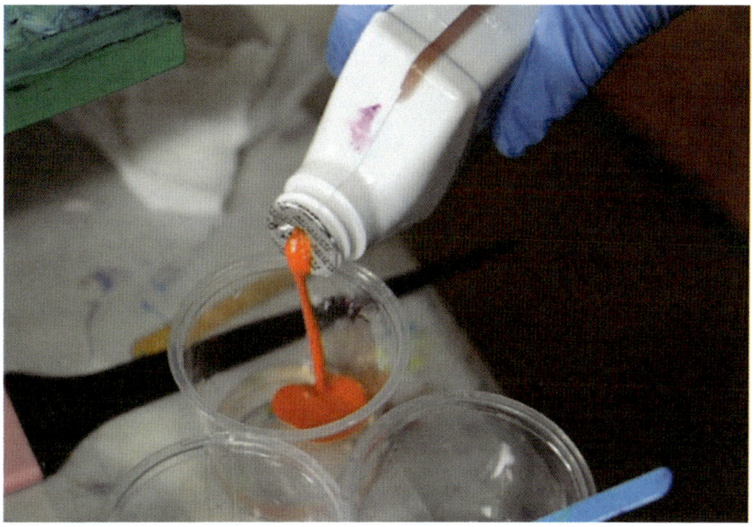

Stir until thoroughly mixed.

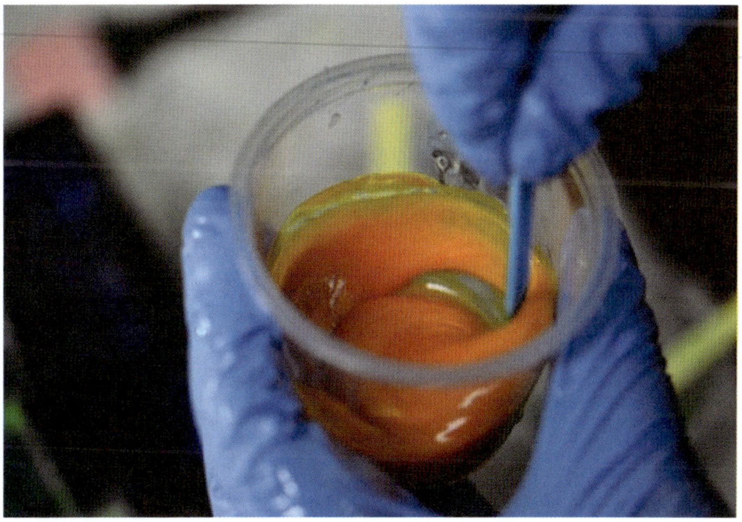

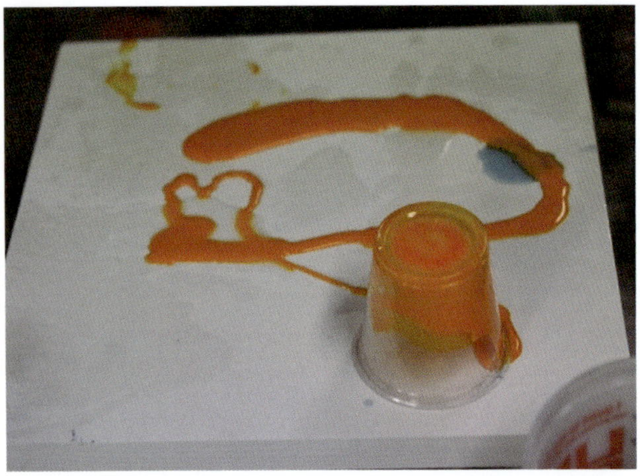

Turn the cup upside down to let the rest of the resin flow out of the cup.

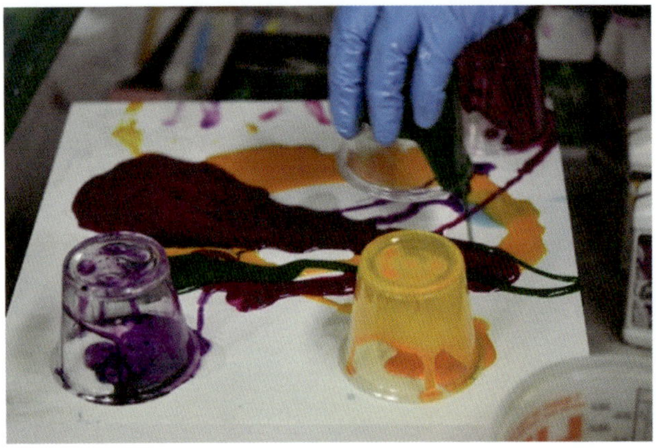

Add as many colors as you like. I'm using orange, purple, raspberry, yellow and green.

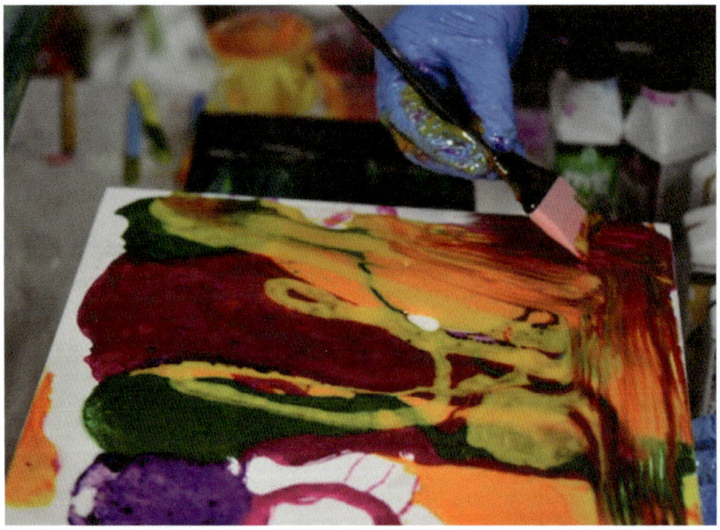

When the paint covers the canvas start moving around to create a design. Silicone hair dye tools work great for design work.

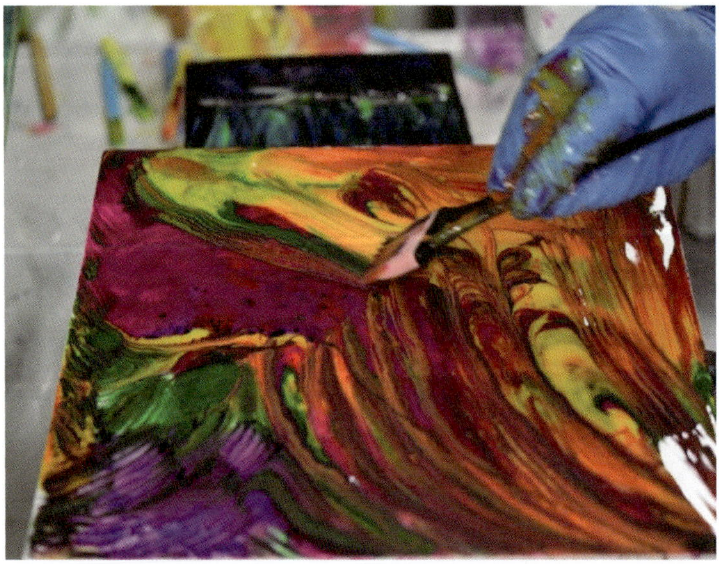

I'm using silicone hair dye tools as my paint brushes.

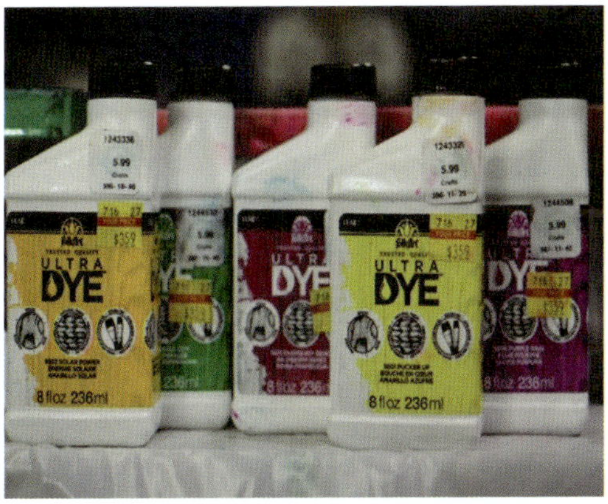

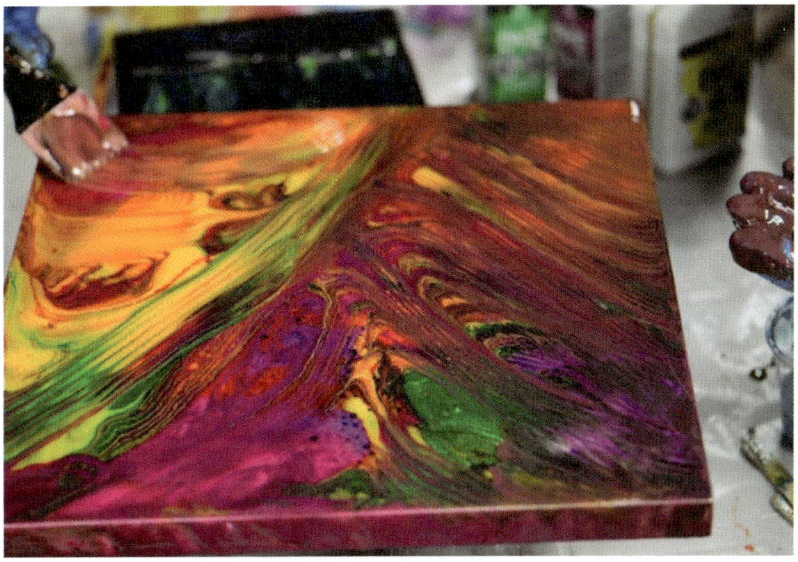

1. Craft dyes.
2. Making more marks with silicone tools.
3. torching for bubbles.

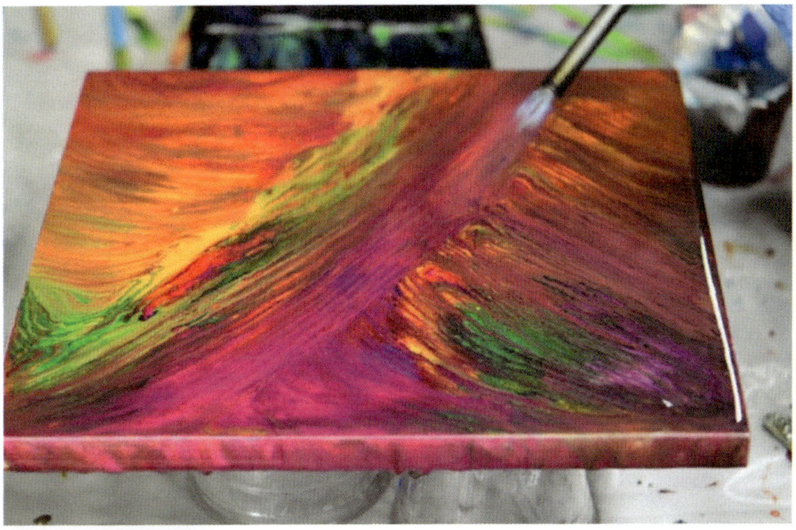

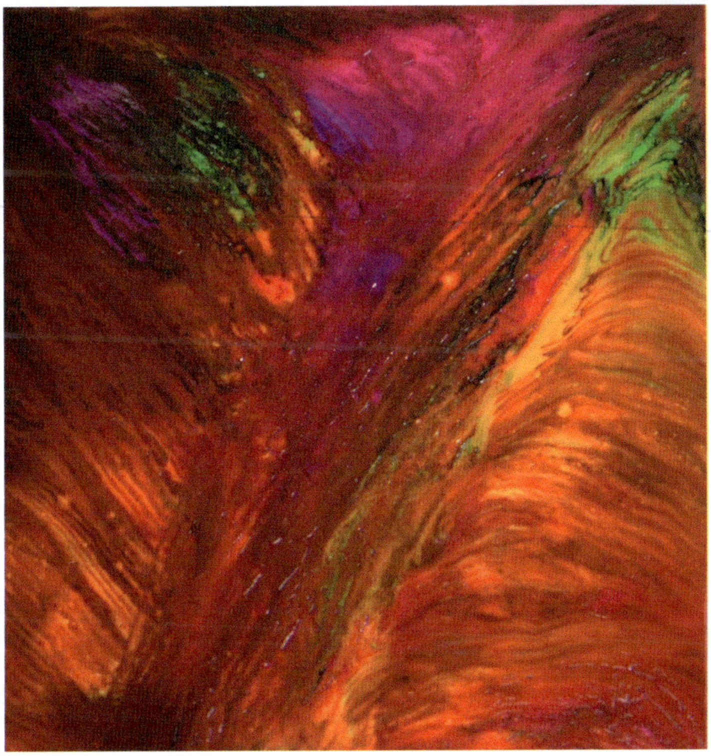

It turned out great. It has wonderful rivers and divots throughout as well as small cells. I will add a top coat of clear resin to give it depth. Layering dyes with clear resin for dimensional art would work great with this colorant.

RESIN PAINTING FOR CELLS

I am using mica pigments for this project. Mica pigments can be added straight into mixed resin. There is no need to premix them. Mica generally does not lump and clump the way that powder pigments do. Stir them well to ensure a thorough mix. I am using silicone oil. For this project, I am using treadmill lubricant to create cells in resin. This is 100% silicone oil sold at sporting goods stores. Dimethicone oil and silicone oil are the same thing. Dimethicone oil can be purchased on Amazon or eBay inexpensively.

When using silicone oil in resin, it is best to use it on the surface rather than mixing it into the paints and pouring it on. It can be sprayed on or dropped from the end of a toothpick or craft stick. It becomes airborne when sprayed and will affect any resin art that is in the area. Greater control is achieved by dropping it from a toothpick or craft stick. To show what happens when silicone oil is sprayed, I am completing 2 pieces. I spray one of them with a barrier between the two. I hold the barrier up for 3 minutes. The painting that I did not spray has massive cells.

The colors that I am using are brown, green, tangerine, powder blue, coffee, rose, ruby, ebony, slate, copper and sage.

Pour the colors on the canvas. Turn the cups upside down to allow all of the paint to fall on the canvas.

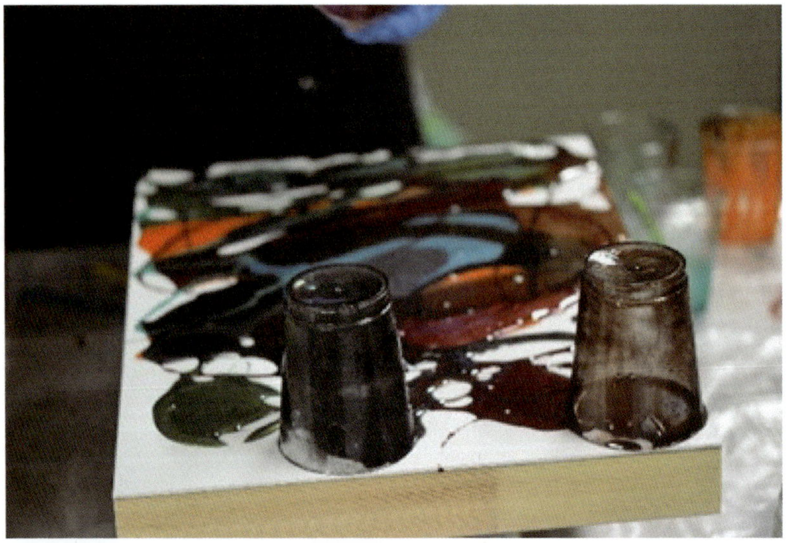

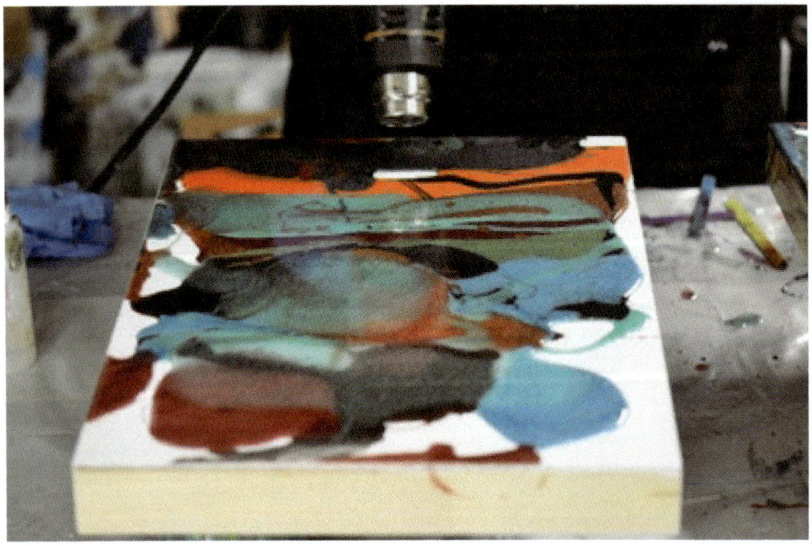

Use a heat gun to move the colors around on the canvas.

A heat gun will heat up the resin and blow it around the canvas. It takes care of bubbles as well, so there is no need to torch.

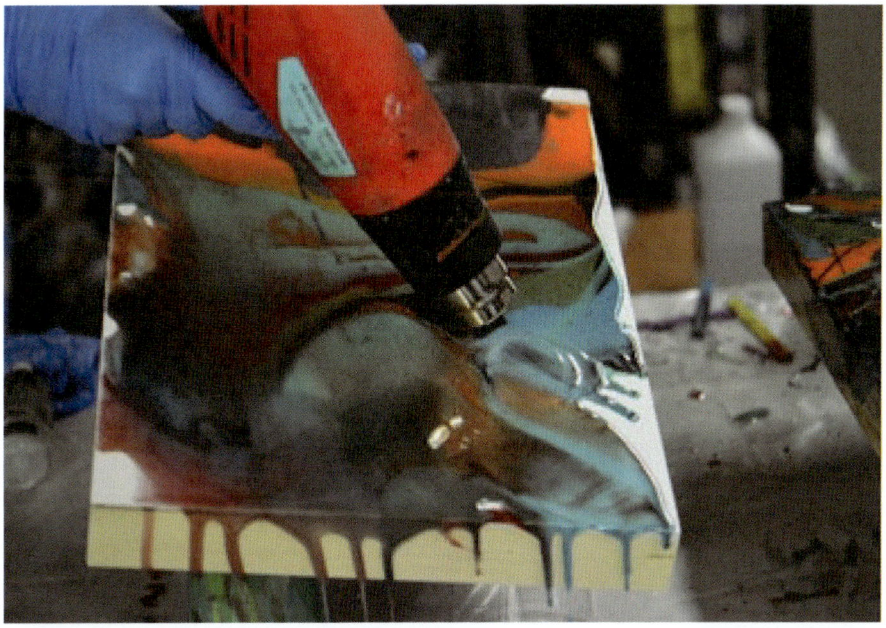

This one has more of the brown colors. I think I will use the silicone oil on this one.

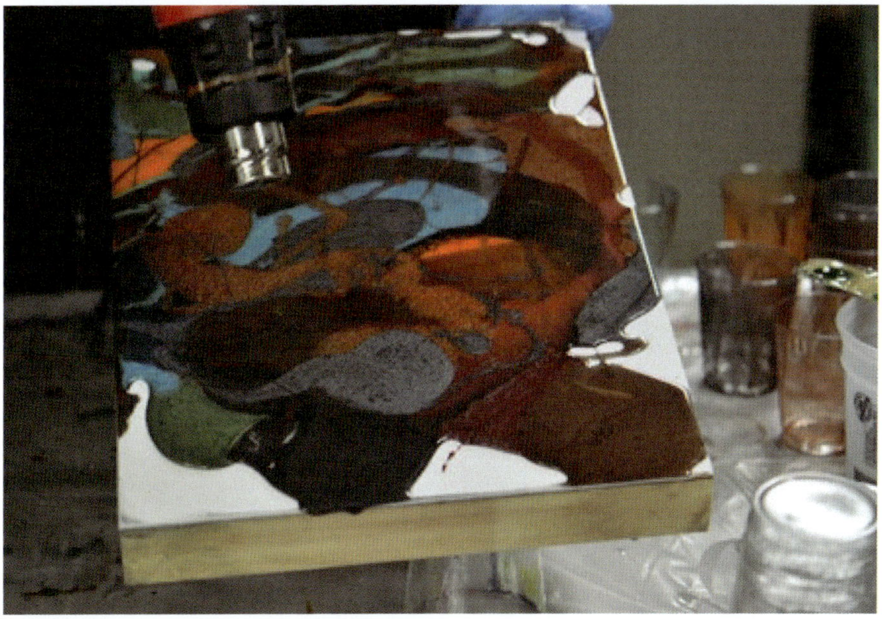

Tilting also moves the paint around and creates effects.

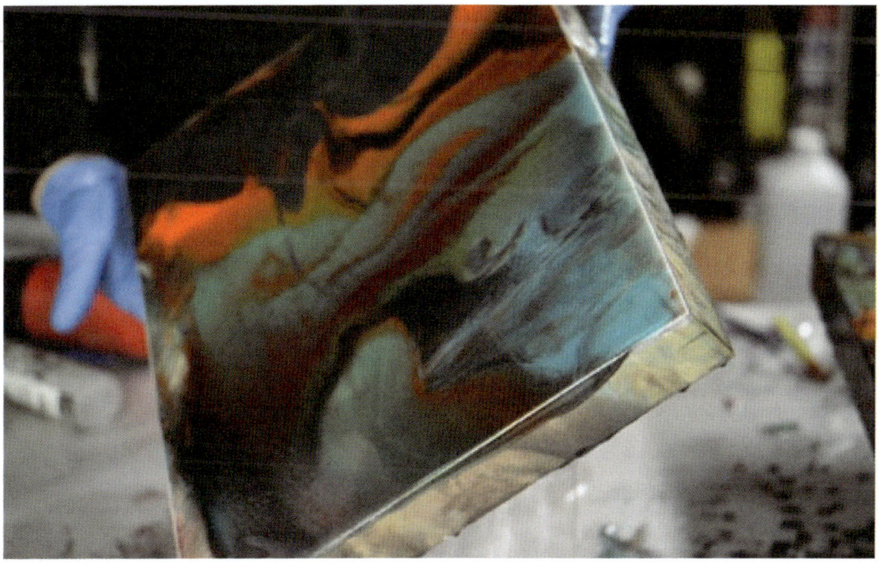

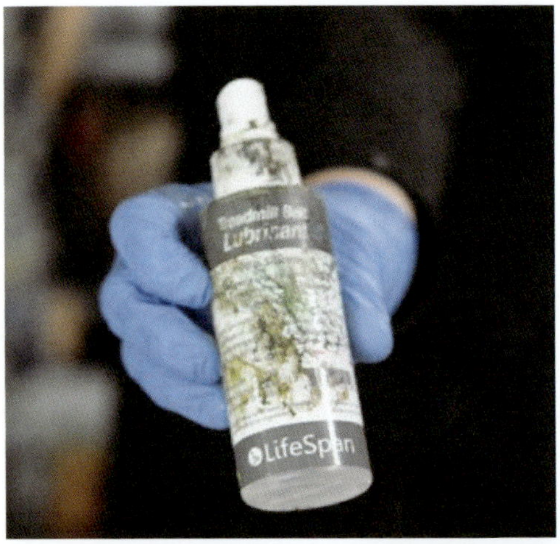

The silicone oil I used. It's a treadmill lubricant.

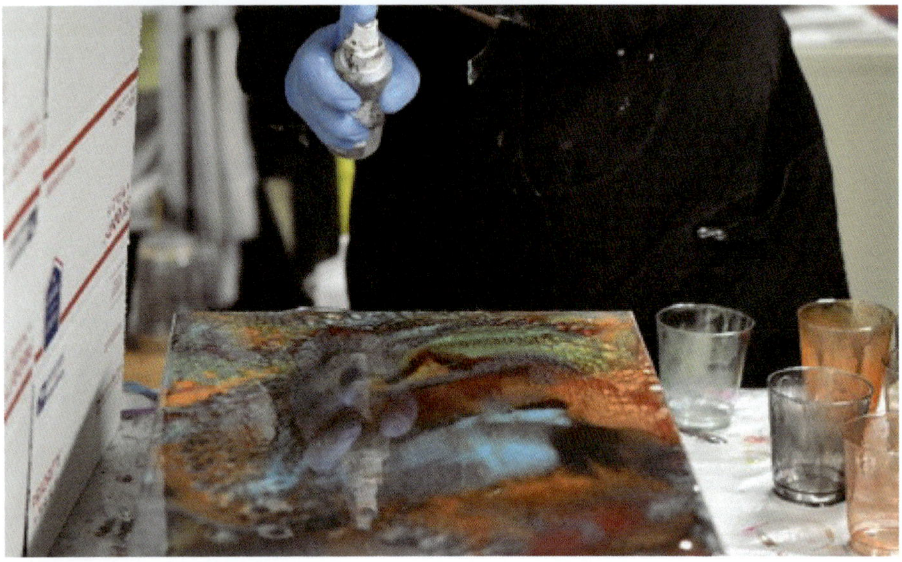

A very light spray is all it takes. The cells happen instantly. I am holding a shipping box between the two paintings to prevent the spray from reaching the other painting.

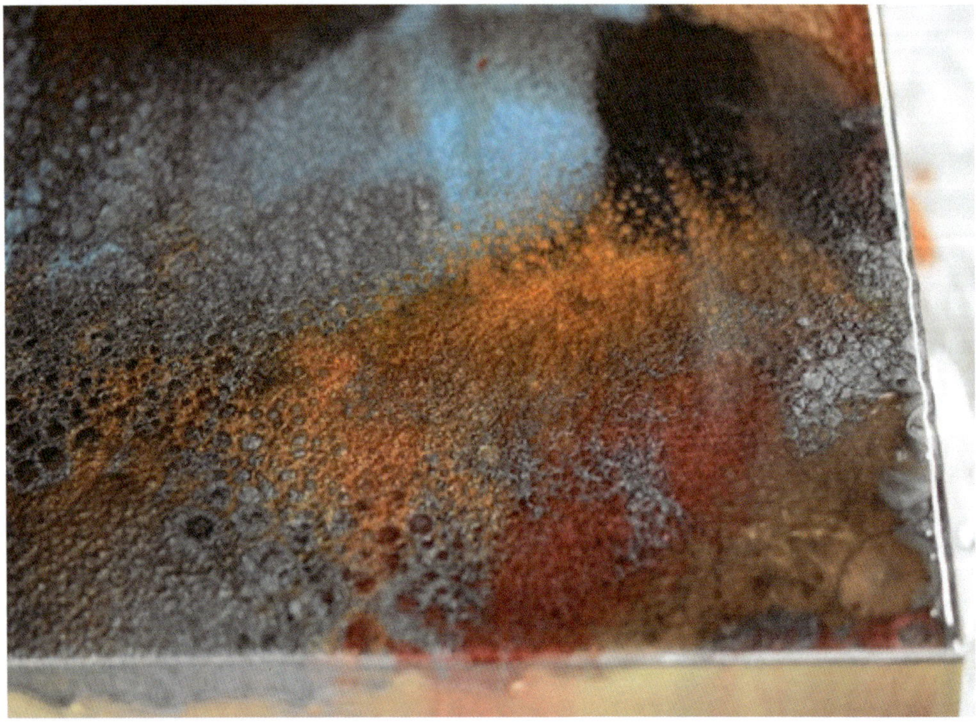

This painting received the spray of silicone oil. It has very small cells.

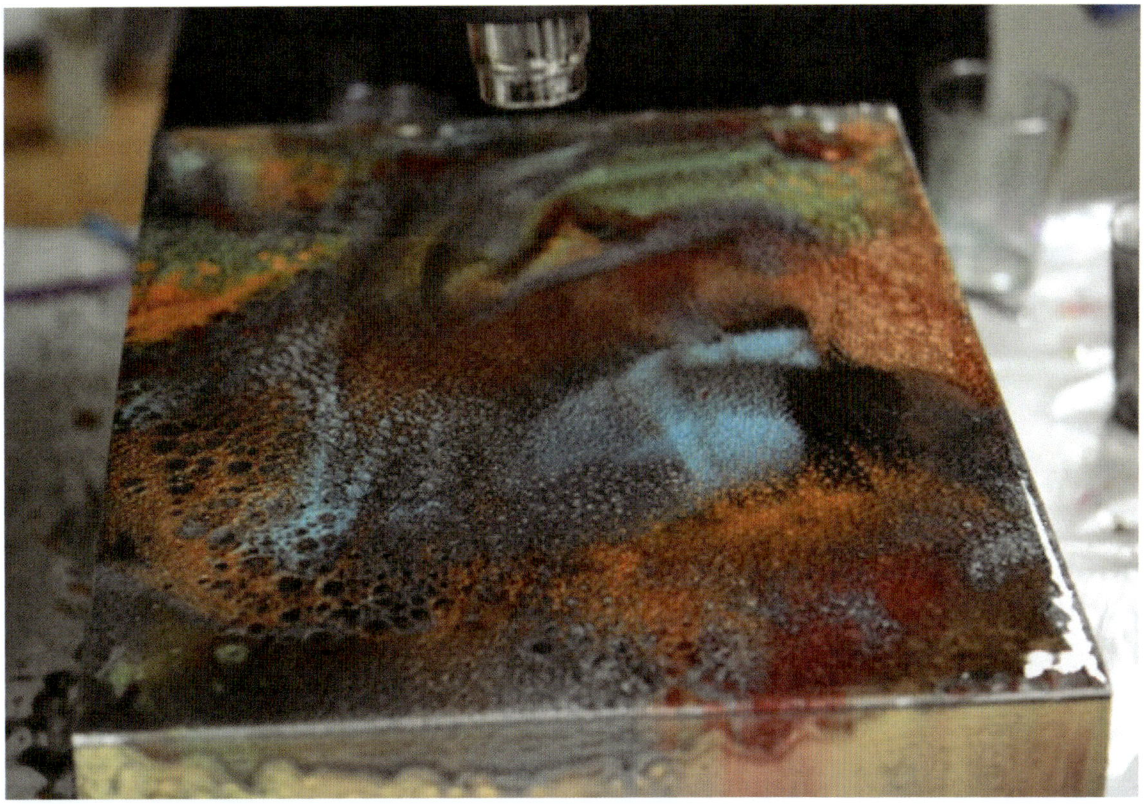

The spray of silicone oil created a very different painting. I go over it with the heat gun to take care of tiny bubbles.

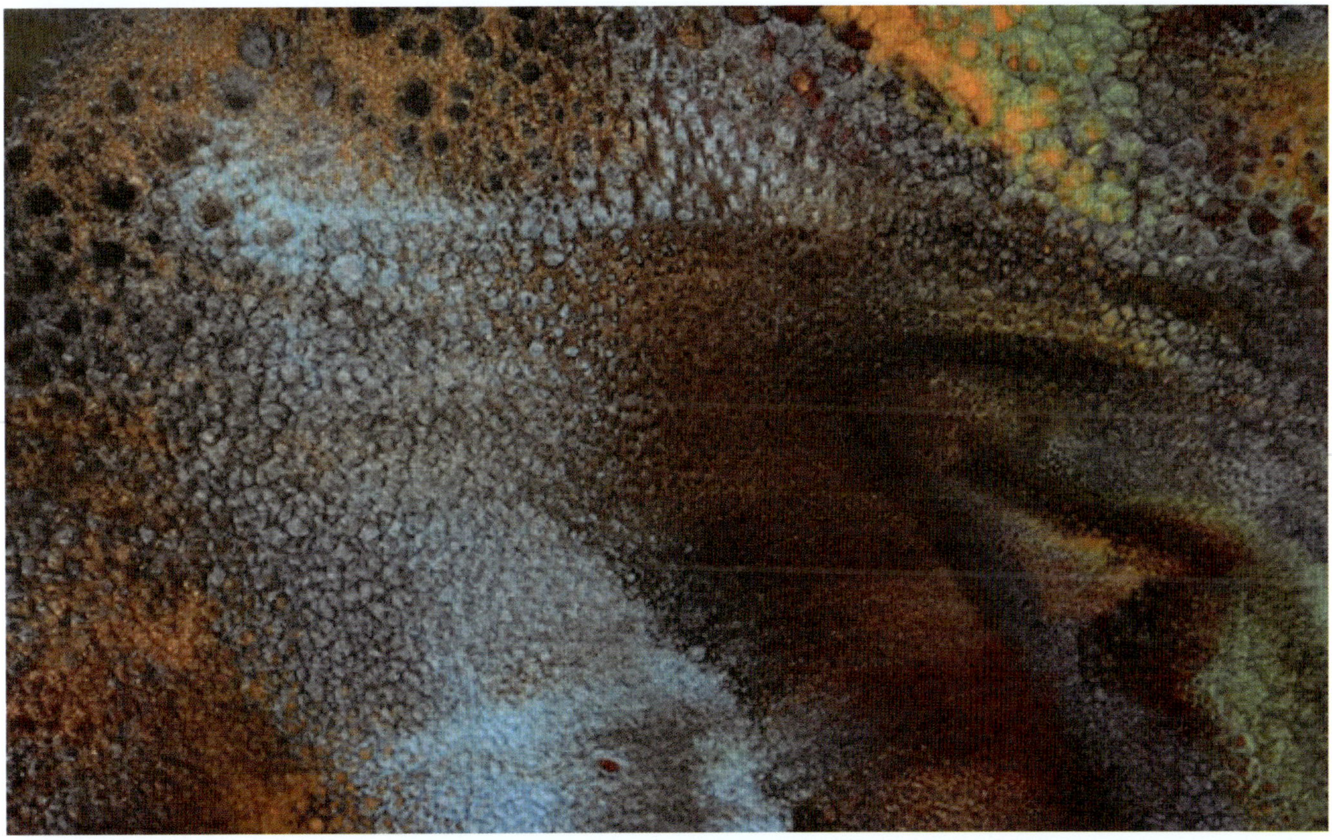

The finished piece.

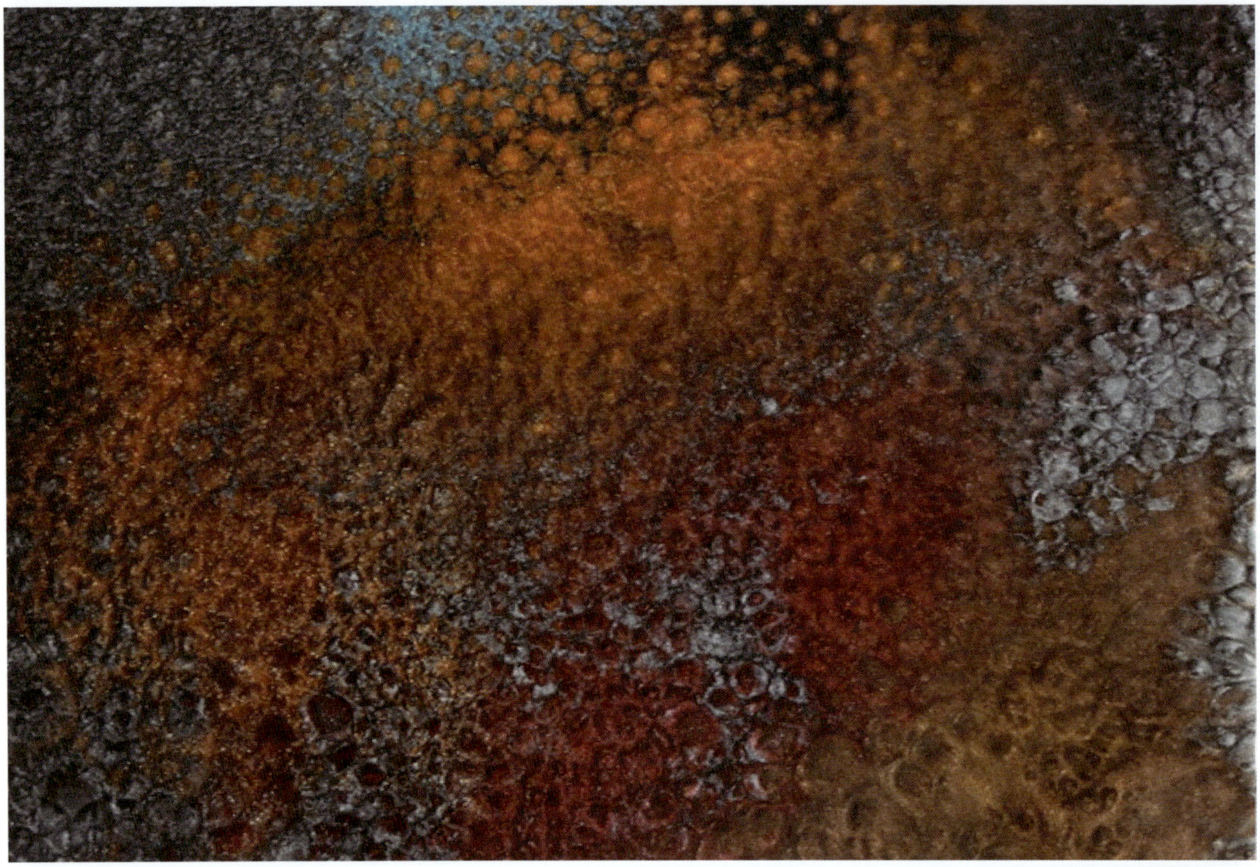

A close-up view.

I did not spray or drop silicone oil onto the second painting. It was on the same table as the one that received the silicone oil. I held a cardboard box between the two and sprayed once onto the first painting. I held the spray bottle low on the painting that I wanted the silicone oil effects. I kept the barrier up for about 3 minutes. Even with the barrier between the two pieces, the silicone oil still reached the other painting. I could see cells forming instantly in the painting that did not receive silicone oil. The cells where larger and more dramatic on the painting that did not receive the silicone spray. Proving that silicone oil goes airborne (when sprayed) and will affect resin art, even if it not directly sprayed onto the surface.

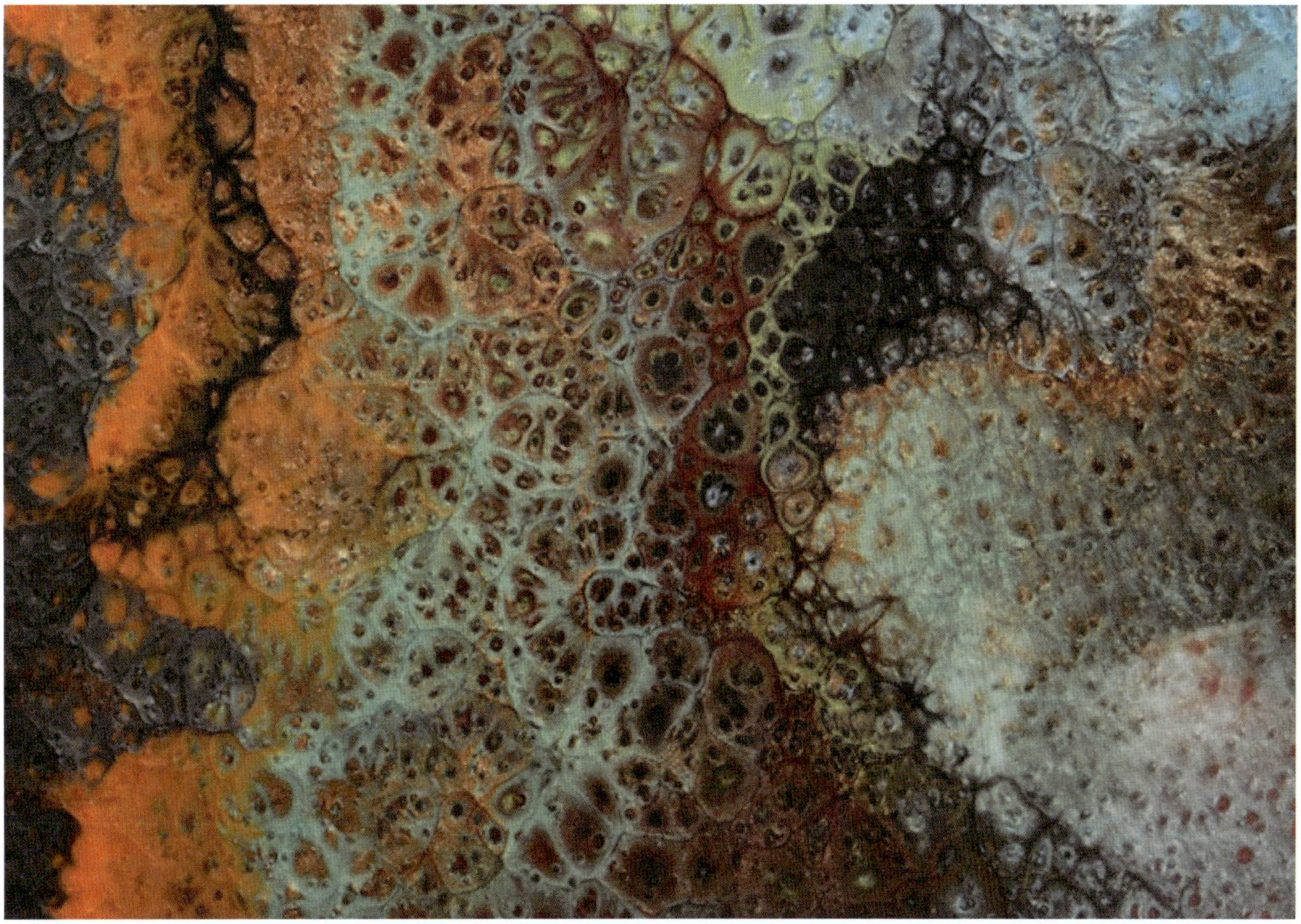

I did not spray or drop silicone oil on this painting. The effects of this one is from the airborne silicone it received. It has larger cells. Larger cells are created when less silicone oil is used in directed locations.

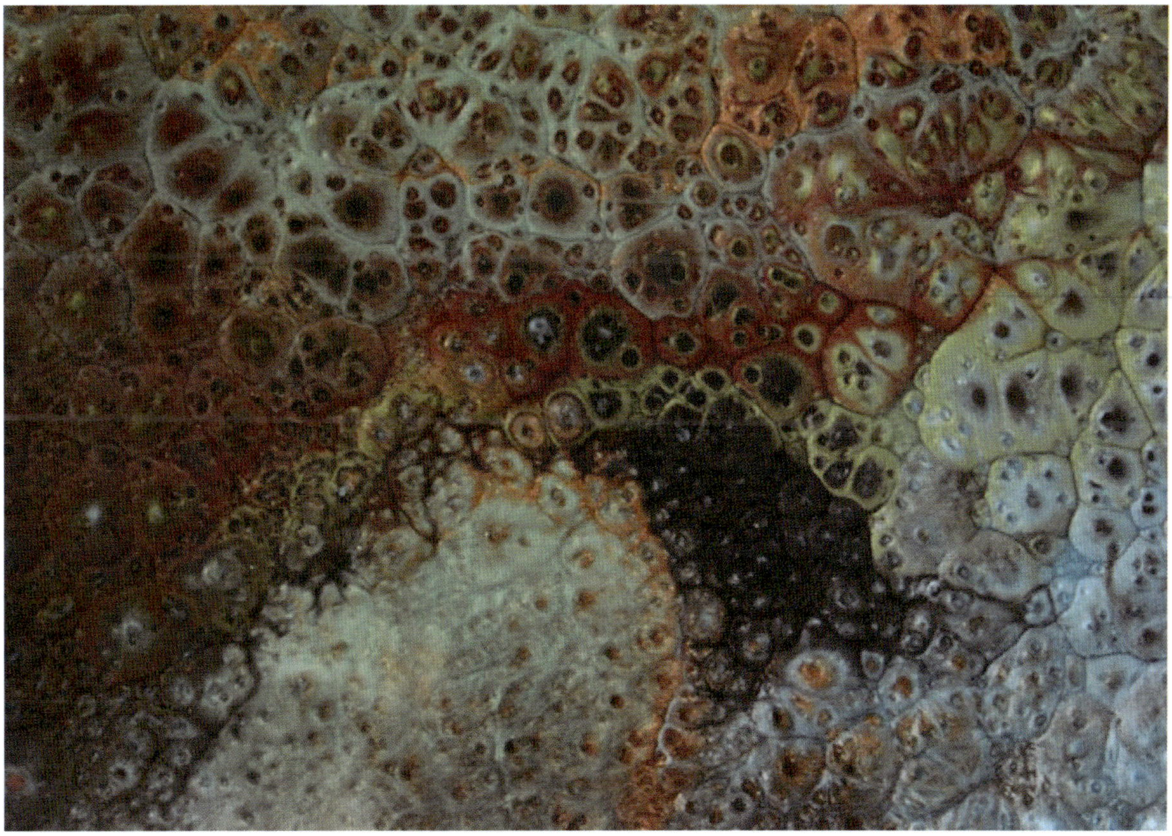

A close-up view.

Remember to cover the resin art when finished. Use a cardboard box or plastic storage bin.

CURING OF EPOXY RESIN

Most resins are cured to the touch in 24 hours and fully hardened in 7 to 14 days. Always read the manufacturer's directions to ensure proper curing. After 24 hours look at what you have. Take note of any areas that need touch up.

Resin continues to go through a curing process for weeks and months after that initial 24 hours. It continues to harden and plasticize. This process is important for strength and scratch resistance of the art. The cured piece could take 2 to 6 weeks to fully cure and harden. If you try to pack, ship or clean the surface before that time you may end up with scratches. For best results allow any project with resin to cure for at least 2 months before trying to ship or clean it.

It may be fully cured within 2 weeks, but if you have a masterpiece on your hands, don't take any chances. Be patient and give it the time it needs to fully cure. If you have an art show coming up, go ahead and hang the piece, just take precautions when moving it. Do not use packaging materials to move it before the full cure time. Avoid cleaning it until the full curing time has finished.

TIP

Never scrape out the last bit of mixed resin from the cup onto your canvas unless you are certain it is properly mixed. If you have stirred the mix thoroughly (scraping the sides and bottom of the cup several times, mixing for the recommended time & until the mixture is free of swirls in the mix) you likely have a thorough mix. Go ahead and scrape out as much resin as possible from the cup. If you are unsure if you have mixed well, pour the resin onto the canvas without scraping the last bit out of the cup. Leave the mixed resin that lags behind in the cup. Any unmixed resin will remain in the cup and not on your canvas. If you do not stir your mix well, and you scrape the last bits out of your cup, there will be uncured spots on your canvas.

TIP

When working with a deep pour, or layered effects are desired, a second pour can be completed 5 to 12 hours after the first one, without sanding. The resin will be cured enough that it will accept the second layer and not heat up from too much liquid resin on the surface. Allow the poured resin surface to sit for 5 to 12 hours and go ahead and pour on a second layer. If a more solid surface is desired (without seepage of one layer down into the layer below) wait 8 hours at least. It is very important to ensure that your area is as free of dust and hair as possible and that you have removed any particles from your first layer. Otherwise you will have a particle deep in your pour that will be impossible to remove.

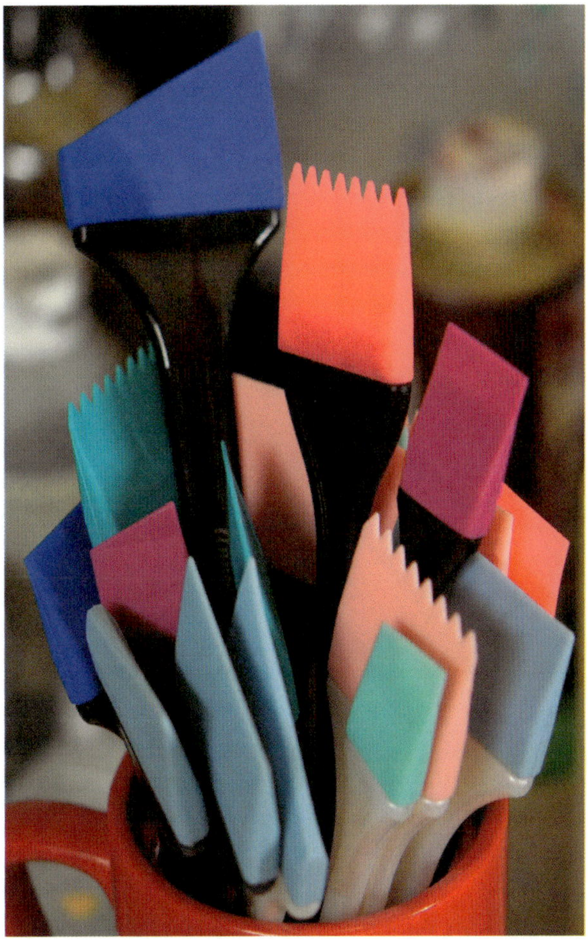

TIP

Silicone Hair dye applicator tools from beauty supply stores or online make great painting tools to use in resin. They are great for spreading resin, moving it around and creating effects in resin. They are easily cleaned with alcohol and since resin doesn't cure to silicone they can be used and re-used many times.

SECTION 12
CLEANUP

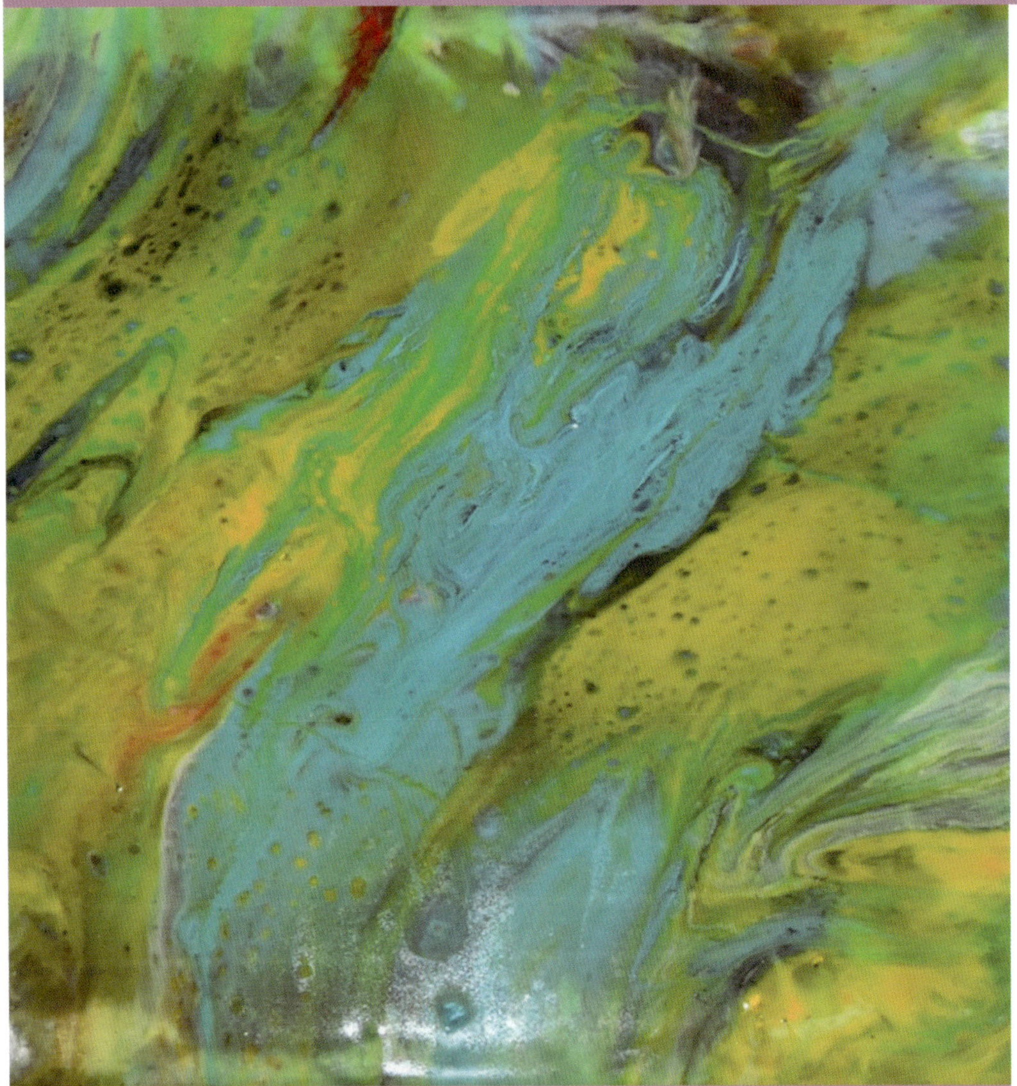

REACHING FOR THE SUN
Resin & Oil Paint on Canvas
12"x12" (31cmx31cm)

CLEAN UP

With gloves still on, wipe down any tools to be cleaned with isopropyl alcohol and baby wipes. Set aside the resin mixing cup to cure. When it's completely dry, simply peel the resin out, and it's clean for the next use. Scrape the excess resin off of the wooden stir stick into the resin mixing cup and place it on top of the cup to dry. It can be used again in a future project as long as it is dry and free of debris. If silicone cups were used, wipe those down with isopropyl alcohol and baby wipes. If plastic stir sticks were used, wipe down with alcohol and a baby wipe. Wipe down silicone spatula, if used.

Remove gloves and wipe down hands and wrists with 91% isopropyl alcohol and baby wipes. Wipe down any areas of skin that may have been exposed to resin. Place the wipes on plastic sheeting to dry before throwing them in the trash. Rub dish soap onto hands and wrists, then rinse well. Wipe down the face with a face wipe or face cleanser. Even though you do not have resin on your face you may have exposed your face to resin particles in the air. If you have concerns about allergies to resin, a shower after resin is an option. Always clean areas exposed to resin with dish soap before showering.

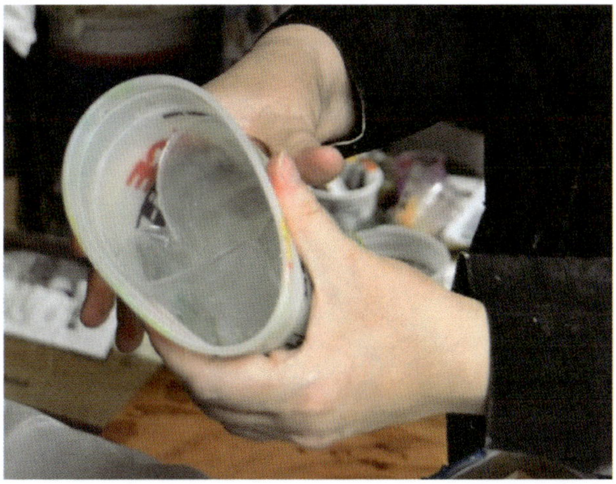

Squeeze the cup to help loosen the resin.

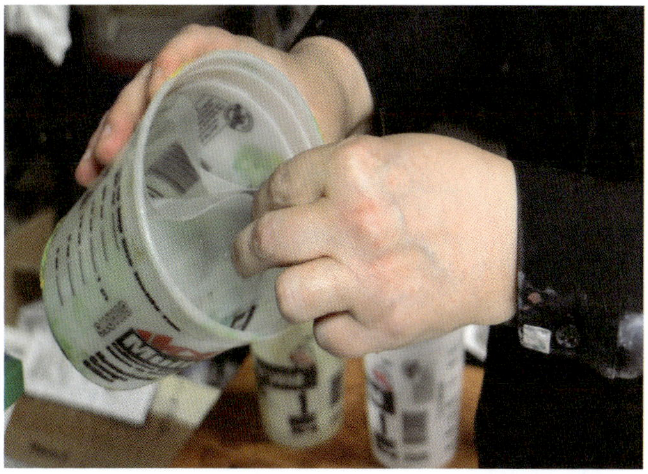

Grab the dried resin and pull it out in one piece.

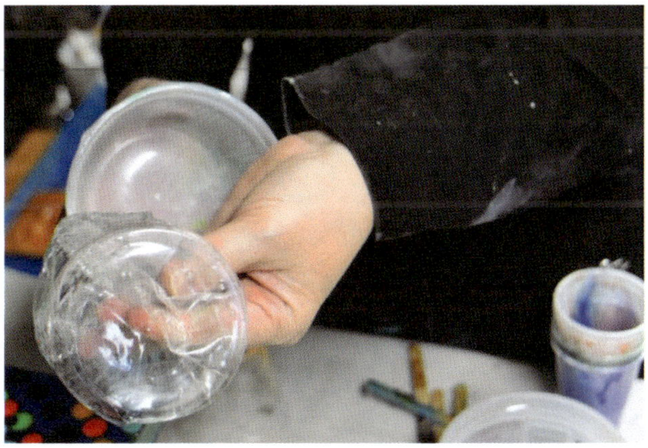

One Large Piece of Dried Resin.

Peeling dry resin from the mixing cup.

Allow the resin to dry in the plastic mixing cup for at least 24 hours. I leave it for several days. After a few days you can peel it out.

SECTION 13
RESIN PAINTING TECHNIQUES

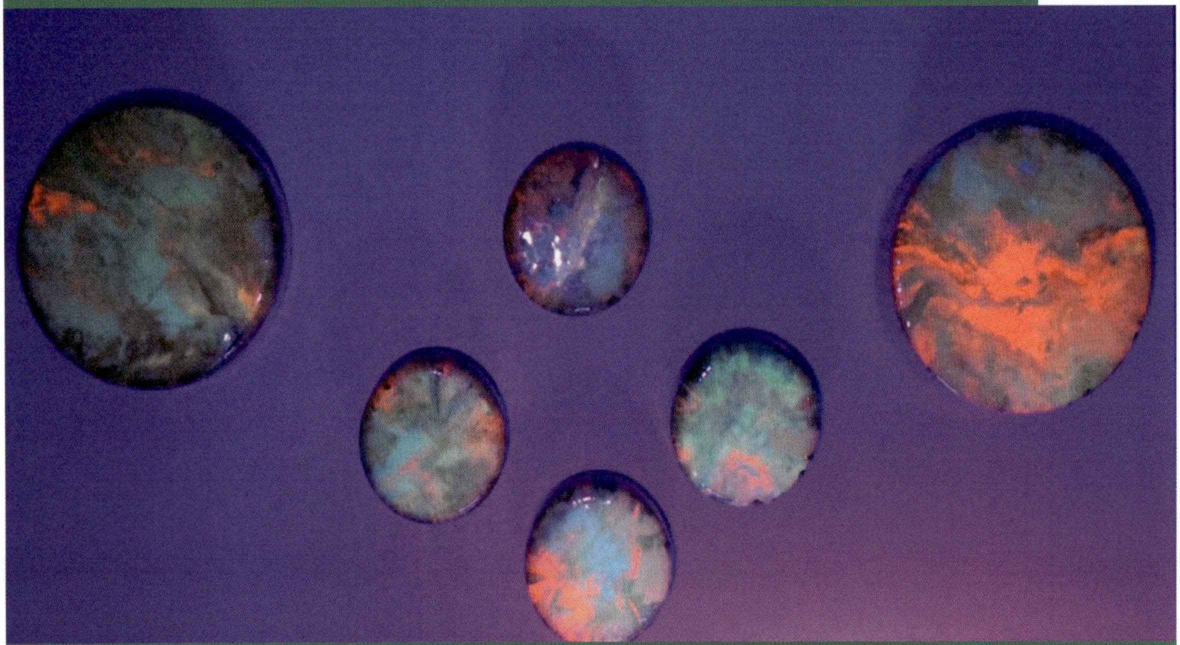

SPACE
Resin, Acrylic Paint, Glow Powder on Wood Bowls
Series of 6 Paintings
10" Round & 6" Round (25cm Round & 15cm Round)

RESIN PAINTING TECHNIQUES

ABSTRACT

Modern abstract is the primary technique for resin art. It is difficult to paint a tree or face using resin alone. Using color mixed with resin and abstracting onto the canvas is the primary technique. Resin moves and flows. It is difficult to maintain the form that you desire when working with resin. It's about putting the resin on the canvas and letting it do its thing.

CELLS & LACING

There are several techniques to use for creating cells and lacing. Cells and lacing are caused by different densities of pigment in paint interacting with each other in liquid form. When a heavier density of paint lands on a less dense paint, the pigments in the denser paint mixes with the less dense paint because it wants to move downward. Given this, if colored resin is placed on top of clear resin the result will be cells and lacing. When an opaque paint is placed on a translucent paint the result will be cells and lacing. Translucent paints are see-through. Opaque paints are not. White color gives the greatest cells and lacing. White is opaque. Place white color mixed with resin on blue translucent paint mixed with resin and allow it to spread. Spread it with a hair dryer, tilt the canvas, or blow through a straw to achieve cells and lacing.

Just remember opaque paints go on top and translucent paints go on the bottom. Metallic paints go on top and all other paints go on the bottom. Lay down translucent paint first. Pour on opaque paints next. If using metallics, pour on metallics last. Use clear resin as the translucent color and pour on opaque paint or metallic paint. Move the canvas by tilting. Use a hair dryer for greatest effect.

There are products that can be used to change the density of resin and create cells and lacing without having to figure out which paints are translucent or opaque. Alcohol, oil, and commercial products made for cells and lacing are some options for cells and lacing. Resi-blast is a commercial product made for producing cells & lacing in resin. Some commercially made pigment paste are purposed for producing cells.

There are 3 types of alcohol that can create cells and lacing. Denatured, acetone and isopropyl. Denatured and acetone can be purchased at the hardware store. Isopropyl can be purchased at the pharmacy and at most grocery stores. A few drops of alcohol mixed into white paint or into any one of an opaque color and dropped onto a translucent color will speed up and enhance cells and lacing. Be careful torching when alcohol is added. It will catch fire. The best part is that alcohol pops bubbles. If alcohol is used, torching may not be needed. Be aware that alcohol is flammable and can ignite when torching for bubbles.

Resi-blast is a product by Eli Chem that is made specifically to create lacing or cells in resin. Resi-blast creates very large cells when dropped from the end of a toothpick onto your desired area of the canvas. It can be mixed into the color cup or dropped onto the surface.

Metallic pigments in resin can create lacing. It creates lacing, it does not create cells. For an interesting effect. Dust metallic pigments over the surface of a completed painting.

Adding a very small amount of walnut oil or linseed oil can create cells. Please do not use vegetable or other kitchen oil as they can go rancid in your painting. A drop or two of an oil mixed into the color cup will do the trick.

Dimethicone or silicone oil. Dimethicone is another word for silicone oil. Silicone oil is used in acrylic fluid art painting and can be used in resin art as well. It works just OK mixed into the cup. It works very well dropped onto the surface with a toothpick. Use a toothbrush or other hard brush dipped in silicone oil, use your thumb to flick the oil on the surface of a completed resin painting to create cells.

Using oil paint mixed with resin creates cells and lacing. Using translucent colors and opaque colors gives the greatest effects.

Spray paints work for cells and lacing because of the chemicals that are used in the aerosol. Some use a type of oil, but most use alcohols. To use spray paints, first spray the paint into a paper cup and then pour into the mixing cup. Spray paint will melt Styrofoam. It's best to do this outdoors. Wear a face mask when using spray paints. The particles are airborne. Pour the mixed resin into the cup and stir well.

Pebeo paints are a type of paint that are made to give cells and lacing. I don't know what is in them. It's a secret formula. Probably some kind of oil. By themselves the paint take some time to dry. When mixed with resin they cure within 24 hours. Pebeo paints can be purchased at some Michael's craft stores.

DIMENSIONAL EFFECTS

Multiple options for dimensional effects:

* Beach style with/without real sand.
* Embedding objects such as glass, beads or rocks into resin.
* Layered mandala painting. Paint mandalas between layers of resin.
* Fluid art painting in between layers of resin.
* Dot painting in between layers of resin.
* Using resin in the stage just before cured to build thick impasto effects. This takes skill and has to be timed just right.
* Using cardboard or Styrofoam to build dimension for resin. I have videos on YouTube using this technique.
* Using ice on top of resin to create purposeful dimples, or cracks, to fill with colored resin on a second layer. Cold water through a straw can also be used.
* Using leftover resin from the table to create mixed media art on canvas. Layer for dimension.
* Layers of clear resin over a painted surface. A tree for example painted in layers between clear resin. A face or form painting between multiple layers of resin.
* Layers of shapes cut from magazines between resin.
* Layering acrylic skins in between pours of clear resin.

PAINTING ON CURED RESIN

There are so many options for painting on a cured resin surface. Here are just some of them:

* Acrylic fluid pours on cured resin: Pour a smooth colored resin surface. Then apply a fluid acrylic pour on top of the cured resin. Maintaining some negative space is preferred but use your own creativity. Let the fluid pour set for at least a week. Apply a clear coat of resin to seal the fluid pour and tie it all together.
* Oil painting on cured resin: Pour a smooth colored resin surface. Apply oil paints to complete your painting. Pour resin to seal oil painting. Generally, oil paintings take a very long time to dry. The drying time depends on the additives you have used in your painting. You can allow your painting to set but not fully cure (the amount of time will depend on the paints and additives you use) and seal with resin before it is fully cured. It will seal as long as the paints aren't wet enough that the resin picks it up. I suggest you let it set at least 2 weeks before adding the resin. It will still be uncured so you want to minimize touching the surface of the oil paint before resin. The resin will cure the oil painting.
* Alcohol inks on cured resin: Start with a cured resin surface. Design with alcohol inks. Let dry and add another layer of clear resin.
* Watercolor on cured resin: Start with a cured resin surface. Paint your design. Let set for at least a week and add a layer of clear resin.
* Charcoal or pencil drawing on cured resin. Really cool effects can be achieved by drawing between layers of resin. Start with a cured resin surface. Lay down your drawing. Consider using a fixative. Resin will cure the surface but will also blur the charcoal or pencil if a fixative isn't used between layers. Flood coat over the drawing.

AIR EFFECTS

Using a heat gun or hair dryer to move the colored resin around on the substrate to blend colors, create cells and create effects.

DIRTY POUR

A dirty pour is done by layering colored mixed resin in a cup, then pouring onto the canvas. There is a myth that you cannot do a dirty pour in resin. But you can. It works very well.

DRAG EFFECTS

Drag a toothpick, hair dye tools, plastic fork or other objects through to create effects. You can create feathering effects or dendrite effects or simply move the resin around the canvas the way your creative self wants.

LAYERED POUR

A layered pour is done by pouring colored resin in layers. Pour one color on top of the other in as many layers as you choose.

SWIPE

Layer colored resin on top of each other and use a silicone spatula or wooden stick and swipe across the paints to create effects. Black or white paint added to mixed resin then poured in a line at one end of the canvas is a popular swipe method. Layer colored resin on the canvas. Pour black or white colored resin on one end of the canvas only. Use a plastic sheet or piece of clean cardboard to swipe down the full surface of the canvas.

TREE RING

Start with a dirty pour and pour in a circular motion when pouring on the canvas. This gives the appearance of a tree ring. The colors will blend together more in resin art than in fluid acrylic art.

WANDERING POUR

Start with a dirty pour or a tree ring pour, but instead of pouring in one spot wander the pour across the canvas in any desired pattern.

SECTION 14
RESIN COATING COMPLETED PAINTINGS

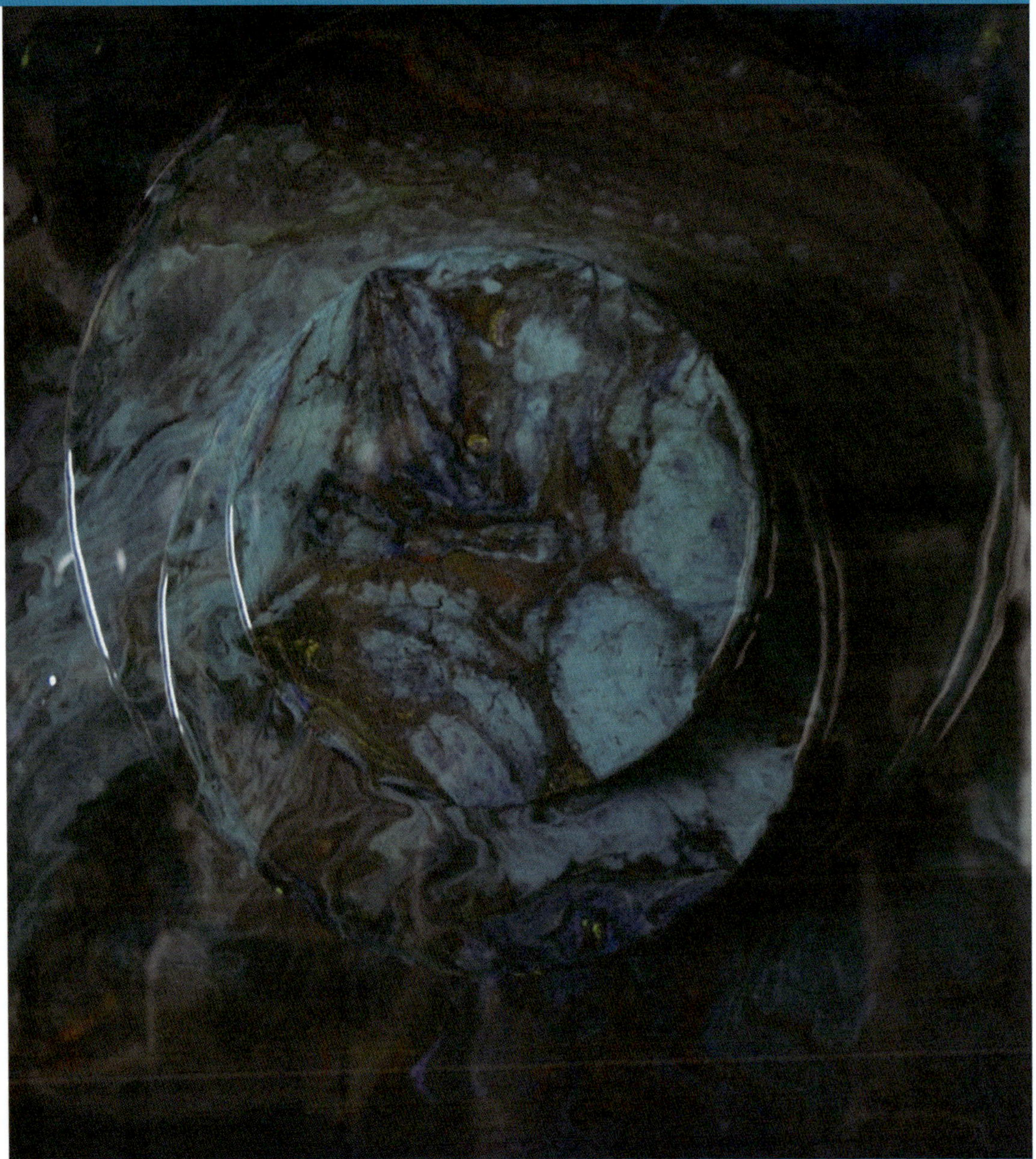

PARALLELS
Acrylic Painting Resin Covered Cradled MDF Panel
16"x16" (40cmx40cm)

RESIN COATING ACRYLIC PAINTINGS

I talked about using acrylic paint mixed with resin in sections 5 and 10. You can make a stable and sturdy resin painting using acrylic paint, as long as no more than 10% paint is used in the resin mix. Let's talk about covering already completed acrylic paintings with resin. Why do it? There are many reasons why one may choose to cover a completed acrylic painting. The number one reason is effect. Acrylic paintings need a sealant of some kind to ensure they last. One can use gloss medium or varnish to seal the work. Resin provides a very high gloss finish. If a doming resin is used, it provides dimension and depth.

A fluid acrylic painting needs at least 2 weeks and as much as 8 weeks to cure before applying resin. However, if you live in an area with high humidity let it cure for 6 to 8 weeks before applying resin. Let it dry for 8 weeks if the painting has been done with thick layers of paint.

The goal is to achieve as much dryness and curing, of the acrylic paint, as possible. I live in a dry climate. I have applied resin to acrylic art 2 weeks after I have completed them. The paintings where done with thin layers of paint. I have never had a problem. Even though I'm in a dry climate, I wait 8 weeks to cover acrylic paintings with thick layers of paint. If there is any chance of mold growing in the area where you live, I suggest waiting at least 8 weeks. It is better to wait and have a successful outcome than to rush it and end up with mold or cloudiness under the resin.

The difference with acrylic art and fluid acrylic art coverage, in resin, is one of working with silicone oil. If silicone oil has not been used, go ahead and resin within 2 to 8 weeks depending on your climate. If silicone oil has been used, the goal is to avoid dimples and pitting in the cure of the resin. The question of, to clean or not to clean, has to be decided when covering fluid art with resin. It's really a question of how best to handle the silicone oil in resin.

If the decision is to clean it before a coat with resin, there are a few methods to try. One way is to sprinkle corn starch on the surface of the painting. Let it sit for about 10 minutes and wipe clean. Clean the surface with a baby wipe. If you still see an oily surface, repeat the process. Another option is to spray with isopropyl alcohol & wipe off. Do not allow the alcohol to sit on the surface, as it will absorb into the paint and change the painting. Another cleaning option is to use dish soap and water to wipe down the surface. Rinse off and let it dry completely before applying resin.

A fluid painting can be cleaned very well and still end up with dimples and pits when covering with resin. For this reason, I prefer to skip cleaning and apply the resin directly. You read that right. This way the resin picks up the silicone oil already on the surface and takes care of any dimples and pits. For this method, apply a thin resin flood coat and massage it into the surface of the painting to pick up the silicone. Pour more resin over the surface to level it out and let cure. See troubleshooting dimples and pits to see how I do this.

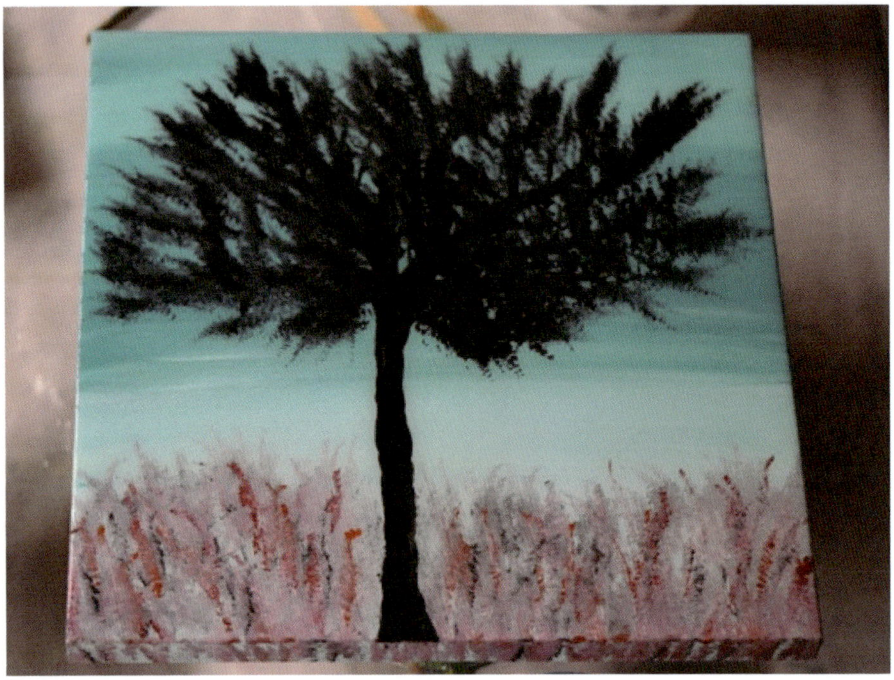

Oil painting with one coat of Art 'N Glow resin in the curing process.

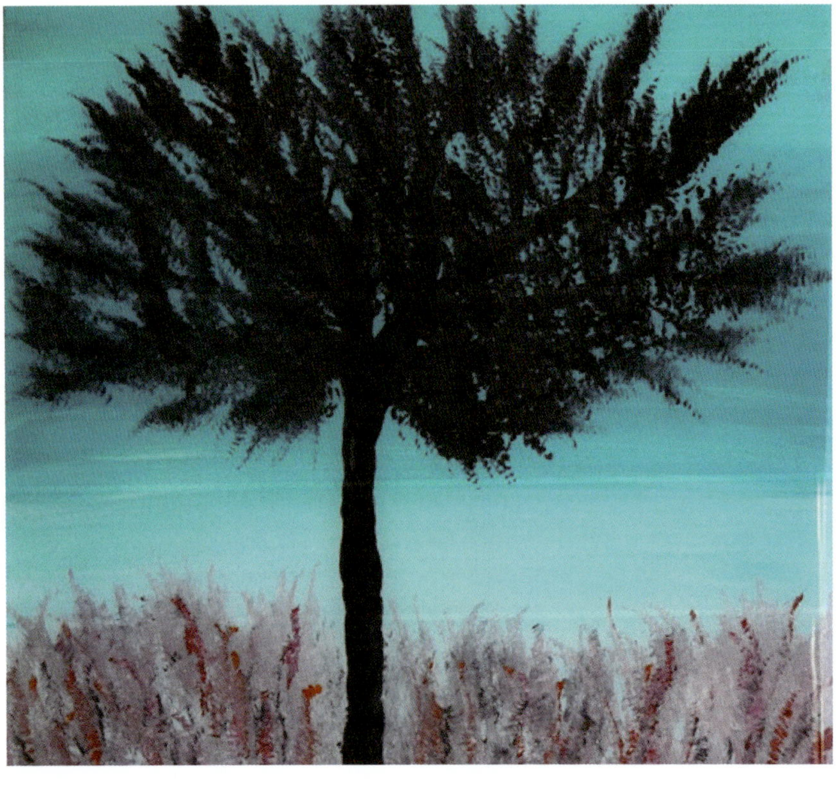

I used 2 coats of resin to cover the thickly painted parts. Here is the finished piece.

I talked about how to mix oil paints into resin for resin painting in sections 5 and 10. Use 10% paint to 90% resin. Mix the paint completely with safflower, walnut oil or linseed oil until all lumps are removed. Then add to resin. For more information see section 10. Here, I'll talk about covering a completed oil painting with resin.

Why cover a completed oil painting in resin? Oil paintings need to be sealed once finished and fully dried. One can use Damar varnish or other oil paint sealant for the task. Using epoxy resin will seal the painting but is not the primary reason to choose this for an oil painting. Only use resin on an oil painting if a high gloss shine is desired for the piece. Resin is modern, where oil paint is classic. Oil paint has vibrant colors only achieved with this medium. When covered with resin it takes it up a notch.

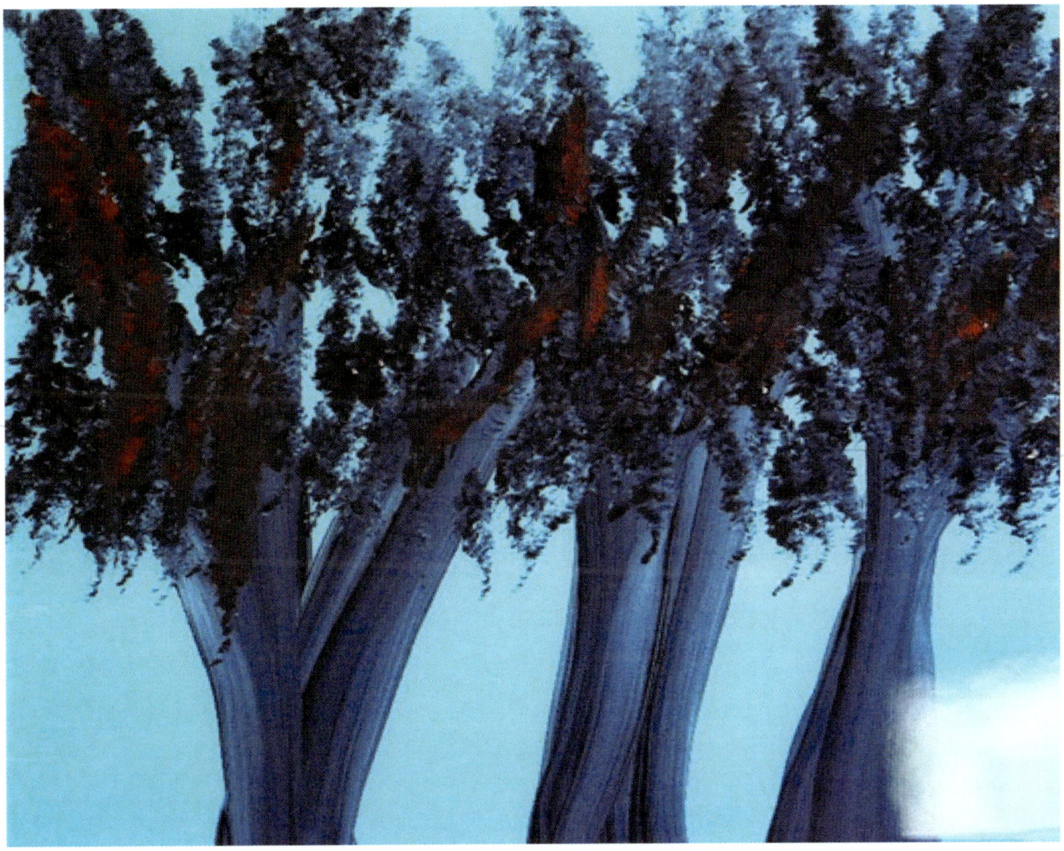

Oil painting covered with Art Resin.

There are many questions to ask when determining the best time to apply the resin. Were thin or thick layers of paint made? What additives were used? How important is it that you maintain the integrity of the strokes in your work? Is it on cotton or wood canvas? An oil painting with thin brush strokes can take a minimum of 6 weeks to dry and a year to fully cure. An oil painting with thick brush strokes can take 3 to 6 months to dry and 2 years to fully cure. Resin can be applied when the oil painting is dry enough to maintain the brush strokes without being picked up by the resin. If thin brush strokes are used the painting is much less likely to blend with the resin and smear your artwork during the resin curing process.

Some oil painting additives can speed the drying process which will allow you to apply resin sooner. Some oil painting additives slow down the drying process and will lengthen the time you need to wait before applying resin. If it is not important that you maintain the brush strokes in your oil painting you can go ahead and apply resin within a few days or a week. The resin might pick up some of the oil paint or at the least turn cloudy from the oil paint, but that may be a look you want. The substrate that your painting is on is important because oil paint absorbs more readily into fabric canvas than it does hard materials. It will absorb into bare wood, but the rate of absorption is a bit slower.

The answer on when to resin coat a finished oil painting is, it depends. It depends on the affects you are going for. If you want the oil painting to be just as painted but to have a resin finish, then wait 6 months to a year before applying resin. If you like the idea that the resin might pick up some of the oil paint and give a smoky forest look go ahead and resin over it within a week or even a few days. Yes, you read that right a few days. Resin will cure oil paint. The oil in the paint seems to make its way to the surface of the resin as it cures, leaving behind pigment. As long as it's a thin layer of paint. If the paint is too thick, the resin cannot seal it in. The result will be pits in your surface where the paint is thick. That is why so many artists say that resin and oil paint do not work together. Resin will provide a fast cure to an oil painting. If the oil painting is dry enough that you are not concerned with losing your brush strokes, it can be successfully covered in resin.

Here is a decision tree:

Thin oil paint with linseed, safflower or walnut oil additive-smoky affects acceptable - resin within a week.
Thin oil paint with linseed, safflower or walnut oil additive-prefer to keep brush strokes – resin in 3 to 6 months. Wait 6 months to a year if you want to be really sure.
Thin oil paint with additives used for quick drying – smoky affects acceptable – resin within a week.
Thin oil paint with additives used for quick drying – prefer to keep brush strokes – resin in 3 months.
Thick oil paint with impasto effects no additives -smoky affects acceptable - wait 3 to 6 to resin.
Thick oil paint with impasto effects no additives - prefer to keep brush strokes – wait 1 to 2 years to resin.
Thick oil paint with impasto effects quick drying additives used – smoky affects acceptable – wait 3 months to resin.
Thick oil paint with impasto effects quick drying additives used – prefer to keep brush strokes – wait 1 year to resin.

Now that you have read through the suggestions on covering completed oil paintings with resin. I'll let you in on a little secret. The oil paintings in the pictures at the beginning of this section where covered in resin 2 days after they were completed. It wasn't cured when I applied the resin. In fact, it was still wet to the touch. But I wanted to test it to see if it would bleed through and give a smoky effect or if the tree would bleed. Nothing happened. I wanted to test for strength as well. Would the resin still be sturdy or would it go sticky and gooey? Would the resin become flexible after curing? The answer is the resin is sturdy. It didn't bleed. It has not gone sticky. I wanted to test brands of resin as well. I used Art Resin and Art 'N Glow. Both brands worked incredibly well. Art 'N Glow is thicker. That is the only difference. A thicker resin will dome more.

I did this style because I thought it would still be interesting if it bled. I would have been OK with that. If it had gone sticky, I would have poured another coat. The only thing that happened is that it took two coats on one of them. The tree, in the Art 'N Glow one, had some high parts or extra thick brush strokes and I had to pour a second flood coat to cover them. I could have left it with one coat. It was covered well and was not peeking through. But I wanted to be sure. I like the look with 2 coats anyway. The second one with Art Resin was painted very flat and did not require a second coat.

I learned it is possible to pour resin over completed oil paintings as soon as you like. The reason is that oil paint is not water based. Any excess oil in the paint will rise to the surface of the resin, and can be cleaned off once cured. It is best to wait a full 6 weeks to clean the oil off the painting after the curing process. In my experimentation with resin and oil paint I have found that resin actually cures oil paint very well. It pulls out the oil and raises it to the surface of the resin, leaving pigment and resin behind. This is only true if the oil paint is in thin layers on the surface. If there are thick layers of paint on the surface you will end up with areas where the resin cures around the oil paint leaving holes. But, if you pour enough layers of resin it will cure even thick layers of oil paint. Taping the sides to create a dam will make it possible to cover thick layers. If there are problems with weakness in the surface, you can pour another clear coat to sturdy it up.

If you have a masterpiece on your hands and you really want to ensure that your painting stays just the way you painted it, I suggest you practice patience and wait 3 to 6 months for your art to at least dry before you resin.

RESIN COATING ENCAUSTIC PAINTINGS

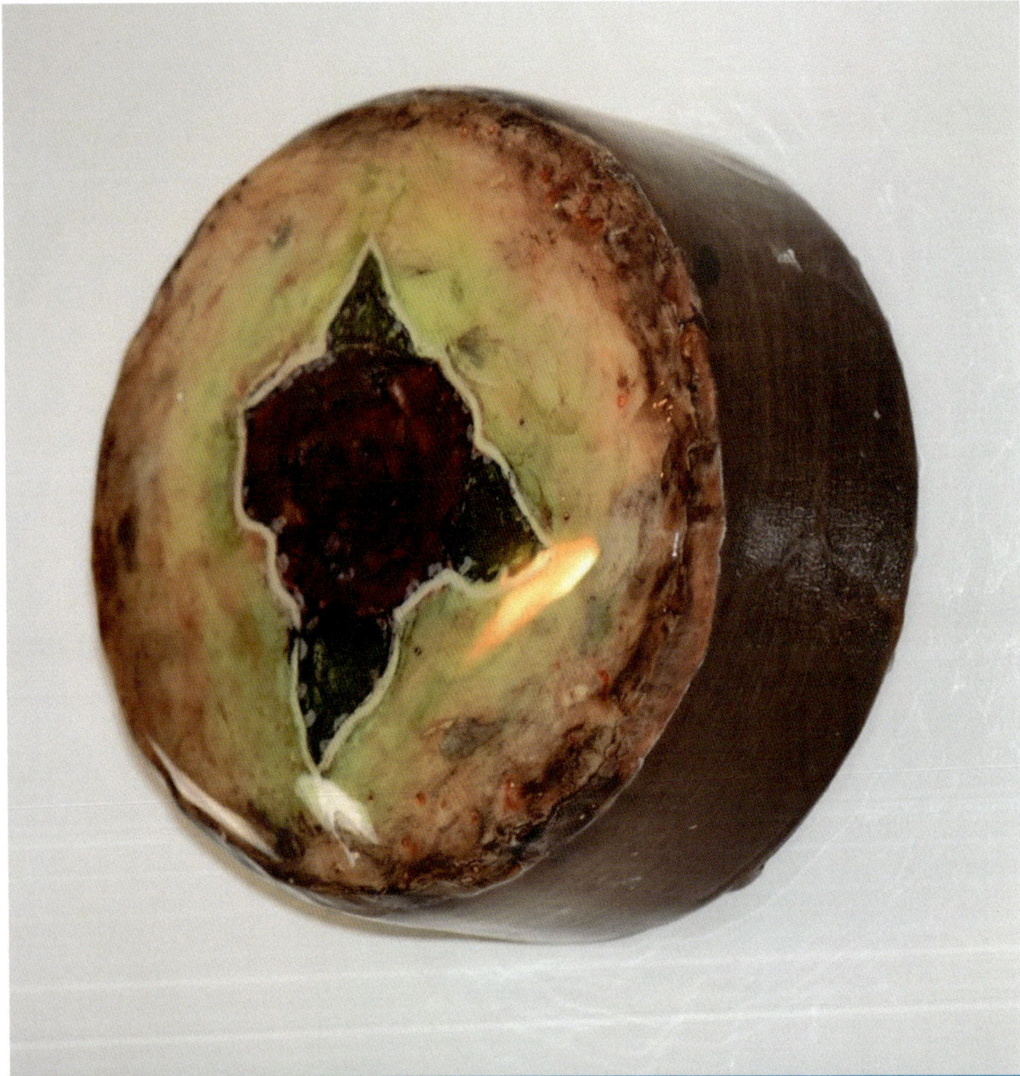

HANGING OUT
Resin Covered Encaustic on Wood Bowl
6"x6" (15cmx15cm)

An encaustic painting is a wax painting. It is one of the oldest forms of painting. Resin and encaustic go beautifully together. It's like they were made for each other. Wax should always be completed on a wood substrate. If not, it peels off.

But here is a story: I wanted to practice a new encaustic technique. I didn't want to waste a wood panel so I grabbed a cheap canvas to practice on. I was given some advice once to never practice on cheap canvases because you never know when you are going to make something great and now it's on a cheap canvas. When I was finished, I really liked what I had done. I should have listened to that advice. Because I know encaustic will not last on canvas I decided to test it out a bit. I banged on it and sure enough the encaustic didn't want to stick to the canvas. So, I covered it in resin. I was still wondering if it was archival now that it was covered in resin. I put it in the freezer overnight. Banged on it and nothing happened. It maintained its integrity. Still not done, I blasted it with a heat gun for a good 10 minutes. The wax was heated below the surface but didn't move. The resin separated from the canvas but within a couple of minutes it settled back into its original shape. I keep it around as a reminder to always choose the right canvas for the work you are doing, even if you are just practicing.

Now back to encaustic and resin. Encaustic has a buttery consistency to me that you just can't get with other painting mediums. It's great on its own. But when covered in resin it is simply stunning.

Encaustic paintings bloom. They go through a process of curing that gives off this powdery substance or bloom on the surface that has to be buffed out over a period of 6 months. They are dry as soon as you complete them. But they take 6 months to cure. Covering an encaustic painting should only occur after the blooming has completed and full curing has taken place. An encaustic can be covered as soon as it's completed and this might even keep it from going through that encaustic blooming. But, for best results, wait 6 months before covering it.

SECTION 15
CLEANING RESIN ART

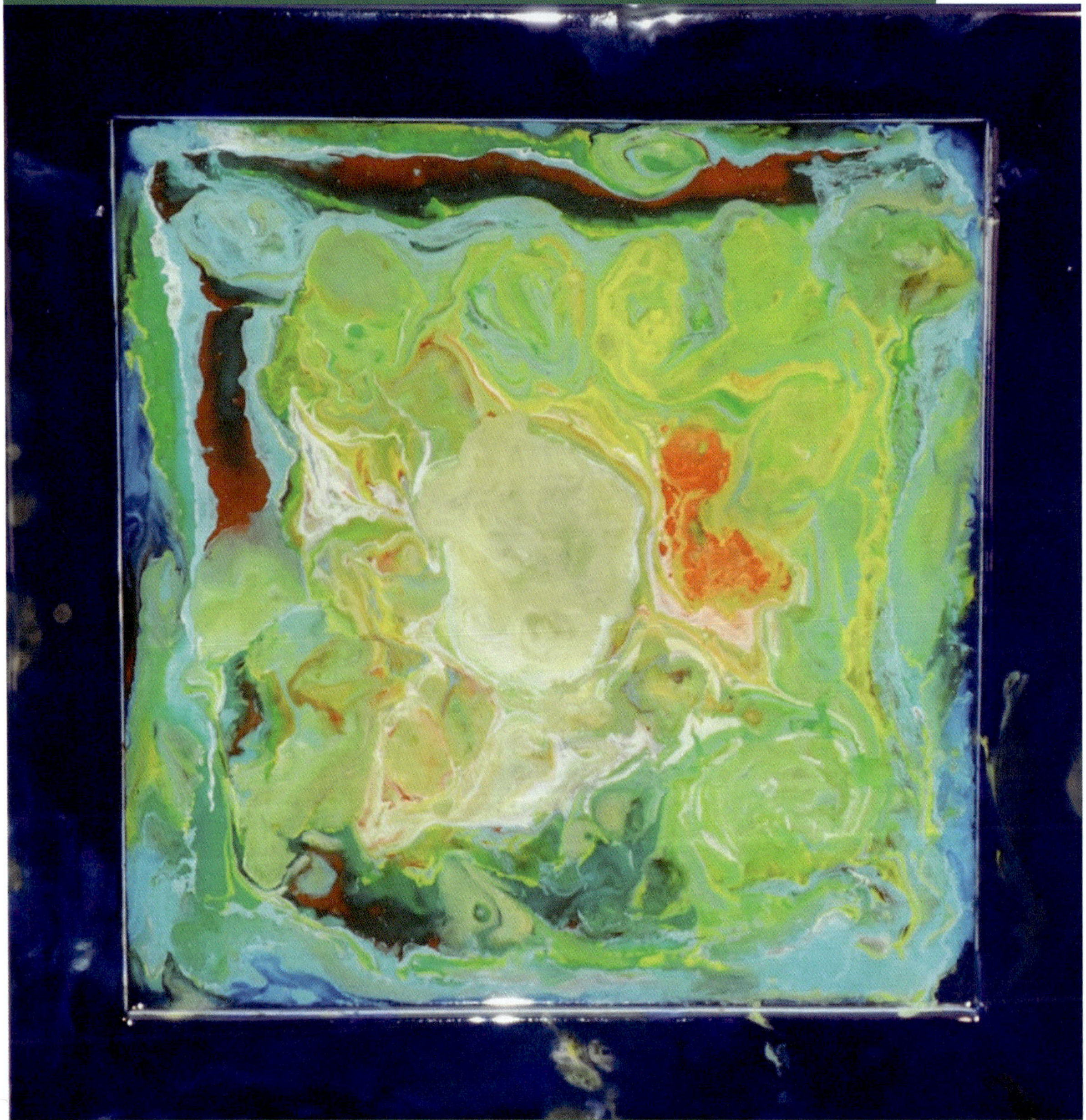

The Healing Circle
Resin & Oil Paint On Handmade Wood Canvas
12"x12" (31cmx31cm)

Once fully cured, resin art can be treated like glass. The best method of cleaning, is with glass cleaner and a microfiber cloth. Paper towels and glass cleaner can be used as well. If using paper towels, make sure it is fully cured. Paper towels can scratch the resin if not fully cured. When cleaning a 3D resin art piece that has hard to reach places, use a hair dryer on cool setting. Blow out any dust and debris from the areas that you cannot reach. Then clean the areas you can reach with window cleaner and microfiber cloth.

Resin art should not be cleaned before it has gone through the full curing process which last usually 7 to 14 days. I prefer to allow resin art pieces a full 8 weeks of curing before cleaning.

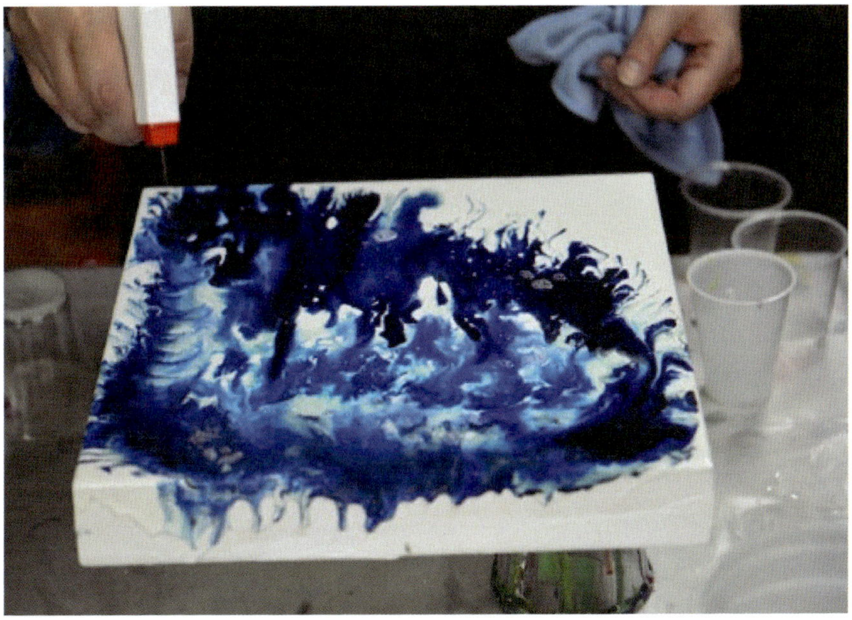

Spray the surface with glass cleaner.

Wipe down with a micro fiber cloth.

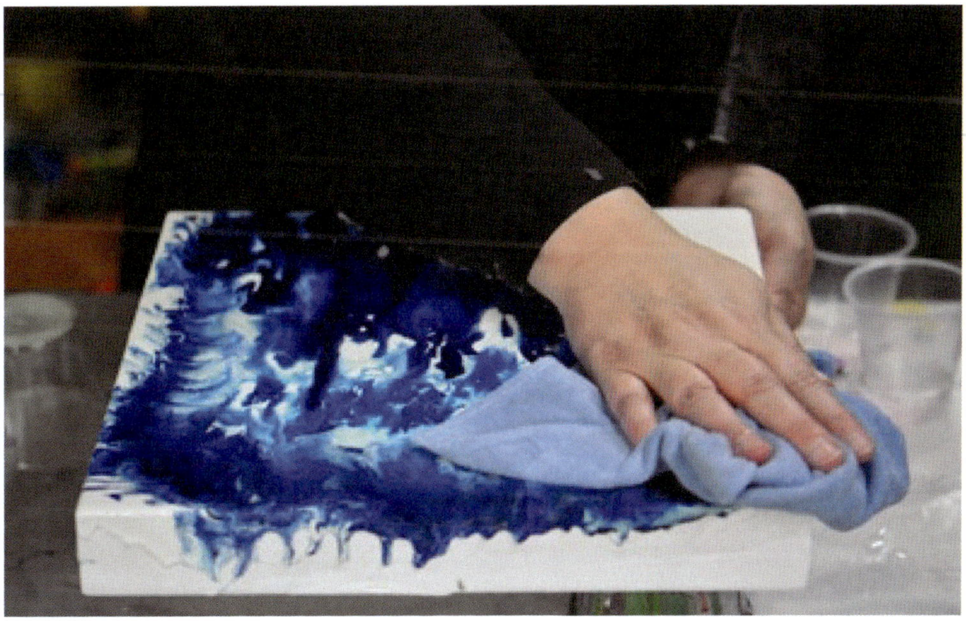

SECTION 16
POLISHING RESIN ART

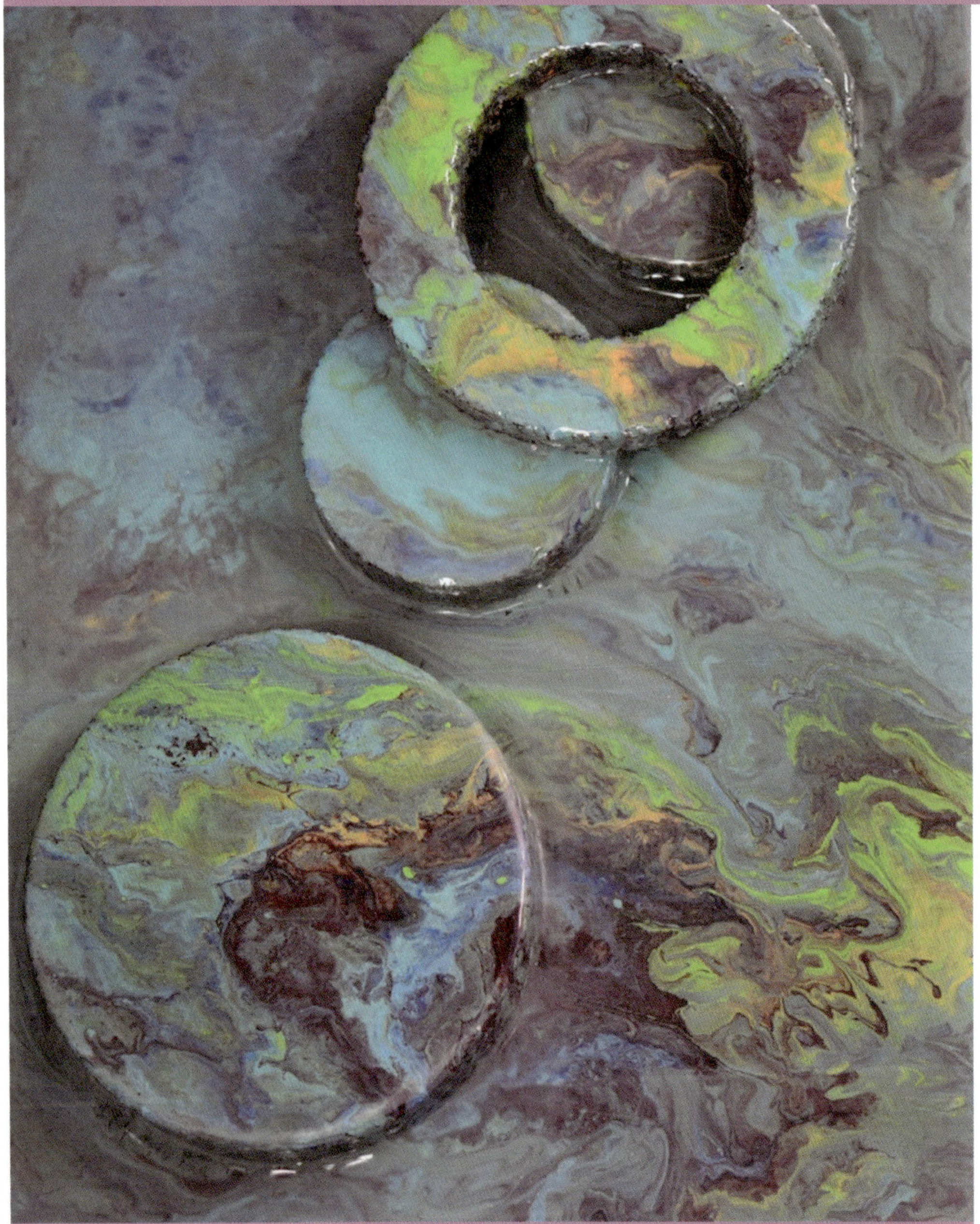

Many Levels
Resin Coated Acrylic Fluid Art on Cradled Wood Panel.
12"x16" (31cmx41cm)

Cured epoxy resin can be polished to bring out the finish or to repair the finish. I personally prefer to sand and pour another coat. Let's say you have a cured resin painting and there is a hair or dust particle in the surface. The particle can be sanded out and a fresh coat poured over to seal the sanding marks and bring back the clear shine. An option is to polish the surface. Polishing provides a shine. The polished shine is milky in nature. The more polishing one does the more shine is achieved but it is impossible to achieve the shine of freshly poured resin.

The process of polishing involves sanding with varying grits of sandpaper followed by rubbing compound, followed by polishing compound. By sanding with varying grits of sandpaper small scratches are worked out of the surface and a natural polish is achieved. The rubbing compound works out any remaining scratches and the polishing compound brings back the shine.

Start with 300 grit for a light sanding and to remove any particles from the surface. Move to 500 grit and sand the entire surface. Move to 800 grit and sand the entire surface. Move to 1000 grit and sand the entire surface. Move to 1500 grit and sand the entire surface. The rubbing and polishing compounds can be applied at this point or continue on to 2000 and 3000 grit sand paper for an even greater polish. When using rubbing and polishing compounds, use a polishing sponge.

I found a sanding attachment for a drill that is used to polish out headlights at my local hardware store. The kit came with sandpaper in 500, 800 and 1500 grits. A sanding block or an electric palm sander works as well.

CAUTION

Wear a face respirator when sanding. Or at least wear a face mask. Sanded resin particles can cause respiratory irritations when airborne.

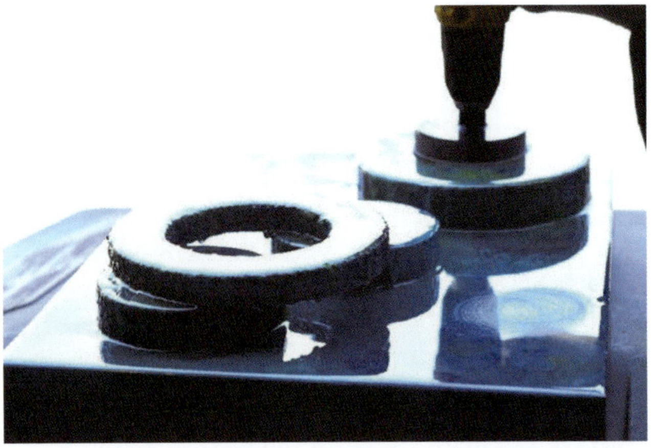

Sanding using 500 grit sandpaper. I am using a sanding attachment on a drill.

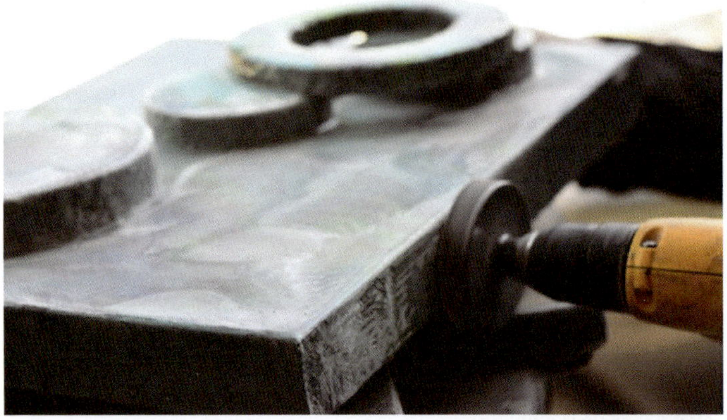

Go over the entire surface.

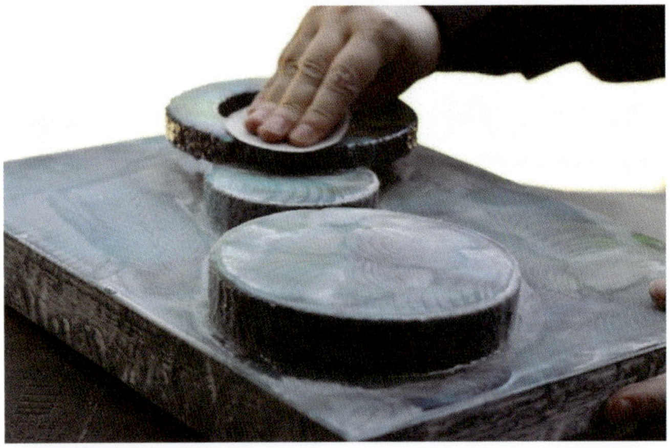

Hand sand in hard to reach places.

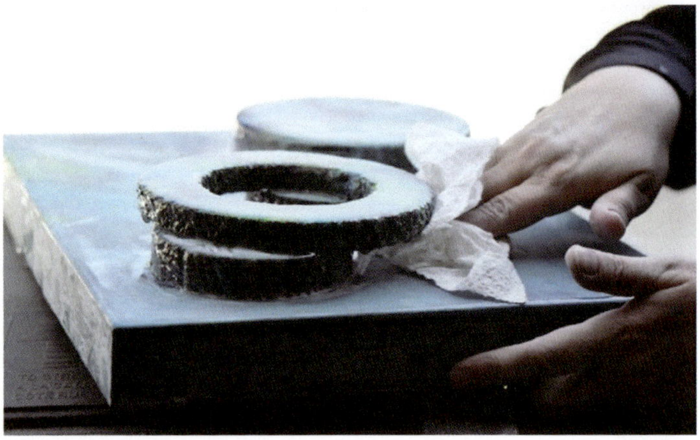

Wipe down with paper towels in between sanding.

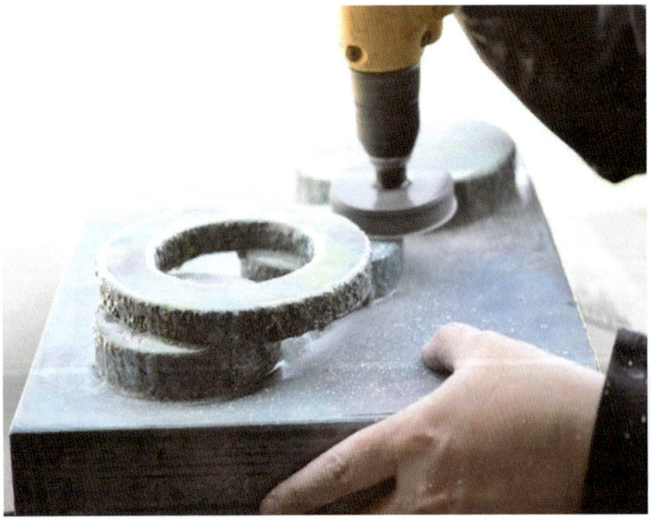

Sanding with 800 grit sandpaper.

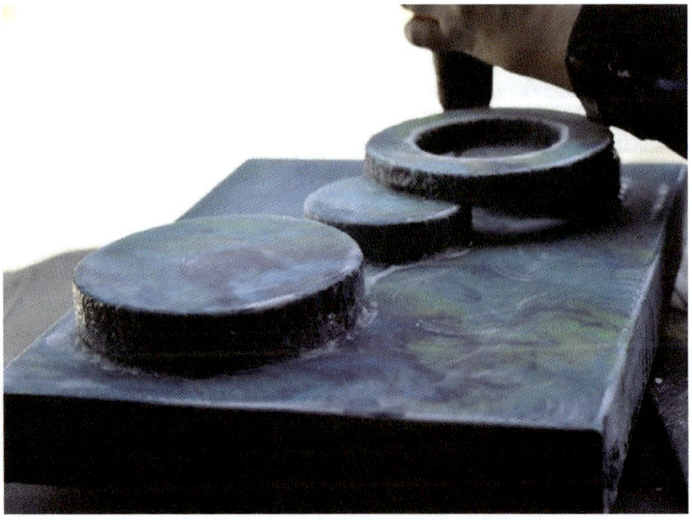

It already looks clearer.

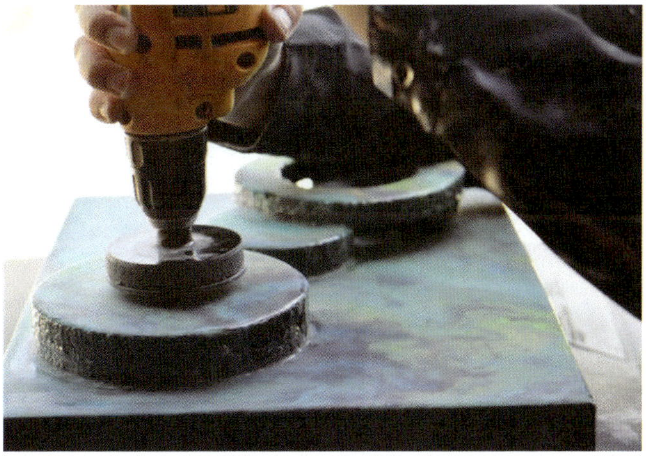

Sanding with 1500 grit sandpaper.

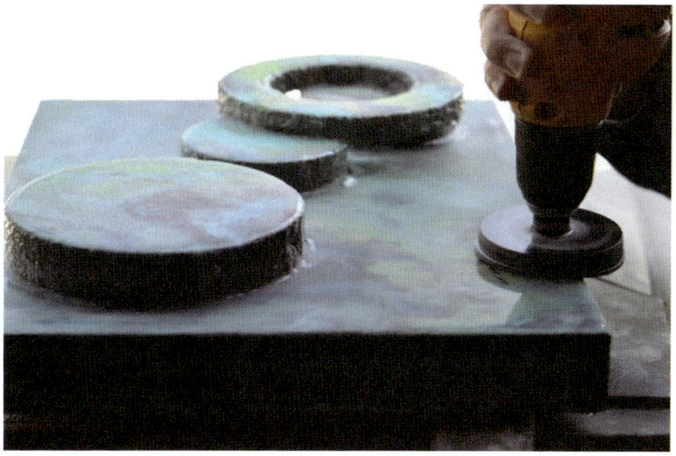

Using 1500 grit sandpaper polishes more than it sands.

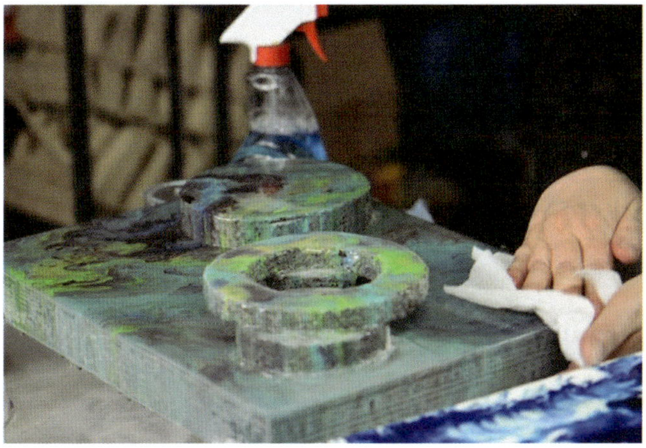

Clean the surface with window cleaner and baby wipes or paper towels.

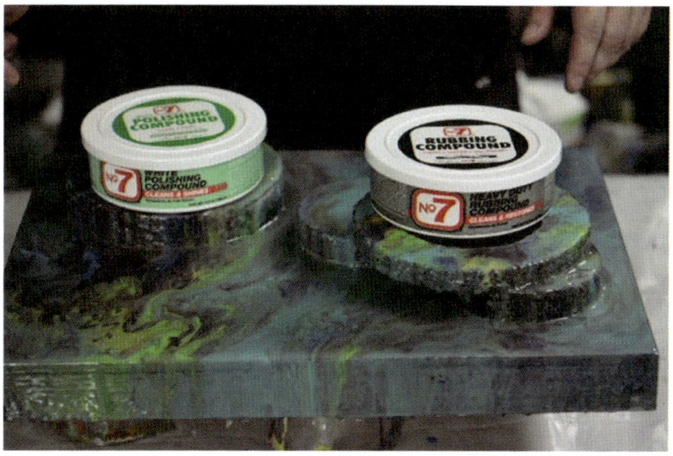

Go over the surface, first with rubbing compound, and then with polishing compound. I picked this up from the hardware store.

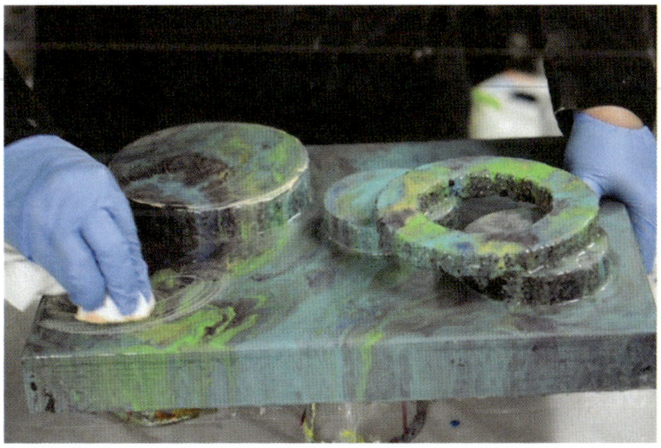

I decided to use a paper towel for the rubbing compound.

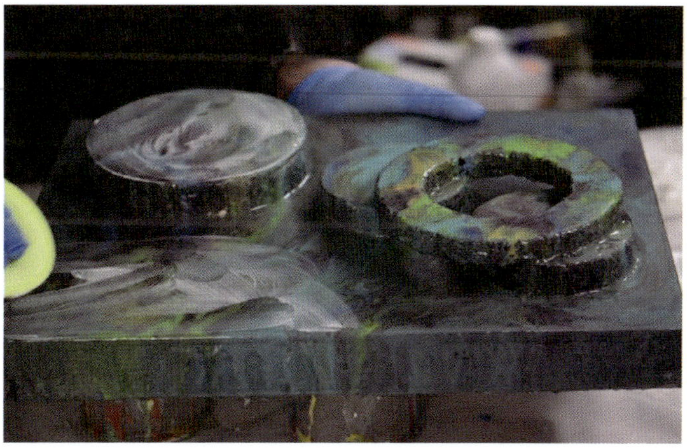

I am using a polishing sponge for the polishing compound.

SECTION 17
TROUBLESHOOTING GUIDE

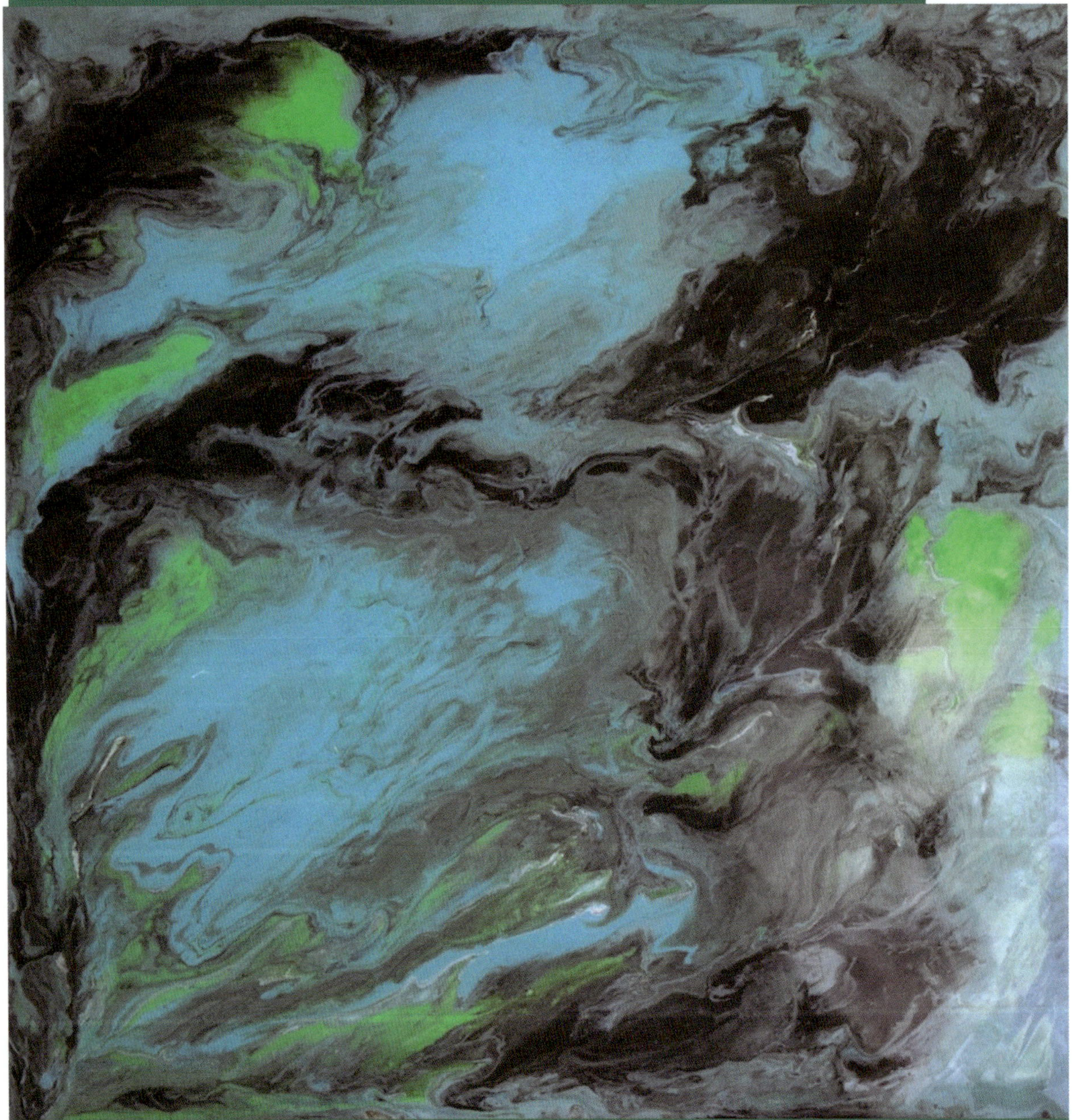

Picking Up Speed
Resin Covered Fluid Art on Wood Panel
8"x8" (20cmx20cm)

EXCESSIVE BUBBLES

Bubbles are going to happen in resin. From the first stir of the hardener & resin, bubbles are created. Every time the resin is stirred, air is being moved into the mixture and bubbles are the result.

A butane or propane torch takes care of them. Lightly move the flame over the surface of the bubbles. What to do if you have run out of butane? Use a heat gun to rid the surface of bubbles. Don't have a heat gun? Use a straw. The carbon dioxide from your breath blown through the straw pops bubbles. Be careful not to breathe in the fumes. Breathe away from the resin and breathe through the straw onto the bubbles. If blowing through a straw is not appealing to you, use alcohol. Spray the surface with 91% alcohol. Spray bottles can be purchased at hardware stores.

Excessive bubbles are another issue altogether. Excessive bubbles can happen because of vigorous stirring of the resin. They can also happen if you have mixed your resin in cold temperatures. Resin is best used when the room is 70 degrees Fahrenheit. To avoid excessive bubbles, stir slowly. If you have stirred vigorously, don't worry, the bubbles will dissipate quickly with the first pass of a torch.

CAUTION

Using a torch after using alcohol on resin may ignite the alcohol. It may cause flames. It is best to avoid using a torch when using alcohol in resin.

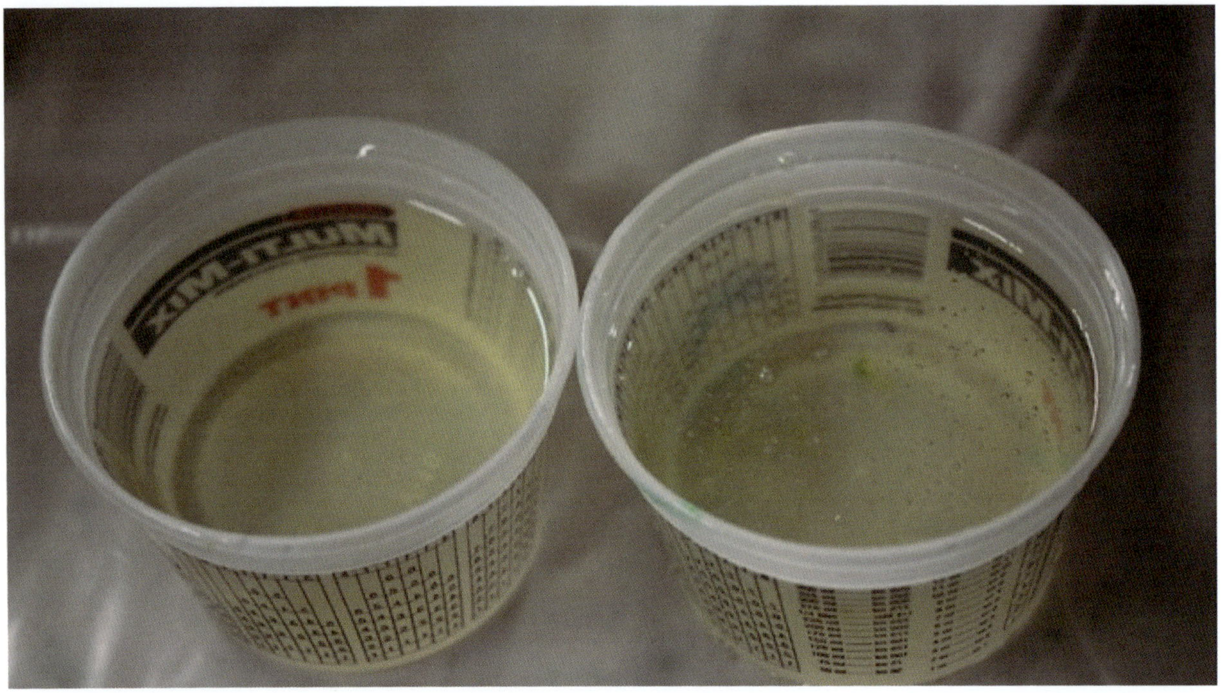

Comparison of slow stirring to vigorous stirring. The cup on the left was stirred slowly. The cup on the right was stirred fast and vigorously.

Vigorous stirring can create excess bubbles in the mix. The one on the left was stirred slowly. The one on the right was stirred fast. A vigorous stirring whips air into the mix and creates excess bubbles. Not to worry, use the resin as you normally would, and torch on canvas to remove the bubbles.

To avoid excessive bubbles from cold weather, always use resin at the correct temperature. The room temperature needs to be a cozy 70 degrees Fahrenheit. The resin and hardener need to be 75 degrees Fahrenheit. If you are going to resin in colder months, heat up the studio. Then place your resin and hardener in a warm water bath for 10 to 15 minutes. This will ensure proper mixing and will prevent bubbles. Keep in mind that the water should be warm not hot. If the water is too hot, the mixed resin heats up too much and too quickly. If this happens the mixed resin will cure within a short amount of time. It can cure within 5 minutes in the cup.

DIMPLES & PITTING

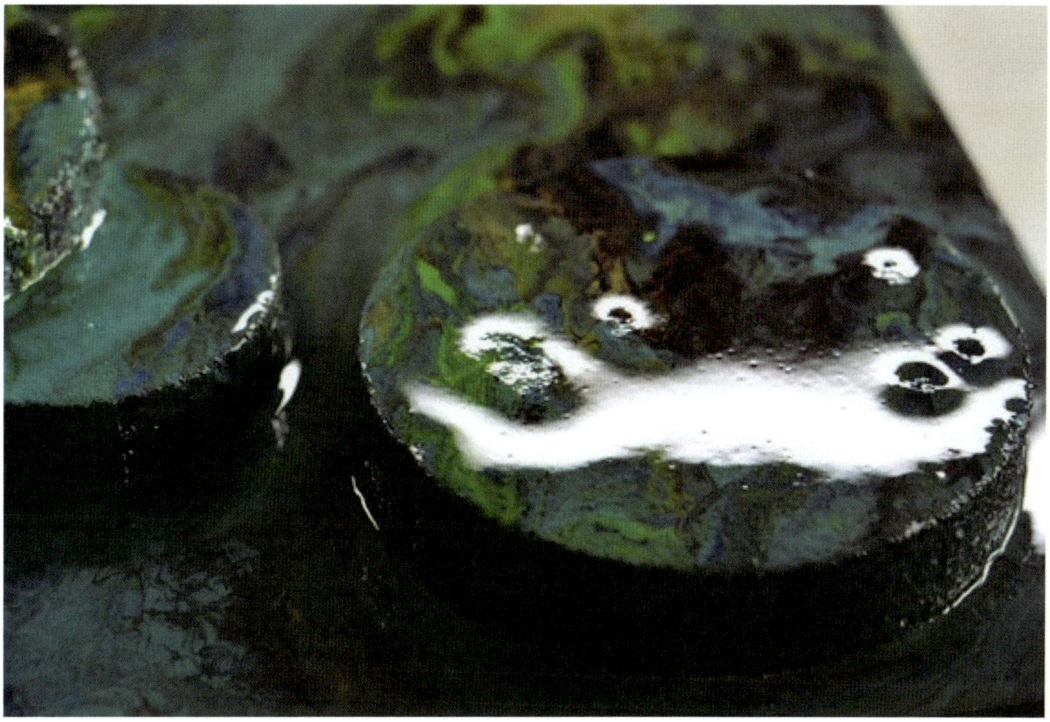

If you ever decide to cover a fluid art piece in resin you will run into the problem of dimples and pitting. That is because the silicone oil used in fluid art, to obtain cells and lacing, repels resin. In fact, dimples and pitting can occur in any resin art piece due to oil on hands touching the canvas, especially the sides. Cleaning the canvas with alcohol and a micro fiber cloth before you resin will help to prevent dimples and pits. Try not to touch it before pouring the resin. However, the most common cause of dimples and pits is silicone oil or other oil in your painting medium that is left on the canvas.

For fluid art pieces, clean with dish soap. Take a wet cloth add a little dish soap and soap up. Wipe down the surface of the painting. Rinse the painting under running water, or use a clean wet cloth to wipe all the dish soap off. Allow to dry completely for at least 24 hours before applying resin.

Cleaning with alcohol is an option. Use 91% isopropyl alcohol and a baby wipe or paper towels to wipe down the surface. Do not allow the alcohol to sit on the surface as it will lift the paint and change the colors of the painting. Lightly wipe down the surface. Check it in an hour. If there is silicone oil remaining on the surface, clean it with alcohol again. Allow the surface to dry completely before you resin. An hour, or so, of dry time is sufficient with alcohol cleaning.

A painting that has dimples and pitting can be saved. There are 2 ways that I do this. The first involves working with wet resin and picking up the silicone oil that is already on the canvas. The second involves doing a light sanding on the piece and then flood coating with a fresh pour of resin.

Because I do a lot of fluid art, which I then cover in resin I have found that the best method is to simply not clean your painting before a resin pour. You read that right. I don't clean my fluid art before I resin. Not anymore. I have found that the method of rubbing the wet resin down to the canvas to pick up the silicone oil is much more effective. Many times, I have cleaned the painting very well only to have pits and dimples show up after the cure. So now I leave the silicone oil on the canvas and use it to smooth out any resulting dimples.

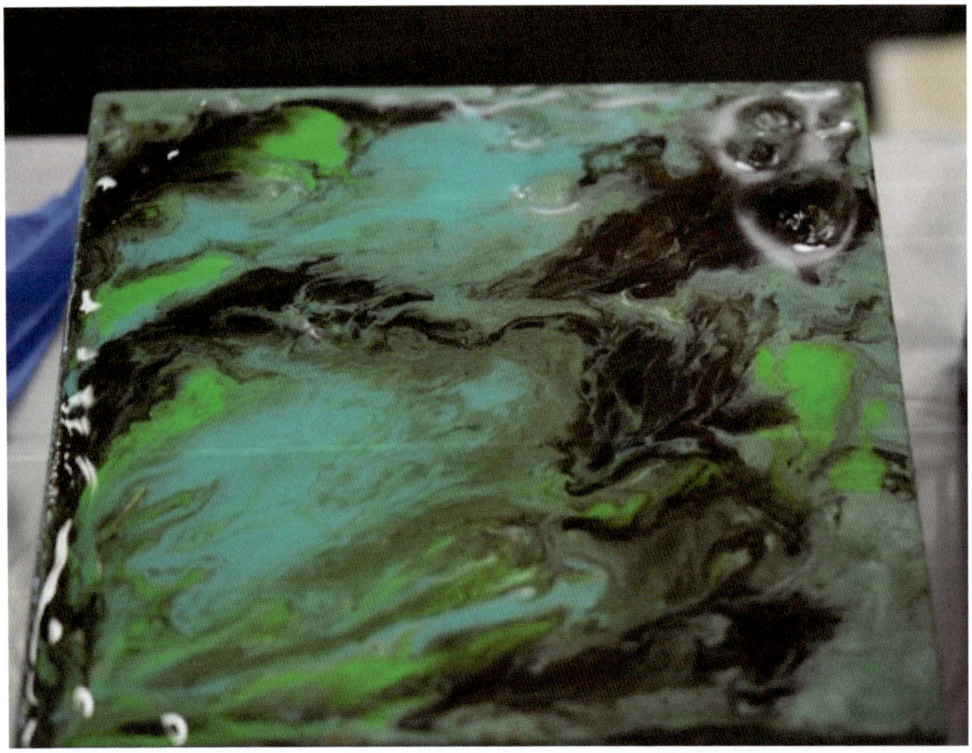

Fluid Art with dimples. A fresh pour of mixed resin. Dimples are forming in multiple areas of the painting.

You are going to need to sit with the piece for a couple of hours. Pour on a thin coat of resin and wait for the dimples to be revealed. Rub the canvas where the dimples are, with a gloved hand. There is no need to massage the whole canvas, only the areas where there are dimples. You may choose to go over the whole canvas. A reason for going over the whole canvas, is if it has multiple dimples or if it's small. Massage for about 20 to 40 seconds. Add an additional layer of fresh resin. Then, sit back and watch for any new dimples to form, or come back in about 5 to 10 minutes. One time usually takes care of the dimples and pitting. If the dimples have reformed, repeat the process. If the surface is particularly stubborn and they keep reforming simply repeat the massaging. You should only need to do this process no more than 3 times. If it happens a 4th time allow it to cure for 5 to 8 hours. Mix up a new batch of resin and pour on a second coat.

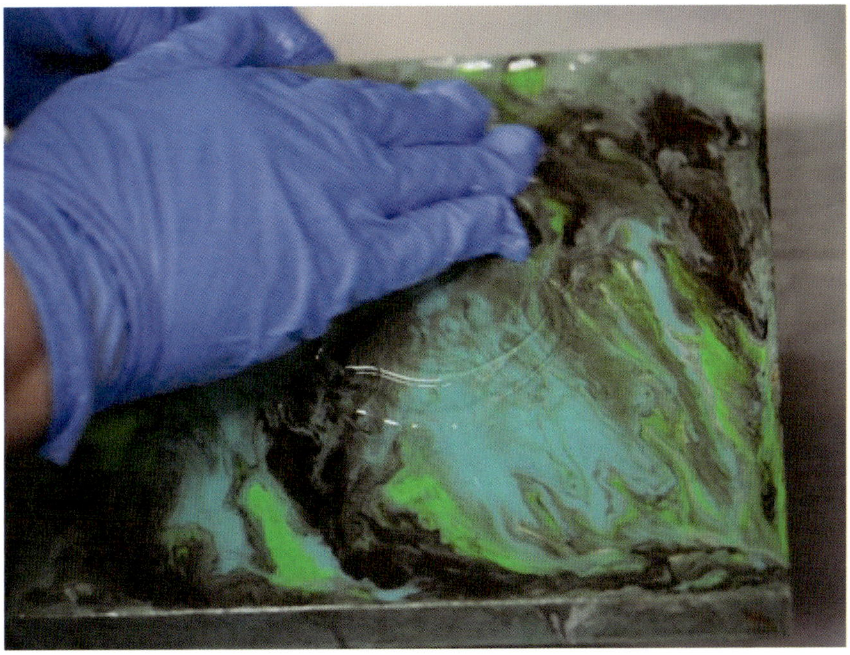

Massage down to the canvas. Press the resin into the canvas and pick up the silicone oil that is on the canvas.

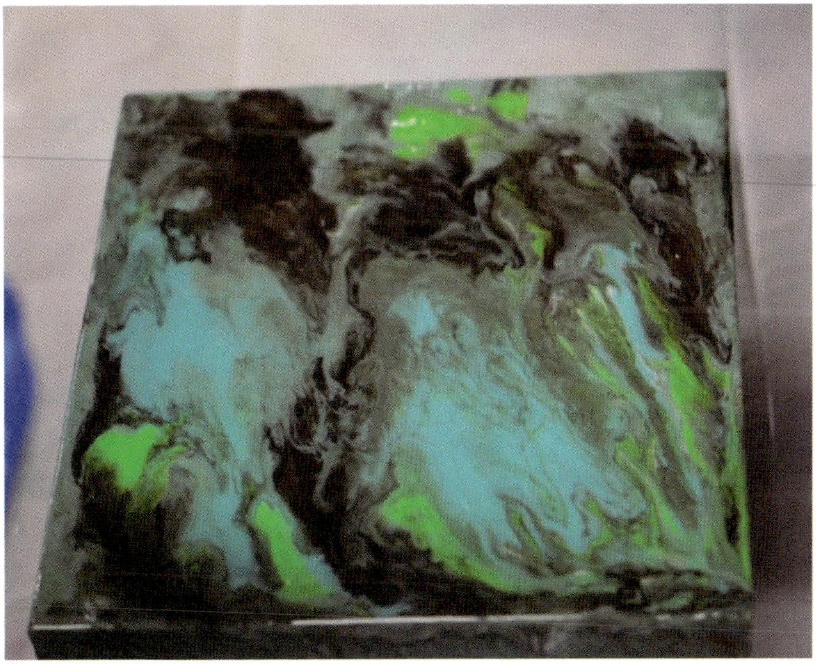

Once is enough to create a smooth surface.

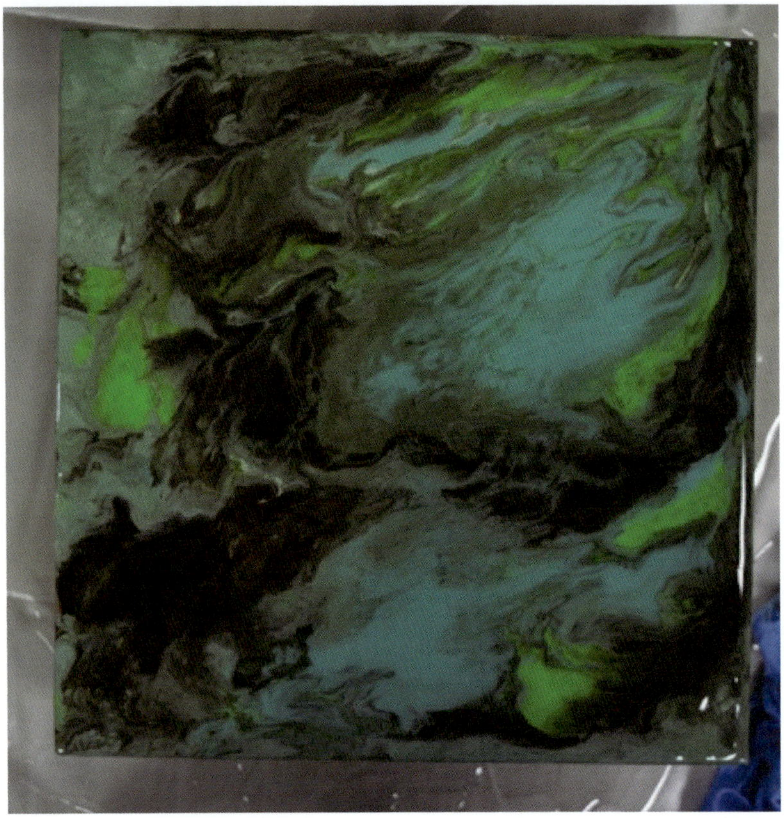

24 hours later and there is no evidence of dimples or pitting.

Another method for removing dimples and pits from fluid art is to add silicone oil to the mixed resin before pouring it onto the canvas. Pour a flood coat of resin on to your canvas. Wait for dimples and pitting to form. In a small disposable cup, add mixed resin. Add a couple of drops of silicone oil to the mixed resin. Pour it on the spots that have dimples and pits. The entire surface of the canvas can be covered in the silicone oil and resin, but lacing or pitting may result in areas that are unwanted. Layer more resin on the surface. Cover the canvas completely in resin and let it cure normally. The idea is that the silicone oil will react with the silicone oil already on the canvas and prevent the repelling process. Use a resin mixing cup to be thrown away as it is difficult to get silicone oil out of containers. It will taint any future mix.

The final method is to go ahead and plan on doing 2 pours on your piece. Pour a flood coat and allow it to cure. Within 5 to 8 hours go ahead and pour a second flood coat. If you choose, allow the piece to cure for 24 hours and do a light sand before pouring the second flood coat.

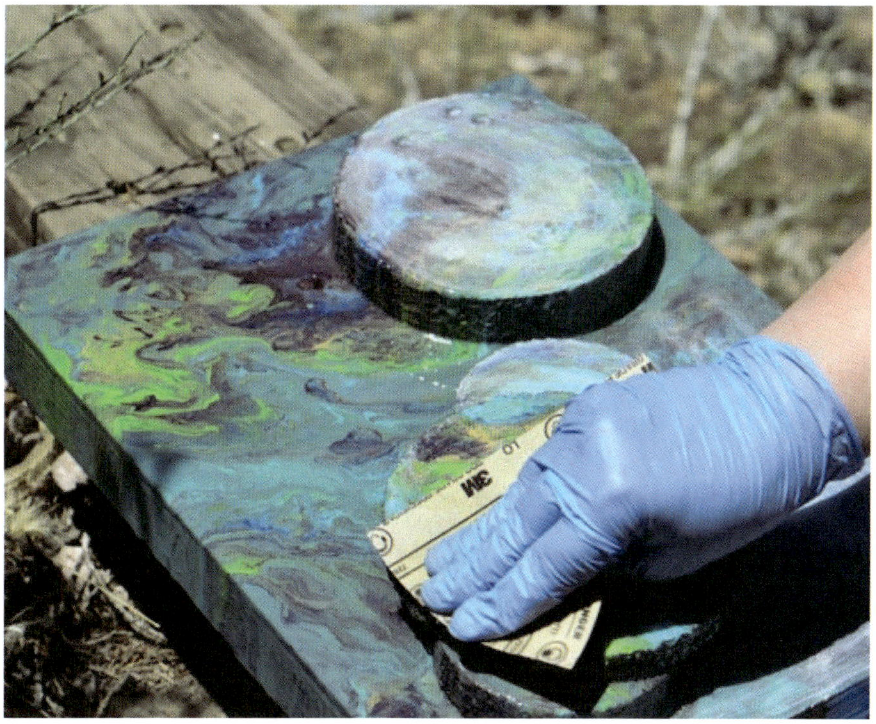

Sanding Painting for Second Pour

But what if I didn't notice the dimpling until it cured, and it's now completely cured this way. No problem. Lightly sand your piece. Clean with 91% isopropyl alcohol. Let it dry completely. Then mix a fresh batch of resin, and pour a new layer. The sanding gives the dried resin tooth. It gives it something to grab onto. This ensures that the resin layers don't separate. The new resin layer will cover the sanding marks completely. It will also cover dimples and pits. Almost any grit of sand paper will work for sanding resin in preparation for another coat, but 120 grit is recommended. If there are still low areas in the piece, repeat the process with another layer.

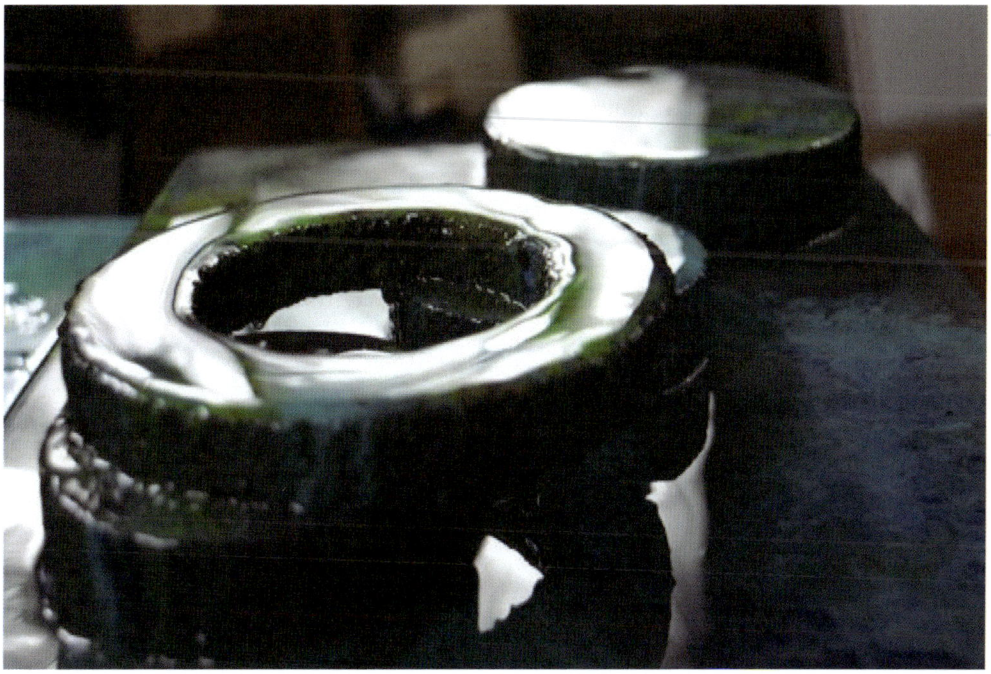

24 hours after a flood coat. No evidence of dimples or pits.

DRIPS & EXCESS RESIN

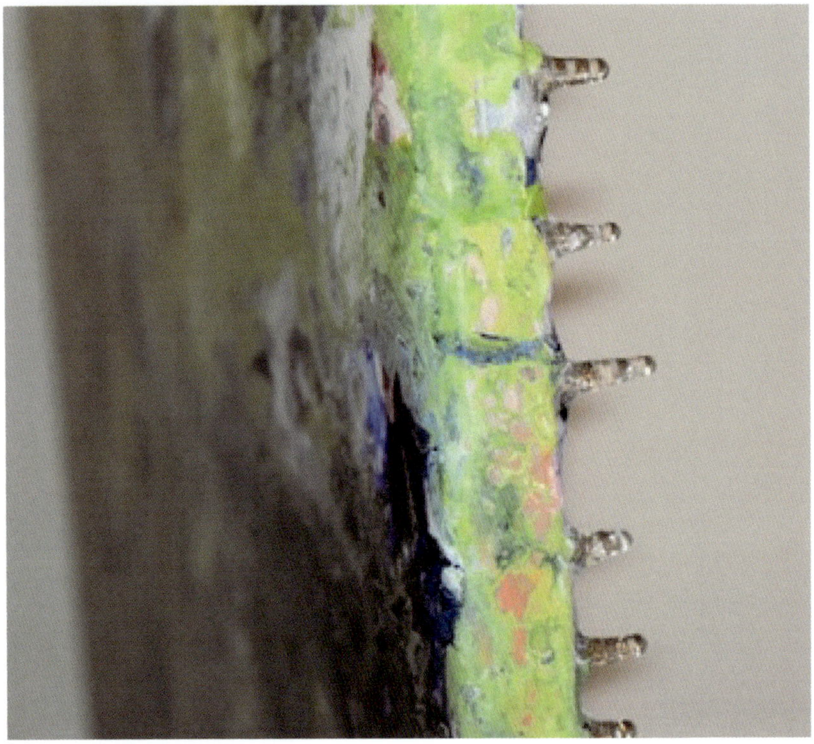

Cured resin in drips on the sides and back of a canvas.

Excess cured resin is a result of resin falling over the sides and pooling in icicles or pooling down into areas underneath the canvas. The easy way to avoid this is to tape off the sides and back. Remove the tape after a couple of hours; or after 4 or 5 hours if you want really clean sides. But if you are like me and you like the drips, and you skip the tape, you are going to have a painting that ends up with a spot or an edge that has too much resin. The way to repair this is to heat the area with a torch and scrape it off with a box knife or paint scraping tool. Some artists choose to sand the areas off. Sanding takes a long time.

Use a torch and a box knife to remove drips and excess resin.

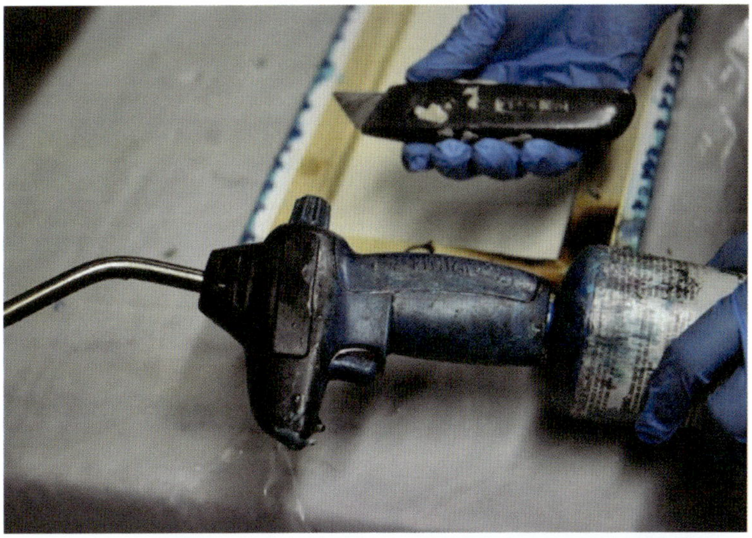

Give the spot a quick sweep with the torch.

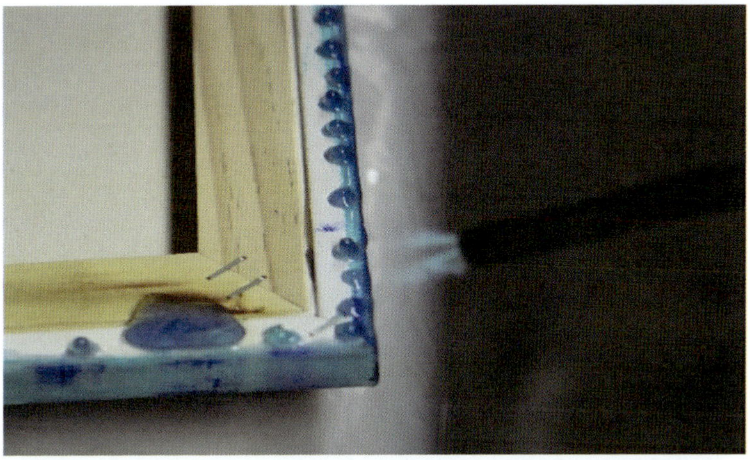

CAUTION

It is important to hold the box knife away from your fingers when using to cut away cured resin spots. It is very easy for the knife to slip and slice into your hands or fingers when held toward you. Turn the knife away from you when cutting.

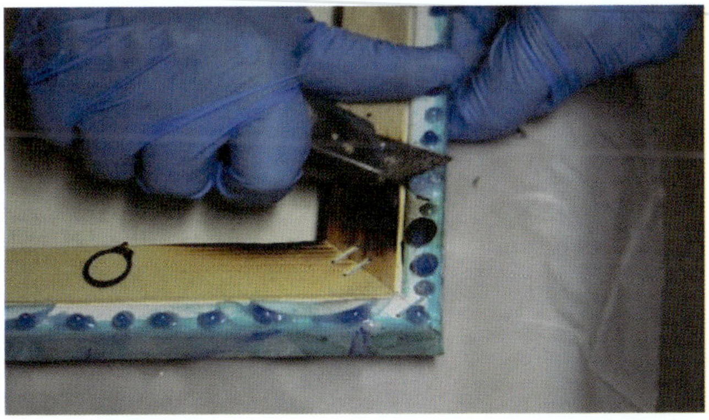

Do not hold your knife this way. There is a danger of cutting yourself if the knife slips.

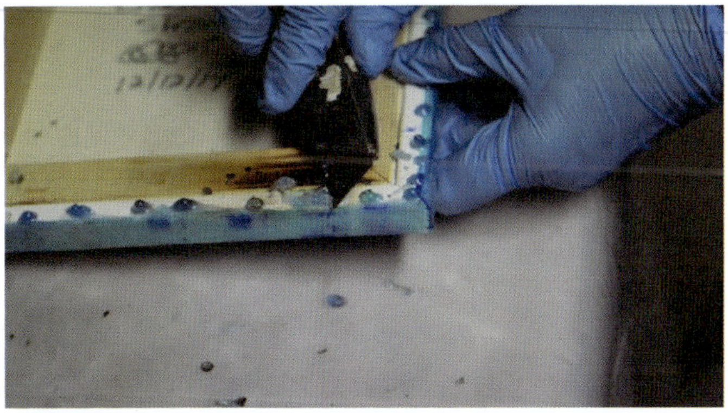

A better way to hold the knife. Hold the knife away from you. Protect your fingers. Trim the now warm resin from the area.

STICKY RESIN

If the resin on the surface has not cured within the proper curing time, chances are the correct mixing ratio was not used. The correct amount of hardener may not have been used. The resin may not have been mixed properly. Too much acrylic paint may have been used in the resin. Sticky uncured resin can happen if resin is used when it is too cold in the room, and the resin itself is too cold.

It's uncured if it's still sticky after 24 hours. It's uncured if, after the required curing time (usually 24 hours), a thumb pressed onto the surface leaves an imprint. The painting can still be saved. It may be enough to simply pour a fresh coat of resin on the surface. If the surface is extra sticky and gooey, scrape off as much of the uncured resin as possible. Don't worry about some stickiness being left on the substrate. Mix up a new batch of resin and pour a flood coat over the whole painting. Allow it to cure for 24 hours, or according to manufacturer's directions. Test after a couple of days for sturdiness. If the surface seems a little too flexible, go ahead and pour another coat.

To prevent this from happening, always use resin in temperatures above 75 degrees Fahrenheit, measure resin at exact ratios and mix well. If you are working in colder temperatures, warm the room to between 70 and 75 degrees Fahrenheit. It is better to warm it to 75 degrees, as the resin will perform better at 75 degrees Fahrenheit. Then place the resin and hardener in a warm water bath.

For a warm water bath, place the resin and hardener in warm water for 10 to 15 minutes. Use warm, not hot, water. The whole bottle can be placed in the warm water. I choose to pour the amount of resin I am going to use into plastic cups and place them in a larger plastic bucket or cup. They are unmixed for the warm water bath. Be careful not to get water in the resin and hardener. Use an old rag or paper towels to wipe down the outside of the cups before pouring the resin and hardener together for mixing. This ensures no water in your mix.

The reason I only warm the amount I am going to need and not the whole container is that I want to maintain the integrity of the resin and hardener for as long as possible. If resin is heated over and over it may destabilize the resin; and heating up the hardener over and over may cause amberization.

TIP

A warm water bath may decrease your work time by about 10 to 15 minutes. By heating up the resin and hardener, the curing process is being sped up. Because the resin is warmer it will begin curing as soon as it is mixed, decreasing your work time. It is important to factor this in to the time needed for the project.

RESIN CURING TOO FAST

If the mixed resin is curing in less than 5 minutes it's probably because an incorrect mixing ratio was used. Too much hardener may have been used. Usually when this happens it hardens in the cup. But if it's already on the canvas and it has cured, it should be perfectly fine in terms of stability. As long as you like the look, it's OK to leave it as is. If you don't like it, sand it down and add another layer.

Resin may cure too fast when too much pigment powder is used. I have found that adding too much pigment powder cuts the work time in half. If an excessive amount of pigment powder is added, it could cause the resin to cure in the cup within a few minutes or as soon as it lands on the canvas.

Resin may cure too fast when too hot of a bath is used to warm the resin and hardener. When this is the situation it will likely cure in the cup before it can be placed on the canvas. If you are able to get it on the canvas, go ahead and use it. Try to make something with it. It should be fine once cured.

CURED RESIN IS FLEXIBLE

Resin art that has cured but is flexible and pliable can happen from not using enough hardener in the mix. It may happen because of the brand of resin being used. Some cheaper brands of resin tend to be more flexible and pliable, rather than hard when cured. These brands usually harden up given a few months' time.

It may have happened because the resin was not mixed thoroughly enough. While mixing, it's important to scrape the sides and bottom of the cup. It's important to stir for the amount of time recommended by the manufacturer. If the mix was not thorough enough, unmixed resin may have landed on the surface in spots and caused the cure to be more flexible.

Flexible cures can occur because too much acrylic paint was used in the mix. When more than 10% acrylic paint is used, the resin will cure flexible. If a fingernail is applied to the surface it will leave a mark. A thumb will likely leave a print. This is due to the water content of acrylic paint. If too much acrylic paint was used in the pour, sand the surface and apply a flood coat of clear resin. The flood coat should harden normally.

If the resin was mixed correctly, choose a better brand of resin. If you like the art, a different brand of resin can be poured as a second coat. It may save it. If the problem is due to improper mixing, pour an additional layer on the piece. A light sanding is required before the new pour. Flexibility can also result from too thin a layer of resin. If the cause is too thin a layer, add a flood coat of resin. A light sanding is required.

COMPLETED RESIN ART HAS YELLOWED

Yellowing is due to the brand of resin you use. The reality is all resin is likely to yellow given enough years. All art yellows given enough years. Some resin brands yellow within months, or within a year or two. Some brands of resin are best used with color. You may only choose to use these brands of resin if you want the yellowing in your art. Other brands of resin say that they are less likely to yellow and claim they can be counted on to not yellow for 20 or more years. If you have a finished piece that has yellowed, and you don't like it, use it for another pour. Resin yellowing is more likely to show on a white or light background. Resin is more likely to yellow when placed in the sun. All art is more likely to yellow when placed in the sun, or near a window that gets direct sun.

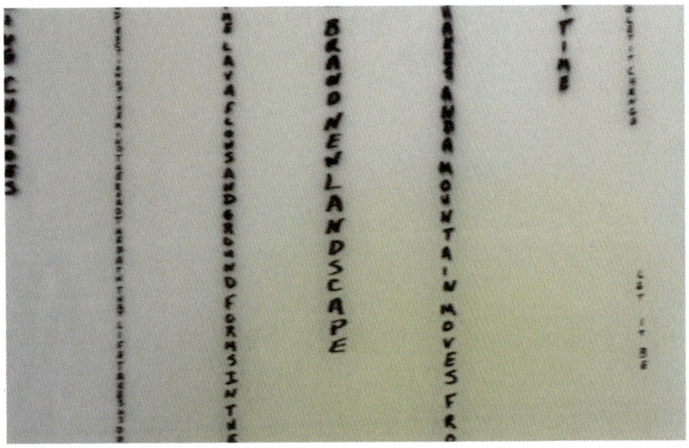

Resin yellowing is more likely to show on a white background.

TORCH OR HEAT GUN BUTTONS NOT WORKING

If resin has cured on the buttons of the torch, or heat gun, there isn't much that can be done to save it. To avoid this, wear multiple pairs of gloves while doing resin work and take a resin covered pair off to do torch work. With layering pairs of gloves, you always have a clean pair on underneath the resin covered ones. Another method is to use plastic food wrap around the buttons of the torch or heat gun before using. Cut the fingers off a glove and slip it over the torch or heat gun & onto the buttons to cover them. If you already have cured resin on the buttons and it isn't working it's best to purchase a new one.

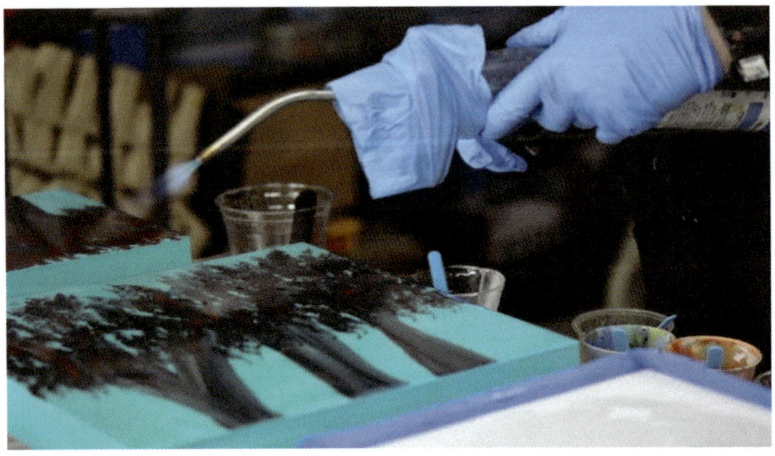

A glove placed over the buttons on the torch will prevent resin getting on them.

COMPLETED RESIN ART SCRATCHES EASILY

There is nothing more frustrating that cleaning an amazing piece of resin art, only to have it scratch. The last thing you ever want is to ship a resin art piece, only to have it arrive to the customer scratched. The most common reason scratches occur in cured resin art is that enough time has not been given for curing before cleaning or packaging. Curing takes 7 to 14 days to full hardness. If cleaning or packing is attempted before that time, scratches will result. Another reason is too much colorant to resin mix. Too much colorant in the resin will weaken the resin and make it prone to scratching. Another reason is a cheap brand of resin is used, that is itself prone to scratching. To repair, lightly sand the surface and pour a flood coat of a quality resin. Allow the new flood coat to fully cure, for at least 14 days. Any scratches in the resin will be covered with the layer new resin.

HARDENER IS TURNING YELLOW IN THE BOTTLE

Resin and hardener have a shelf life of about 6 months once opened. Once exposed to oxygen, discoloration begins. The hardener will most likely go through amberization if not used within 6 months. It can still be used even if it turns yellow. It may not even be yellow on the canvas. It will likely be crystal clear, once mixed with resin and used on canvas. I have used resin and hardeners years after they have sat on a shelf in my studio. I have used them well over a year after the bottle was opened. The cure was more yellow with one resin; and required a warming bath with another resin. If you are unsure, use it with colorants or in a project that yellowing is OK. Just don't throw it away. It will still provide a sturdy resin surface for the right project.

RESIN HAS CRYSTALLIZED IN THE BOTTLE

Resin and hardener have a shelf life of about 6 months once opened. Once exposed to oxygen resin begins to oxidize and this leads to crystals forming in the bottle of resin. I have used it in this state. I warmed the bottle in a warm water bath and mixed it normally. It cured crystal clear with no specks in the work. The bottle of resin was over a year old. If this happens don't throw it away. It will still provide a sturdy resin surface for the right project. It is important to note that if the resin has crystallized in the bottle it requires warming up to be used. If used without warming it will not cure properly.

SECTION 18
FREQUENTLY ASKED QUESTIONS

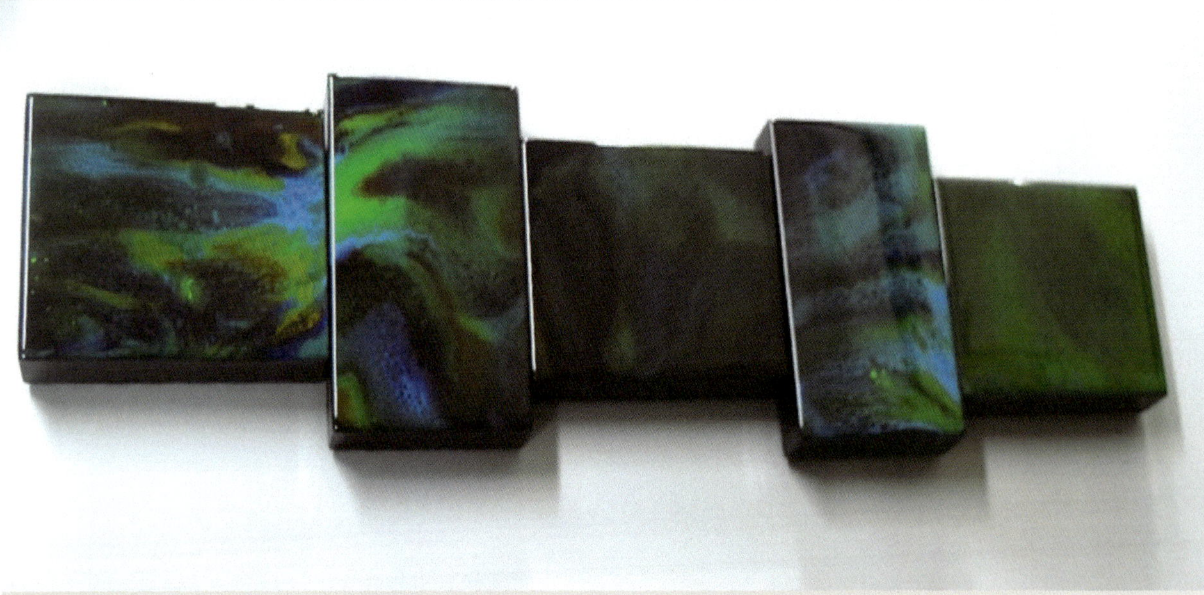

Alchemy
Resin & Oil Paint on Series of 5 Wood Panels
5"x7" (13cmx18cm)

CAN I USE FOOD COLORING IN RESIN?
No. I don't recommend it. Food coloring contains water. The resin will cure flexible and rubbery. Food coloring will fade in a short amount of time. It is best to use artist grade pigments, paints & micas in resin work.

WHERE DO I PURCHASE SUPPLIES IF I DON'T HAVE AN ART STORE NEAR ME?
Everything that is needed for epoxy resin art can be found Online. Amazon, eBay and art supply websites. Every supply needed can be purchased on Amazon or eBay. Hardware stores will ship to your home. Blick art supply and Jerry's Artarama sell Online and ship to your home. Epoxy resin manufacturers sell and ship from directly from their website.

CAN I USE TWO DIFFERENT BRANDS OF RESIN WHEN MIXING? I HAVE RAN OUT OF THE BRAND OF RESIN I WAS USING FOR A PROJECT AND NEED TO DO ANOTHER LAYER. I STILL HAVE SOME HARDENER LEFT. CAN I USE A DIFFERENT BRAND OF RESIN MIXED WITH THE HARDENER?
Resin brands can be used in layers, once the first layer is cured. It's not a good idea to mix brands of resin and hardener. Do NOT use the hardener from one brand and the resin from another brand to mix together for a project.

YOU RECOMMEND SANDING BEFORE POURING A SECOND COAT OF RESIN. I AM CONCERNED ABOUT SCRATCHING UP THE ART. WILL THE SECOND COAT, COVER THE SCRATCHES?
Yes. The purpose of sanding before pouring a second coat is to create scratches in the surface. The scratches create micro openings in the surface of the substrate that allow for bonding of the second layer. This prevents peeling away of the layers. The scratches themselves will be clear, as the resin from the second layer bonds into them and with the first layer.

WHICH IS BETTER, A HEAT GUN OR BLOW TORCH?
It depends on what it is being used for. A torch is better for taking care of bubbles. A torch can be directed at a single area and does not blow the resin around. A heat gun uses air. Use a heat gun when heating up the resin and moving it around the canvas is desired.

WHAT IS THE DIFFERENCE BETWEEN CASTING RESIN, ART RESIN, & COUNTER TOP RESIN?
Casting resin is used for molds & jewelry. Art resin is used on canvas. Counter top epoxy or resin is used for covering tables and counter tops but is often used in art.

WHAT IS MEANT BY DOMING RESIN?
A doming resin cures round or domed. A flat resin cures like a flat piece of glass. A resin that is thicker in consistency is more likely to dome. The thicker the resin the higher the dome. The reason is, that more of the resin is allowed to sit on the surface of the substrate as it cures. It cures up rather than falling off the canvas. A doming resin provides dimension and depth to art.

HOW DO I STORE RESIN WHEN I AM NOT USING IT?
Keep it upright in its containers. Keep it in a shipping box for best results. It helps to create a dark space for the resin. Then place them in plastic container if desired. Store in temperatures above 70 degrees Fahrenheit if possible. Most resins have a shelf life of a year, when unopened, and 6 months after opening. Still use the resin from an expired or old bottle. Just use it with color.

WHAT ABOUT USING MOLDS IN RESIN?
Silicone molds are best for resin use. Concrete molds and many plastic molds may leave the resin permanently cured in the mold. A mold release made for resin can help if these types of molds are used.

HOW DO I PHOTOGRAPH RESIN ART?

Resin art is very difficult to photograph. The shiny surface creates a glare that shows up in your pictures. It is very possible to take great pictures of resin art, regardless of the device used photographing it. Use a room with minimal windows. If possible, purchase a photography light. Photography lights can be purchased fairly inexpensively Online. This is a light with an umbrella that directs the glow towards the art. It provides a soft light that is better for art.

When using a phone or tablet, aim from the top of the painting down, rather than straight on. Look for glares or mirroring on the surface of the picture. If you see them, change the angle. Try aiming from one side of the painting toward the middle, rather than straight on.

When using a professional camera, like Nikon or Canon use a polarizing filter. The best lens to use for art is a 60mm. Regardless of the kind of lens you use, a polarizing filter will knock out the glare from resin paintings. This is the kind of filter that looks like the lens of sunglasses. They are offered in different strengths. Find them for outdoors or for bright florescent lighting. I use one made for bright florescent lighting. It's a little darker, but not so dark that I can't use it indoors. It has been great at preventing glare. I have a Nikon 5600 camera with a 60mm lens. I also use a variable 18 to 55 lens from time to time.

WHAT IS THE BEST WAY TO SHIP RESIN ART?

You have created a beautiful piece of art and someone on the other side of the country, or in another country wants to purchase it. It is important to package the artwork well for shipping. Bubble wrap will ensure that it is not damaged in transit but it may leave marks on the resin if not handled properly. First, allow the resin to sit and cure. Resin takes 7 to 14 days minimum to fully cure. Allow the resin art to sit for at least 8 weeks before shipping, to ensure proper curing. When you can clean the resin art with glass cleaner and a soft cloth and it doesn't scratch, it's cured. I choose to wait a full 8 weeks before cleaning, wrapping packaging and shipping resin artwork.

Wrap the resin art in something that won't stick to it, before wrapping it with bubble wrap. I suggest Glassine. It can be found in art stores or on Amazon. Glassine is made for storing and protecting art. It protects the surface of the art. You can use wax paper or parchment paper if you can't find Glassine. Last, wrap in bubble wrap several times. Leave enough packing on all sides in the box. With extra packaging, if the box is crushed or banged it won't get to the painting. If there is any room left in the box, fill with packing peanuts or more bubble wrap. Make sure that the art has no room to move around in the box. A well packed art shipment will contain bubble wrap at the bottom and at the top and on each side of the art piece.

The shipping label should be printed clearly. Include your return address. If there is a problem with shipment it can be returned to you. If the customer changes their mind, they can refuse the shipment and it will be returned to you. If you do not include your return address, it will be lost and you will not be able to get it back.

WHAT IS THE BEST METHOD FOR PRICING ART?

Your work is valuable. Don't undervalue what you do. Your work may be a hobby and it's great just to share it with others. However, you put time and money in your art. That is worth something.

There are a few different ways to price art. One way is to calculate cost of materials plus cost of time painting. Some artists multiply this number by 2 or 3. If you are placing your art in a gallery, factor in the cost of the gallery commission. Another way is to add the dimensions of the painting and multiply it by your chosen dollar amount. For a 10x10 painting: 10+10=20x$5.00=$100.00. 10+10=20x$10.00=$200 and so on. This method ensures exact pricing across your art work and is easier to do than materials pricing. The key is to use a pricing standard that covers your cost of materials and time doing the art.

The most consistent way to price your art is by square inches. It's easier than you think to use this method. The formula is side multiplied by side equals square inches multiplied by chosen dollar amount. For a 10x10 painting: 10x10=100square inches. 100x$1.00 = $100.00. Set a chosen price per square inch that will cover the cost of materials and time completing the art. If you have the piece in a gallery add the cost of the gallery commission to the price per square inch.

The goal with pricing art is consistency from piece to piece. It's helpful to avoid pricing one piece of art at .25 and another at 1.00. If your prices are all over the place, it's difficult to know if you are covering the cost of supplies and customers may assume that the lesser priced piece is less valuable in some way.

Resin cost anywhere from $60 to $300 per gallon. Good paints are $6 to $50 per tube. Good pigments are $10 to $50 per container. A 10x10 canvas can easily use $40 in paint & resin. A 48x70 canvas can use $200 in paint & resin. The small canvas itself will cost $15 and the larger one will cost $250. That is a total of $55 in materials on the small one and $450 in materials on the large one. If you want to make any profit on your art, it's easy to see why artists double and triple materials + time spent. Especially if you are selling at art shows and festivals with added expenses.

Extra expenses that artists often forget to add to the cost of the sale are shipping cost, website and advertising cost, utilities in the studio, packing materials, and art show fees. These are fees that accumulate over time. They may not be associated with one particular art piece but should be a factor when setting prices in art. I spend thousands on the business and practice of art every year. When a sale occurs, it helps to pay for some of the cost.

WHAT DO I DO WHEN SOMEONE ASKED ME TO DO SOMETHING SPECIFIC FOR THEM?

COMMISSIONS

Someone wants you to do a specialty painting for them. Congratulations, you are now a professional artist. There are a few things to consider when taking on a commission. A contract for the work is important. A contract to include details such as the size of the art, chosen medium, the chosen colors, the total price, and the number of attempts the artist will make to complete the contract. The contract needs to state what happens if the customer does not choose to buy the art. Most contracts state that a non-refundable deposit is to be provided at signing. If the customer decides not to buy the art you keep the deposit.

When setting up a commission it's important to ask the customer lots of questions. Ask about the space they want the art to be placed, which of your completed art pieces they are drawn to, the colors in the space they will be placing the art and their budget for the art piece.

If the customer wants a piece of art that you struggle to see working, be willing to talk to the customer to find a color combination that will work. Do a small painting as a test to see if the colors work. Ask the customer if they will consider the addition of another color. Offer a color combination that you know will work.

Communication is a key component in completing a successful commission. The reason that most commissions don't work out is lack of proper communication on what is expected and desired for the art. A customer has a vision and is trying to communicate that vision to you. It's your job to interpret it as best you can on the canvas.

HOW AND WHERE CAN I SELL RESIN ART?

The best advice I can give you is don't undervalue your work. Some resin artists sell their art at such low prices that they don't even cover the cost of their art supplies. See pricing.

Where can you sell your art?

- ☒ Create a website
- ☒ Etsy
- ☒ Amazon Handmade
- ☒ Shopify
- ☒ Online gallery
- ☒ Local gallery
- ☒ Art shows
- ☒ Craft festivals
- ☒ Local restaurants
- ☒ Local coffee house
- ☒ Facebook
- ☒ Instagram

For selling art Online you will need a PayPal account. Find everything you need to know on their site. If you choose to sell at art shows or craft festivals, accepting credit cards allows for more sales. There are plenty of credit card devices and companies to choose from, but squareup.com has a device that pares with your phone, making it easily portable. PayPal also has a credit card device.

Many artists are listing their art on sites like Etsy and Amazon Handmade. There is massive competition on these sites and marketing to capture customer's attention and set yourself apart is necessary.

I created my own website when Etsy wasn't generating sales. My website has thrived. With a website, you have access to Google ads and search links which generates traffic to your site. Posting on social media sites like Instagram, Facebook and Twitter also drives traffic to your site. Many artists are selling their art on these social media sites without having a website.

Craft festivals and art shows are the best places to sell art. There is an expense in taking part of these events. The cost of having a booth at an art show or craft festival can be anywhere from $100 to $1000, depending on the venue. If you choose to have a booth, follow the venue guidelines. Be prepared to accept credit cards. Make it comfortable for your customers. Give out business cards. Talk to your customers. Consider giving out free items. A book mark or business card can keep customers thinking about your art after the festival. Especially if the book mark or card offers a discount on art at your site.

SECTION 19
RESOURCES

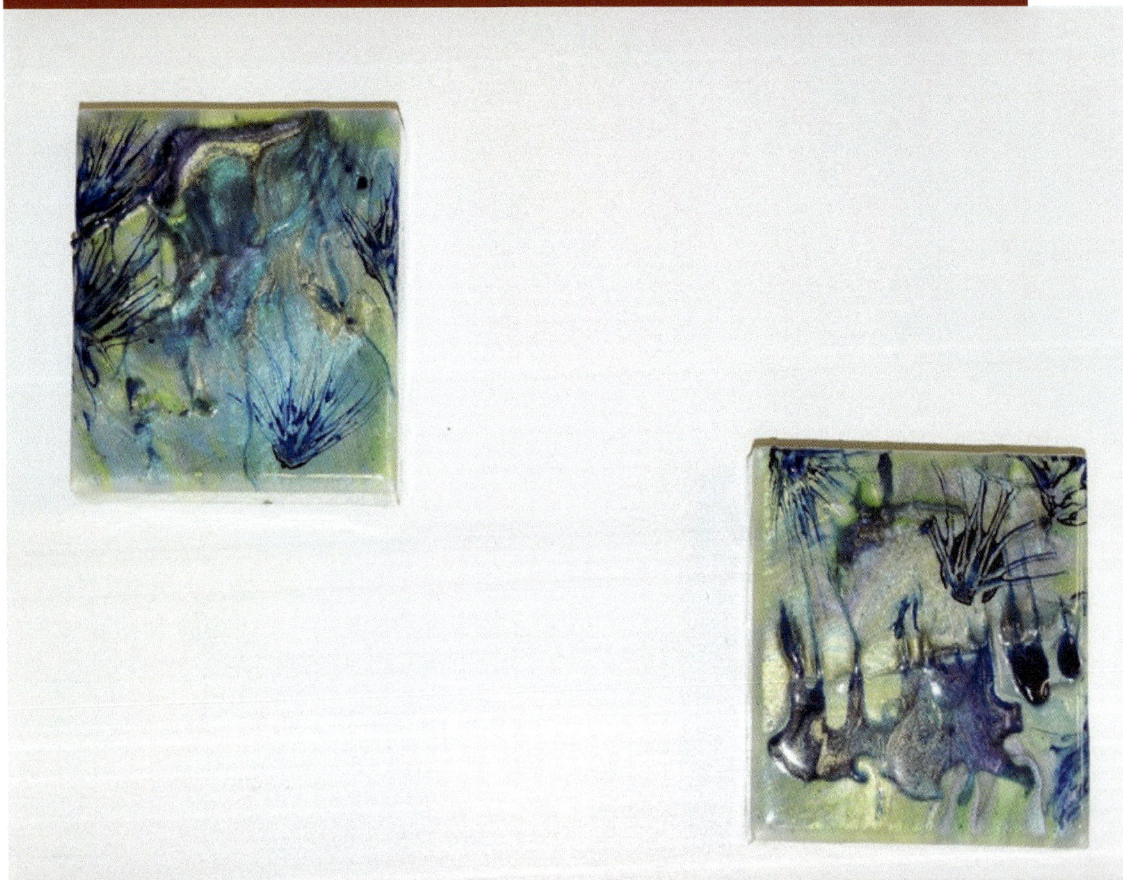

Sea Flowers
Resin, Mica, Ink on Canvas
5"x5" (13cm x13cm)

A few suggestions on where you can find supplies.

EPOXY RESIN

artnglow.com
artresin.com
elichem.co.uk
promarinesuppplies.com

DEPARTMENT STORES

Eye Shadow
Blush
Clear Packing Tape
Masking Tape
Craft Sticks
Alcohol
Plastic rulers

ART CRAFT & HOBBY STORES

Acrylic & oil paints
Gesso
Stamps & stencils
Linseed, walnut, safflower oils
Pouring medium
Polymer medium
Canvas
Gesso board
Enamel paint
Alcohol ink
Acrylic ink
Styrofoam for crafts
Craft sticks
Some brands of epoxy resin
Craft dyes
Inks

HARDWARE STORES

HVAC tape
Masking tape
Plastic sheeting
Paint mixing cups
Some brands of epoxy resin
Butane or propane torch
Heat gun
Nitrile Gloves
Kilz paint primer
Pharmacy
Long tweezers
Eye shadow
Blush
Gloves

ONLINE RESOURCES

Art 'N Glow

artnglow.com

- Resin
- Glow paint
- Glow pigment

Master Cast 1-2-1

elichem.co.uk
A UK based company that ships all over the world.
Resin- a few different kinds
Resi-Tint - colorant
Resi-Crete - texture
Resi-Blast- for cells and lacing

Art Resin

artresin.com
Resin
Resin tint
A great resin calculator

Ampersand

ampersandart.com
Clayboard panels, Gessoboard panels, Ampersand canvas.

Blick Art Supply

dickblick.com
Art supply store.
Wood panels, canvas.
Acrylic paint, oil paint, inks & pigments.

Golden Acrylic Paint

goldenpaints.com
Acrylic paint and mediums.

Amazon

amazon.com
Epoxy resin (Mastercast, Art 'N Glow, Art Resin, Pro Marine, East Coast, and most other brands)
Pigment powder
Mica powder
Nitrile gloves
Silicone hair dye applicator tools
Most art supplies
Plastic craft sticks
Plastic rulers for stirring resin

Winsor & Newton

winsornewton.com
Oil paint

Home Depot Hardware Store

homedepot.com
Hardware supplies
Plastic sheeting
Paint mixing cups

Liquitex Paints

liquitex.com
Acrylic paints and mediums.

Ranger Craft Supply

rangerink.com
Alcohol ink and embossing supplies.

Jerry's Artarama

jerrysartarama.com
Art supplies, wood panels, canvas.
Acrylic paint, oil paint.

Gamblin Oil Paint

gamblincolors.com
Oil paint.

Acknowledgments

A heartfelt thanks to Jon for your support and help with all of my art. For giving me your honest critique of each artwork that I show you and for your patience in helping me with an extra pair of hands when I need it. Thank you for your constant willingness to edit anything that I ask you to edit. You are the best. Thank you, Christina for your support and for covering me in the office while I spent time writing this book.

Thank you to all the artists in the resin artists groups who asks troubleshooting questions and create a space to share work. Thank you to artists and collectors of art everywhere. Art is so important. To Alex at Art 'N Glow Resin for a detailed data sheet about your resin, and for making yourself available to me. To David at Pro Marine for quickly providing detailed information about your resin. To Rebecca at Art Resin for your quick response to my request for information, and for making yourself available to me.

FINAL THOUGHTS

Resin makes beautiful art. Practicing safety is crucial when working with this medium. If you have found this book and are starting a journey in the wonderful world of epoxy resin art, enjoy the ride. Look for resin art groups and join on Facebook, Instagram, or other social media. These groups are filled with support and information that is helpful as you work. You will find me on these groups. I look forward to seeing what you create.

You can find more information about me and my art at https://strongartcreations.com

Index

G

H

I

L

M

N

O

P

R

S

T

V

W

Y

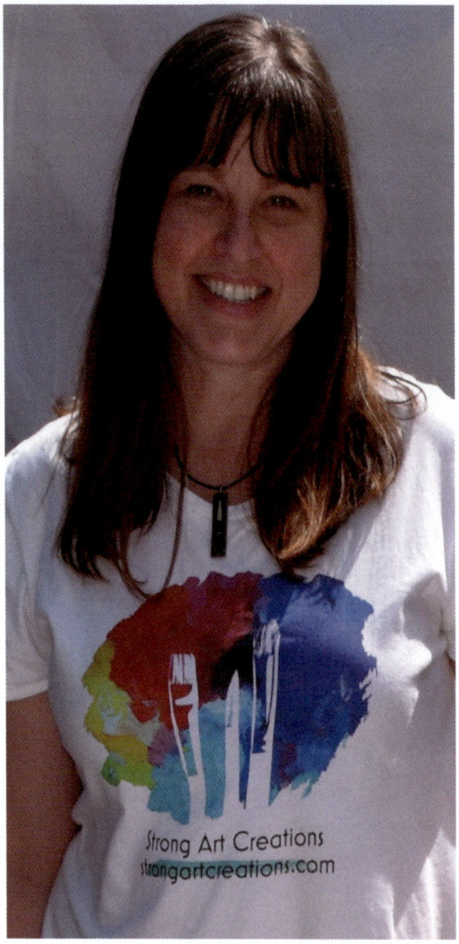

Charlotte is a psychotherapist with a full-time practice, she also finds time to fully research art technique, and creates art at night and on weekends. She sees art as meditation and spiritual practice. She is self-taught as an artist and has logged thousands of hours studying the form and practice of brush stroke, paint formulary, and the archival nature of art. She strives to ensure that all of her creations are archival and will stand the test of time. She loves to experiment and push the limits of the ordinary. Charlotte works with encaustics, oils, acrylics and resin on canvas and in jewelry. Most of her work is abstract, however she has completed portraits and landscapes. Charlotte is also a writer. Having written her first film script, she is now embarking on a second film script. Her two rescue dogs, Sisko and Dax, are her muses. Their phenomenal spirits are constant sources of inspiration. Born in Florida, and after living in New Mexico, for a time, she settled in California. Where she has lived and practiced her art for the past 20 years. Visit Charlotte online at https://strongartcreations.com

Photographers
The photos in this book where taken by Jon Koch & Charlotte Strong

44900366R00086

Printed in Poland
by Amazon Fulfillment
Poland Sp. z o.o., Wrocław